SPECIAL EDUCATION

Yearbook of the European Association for Education Law and Policy

Volume 5

The titles published in this series are listed at the end of this volume.

# Special Education

## Yearbook of the European Association for Education Law and Policy

Edited by

Jan De Groof

and

Gracienne Lauwers

KLUWER ACADEMIC PUBLISHERS
DORDRECHT / LONDON / BOSTON

A C.I.P. Catalogue record for this book is available from the Library of Congress.

ISBN 1-4020-1545-3

Published by Kluwer Academic Publishers,
P.O. Box 17, 3300 AZ Dordrecht, The Netherlands.

Sold and distributed in North, Central and South America
by Kluwer Academic Publishers,
101 Philip Drive, Norwell, MA 02061, U.S.A.

In all other countries, sold and distributed
by Kluwer Academic Publishers,
P.O. Box 322, 3300 AH Dordrecht, The Netherlands.

*Printed on acid-free paper*



Printed in the Netherlands

# Table of Contents

# Introduction

> People with disabilities should be at the centre of the European Year, which is about raising awareness of the rights of disabled people to full equality and participation in all areas. It is about tackling barriers that people with disabilities face, wherever they occur. The European Year is also about raising awareness that disability is an issue of concern to all of us.[1]

Special education in Europe has developed considerably during the past ten years.

The 1990 Jomtien Conference on Education for All and the 1994 Salamanca Declaration have significantly contributed to the ongoing work in most EU Member States on including disabled children into mainstream schools.

The Amsterdam Treaty included a new Article 13, which gave the European Union the right to legislate against additional types of discrimination, in the labour market and in society. Combating discrimination on the basis of disability became one of the founding principles of the European Community.

> Without prejudice to the other provisions of this Treaty and within the limits of the powers conferred by it upon the Community, the Council, acting unanimously on a proposal from the Commission and after consulting the European Parliament, may take appropriate action to combat discrimination based on sex, racial or ethnic origin, religion or belief, disability, age or sexual orientation.

This is the basis on which the 2000 EU Directives, which opposes discrimination in the labour market and in society as a whole, was prepared. The Employment Directive (2000/78/EC) lays down an anti-discrimination principle of equal treatment in the context of sexual orientation, religion or belief, disability and age. It has to be implemented by 2 December 2006 in relation to disability.

Although there are currently no specific proposals for changes to mainstream disability legislation or policy in the European Union, special needs education is an area, which is receiving increased attention from the European Commission and the Member States.

In November 1996, the European Agency for the Development in Special Needs Education, was created as a separate agency for special needs education, supported

1 Commissioner Anna Diamantopoulou.

by the Ministries of Education in 15 participating EU countries, Norway, Iceland, Switzerland and the European Commission.[2] The European Agency provides an important example of how governments develop co-operation without the participation of the European Commission.

The year 2003 has been designated as the European Year of Disabled Citizens.

> 2003 has been named the European Year of People with Disabilities and a number of related conferences and events will be taking place under the Greek Presidency. An informal meeting of Employment and Social Affairs Ministers will be devoted to the social policy agenda from a disability perspective. Disability questions will be integrated into the agendas of all Ministerial Councils that will be held in Greece.[3]

The EU Charter of Fundamental Rights will provide an important legislative base for future developments in special needs education.

> Any discrimination based on any ground such as sex, race, colour, ethnic or social origin, genetic features, language, religion or belief, political or any other opinion, membership of a national minority, property, birth, disability, age or sexual orientation shall be prohibited. (Article 21 Charter)

Education of children with special educational needs has also become a main feature in the accession negotiations with the countries from Central and Eastern Europe, especially discrimination in access to mainstream educational systems faced by Romani children in the candidate member states[4] and the segregation of Romani children in separate classrooms, separate schools, or special schools for the mentally and/or physically handicapped.[5]

Legislation specifically prohibits discrimination in access to education and special programmes are being elaborated to guarantee access to education in Bulgaria, Hungary,[6] Latvia, Lithuania, Romania[7] and the Czech Republic.[8]

2 http://www.european-agency.org/

3 Statement on the key priorities for the Greek Presidency (first half of 2003).

4 *Monitoring the EU Accession Process: Minority Protection*, Open Society Institute, 2001.

5 *2000 Regular Report* on Bulgaria, the Czech Republic, Hungary, Poland, Romania, Slovakia and Slovenia.

6 In Hungary, although since 1993, a special allowance has been allocated on a quota basis to schools to develop remedial "minority education programmes" exclusively for Roma, this form of education was deemed to exploit to segregate Roma pupils." (Reports on the Activity of the Parliamentary Commissioner for the Rights of National and Ethnic Minorities, Office of the Ombudsmen, Budapest, 2001, pp. 47–52.)

7 Order of the Ministry of National Education no. 4542/18.09.2000 on the Access of Young Roma in Vocational Schools, High Schools, Colleges and Faculties and Universities.

8 In the Czech Republic, a 2000 amendment to the Law on Education removed a legal prohibition which barred graduates of special schools from taking the entrance examination for secondary school. However, in practice students who have attended special schools are

However, there is no coherent system of sanctions in place in any of these countries, and successful application of these and related laws is extremely rare. To date, governments in the accession region have not done enough to remedy these unlawful practices.

In Bulgaria,[9] separate education is primarily rooted in residential segregation. In the Czech Republic,[10] Hungary,[11] Poland and Slovakia,[12] the separate education system is grounded in a test-based assignment system that purports to provide special assistance to (mostly Romani) children with special needs. Romani children are deprived of equal educational opportunities because of the inferior quality of the curricula in most special classes and schools; the absence of monitoring systems to ensure that placements, once made, continue to be appropriate; and the fact that very few students ever return from special schools to mainstream education, which in its turn entrenches further the patterns of discrimination and segregation.

Against this background, we welcome the designation of 2003 as the *European Year of Disabled Citizens* and we hope that this book help highlight of how the needs of people with disabilities, particularly in the areas of education and training, are met in Europe, the USA, the Russian Federation and South Africa.

Jan De Groof
Gracienne Lauwers

January 2003

---

ill-equipped to succeed in the entrance exam. (Law no. 19/2000 Coll. amending Law on Schools No. 29/1984, Article 19, Section 1 of the School Act.)

9 A majority of the 19,000 students in 130 Bulgarian schools for the mentally deficient are estimated to be Roma. (Figures provided by the Bulgarian Helsinki Committee.)

10 ERRC, *A Special Remedy: Roma and Schools for the Mentally Handicapped in the Czech Republic*, 1999.

11 42 percent in Hungary, rising to 94 percent in the north-eastern part of the country (Data of the Hungarian Ministry for Culture and Education, 1993).

12 In Slovakia, more than half of Romani students attend special schools (Wide Open School Foundation, "Strategic Plan 2001–2003", Slovakia, 2000, p. 11).

# Part 1

LODE DE GEYTER[1]

# Trends and New Thinking in Europe on Special Needs Education[2]

## 1. Special education: an enormous variety

Special education varies from a very specific educational type depending on the pedagogical needs of the pupils, over a special type of education for some kinds of handicaps to a specific educational type for severely handicapped persons integration.

In Flanders (Belgium) eight different types of education have been set up on primary level, and on secondary level four training forms, according to the pupils' capacities linked to their future social and professional integration, are organised.

In Germany the organisation of special education consists of ten different educational types and in the Netherlands there are even fifteen types.

In other countries (Denmark, France and Luxemburg) schools and centres with a big variety of pedagogical-didactic offer for motor, sensory and mentally handicapped children and adolescents are organised. The specialised institutes in France depend on the Ministry of Education, health or Social Affairs according to the kind of handicap. In many other countries, the organisation of special education on nursery level is not under the authority of the Ministry of Education. In some other countries special education aims especially at the training of severely handicapped children and adolescents.

Although there is an enormous variety in pedagogical offer, methods, staff, countries, kinds of handicaps, types of educational organisations, we try to achieve 1 common GOAL: (here I am referring to art. 3 of the Law "On education for children with disabilities in Russia"). Special education allows handicapped persons to

[1] Pedagogical/legal advisor of the Catholic network coordinator integrated education.

[2] Reprint. De Groof J., Lauwers Gr., *A New Framework of Special Education in the Russian Federation*, Garant, 2000, 21–25.

*Jan De Groof and Gracienne Lauwers (eds.), Special Education*, 3–7.

develop their capacities in order to get adjusted and integrated into the social environment, to be prepared for professional activity, self-service, self-support and family life.

As formulated in the Law: Special Education allows disabled persons to get education in the adequate less restrictive educational environment aimed at ensuring their social adaptation and integration.

## 2. Integrated education: national differences

In all state-members of the European Community the integration is encouraged and aimed at, but in very different ways and forms.

All combinations are possible. In Luxemburg, for instance, all visually impaired children are integrated individually in all education levels. In Flanders (Belgium) children with all kinds of handicaps can be integrated in a permanent or temporary way, receiving additional help from special education.

In the Netherlands special attention is given to the integration of children with serious learning difficulties or behavioural problems. In Italy the integration is particularly individual. In Greece and Portugal the system of special classes in regular schools is very common, even in Ireland. Also in Spain, France, Great Britain and Denmark the individual integration into a normal setting is preferred.

In the European Community three options within three regions can be distinguished:

### *(a) Northern Europe*

In Denmark they promote "the school for all", "together to school". This is a political choice based on social points of view and values, but also on the enormous referring to special education in the seventies. Even non-educational factors play a role, viz. the geographical situation of their country. Because of the lower density of population the choice of a neighbouring school is not so easy.

They speak more about non-segregation instead of integration, up to the age of 14. Later, in secondary school, there are more severe curriculum demands, which can lead to a bigger drop-out of the integrated pupils.

### *(b) Central Europe*

In Germany, Belgium-Flanders and the Netherlands they state that integration can succeed only if the normal school profoundly changes its system. Three forms of integration are organised in those countries.

First, additional help to a handicapped pupil and the team in the normal school given by a teacher or therapist from the special school within a collective responsibility for the child with a handicap. The transfer of the mutual know-how towards the child is important.

Second, the "Zieldifferente Integration": one recognises that some children have specific needs. In respect to the variety they can participate in the mainstream in the regular school. The curriculum is adapted and the basic programme is filled in otherwise if necessary.

Third, the "Co-operating-Schools": a system of co-operation between special and regular education, whereby the know-how about special education of children with special needs is transferred to normal education.

### *(c) Southern Europe*

Special supplies, within education, have hardly been set up in the past. In Spain they try to give an answer to children with special needs in the normal primary school. This is achieved through organisational-measures, but also through adapting elements of the contents. Every schoolday they foresee two free moments. With a little extra help, children arc ablc to make learning progress in their own way and at their own working speed. (Here I am referring to art. 1 of the Law.)

I am very happy that the integrated education has become such an important matter in this Law in which you promote the I.E.D. and the fact that the normal education must provide special conditions. You are fully right, although I think that creating these "special education conditions" is a collective responsibility of regular and special education.

Integrated education, as we define it, is only a means to achieve one goal: the integrated co-operation of the two educational systems (special and ordinary school), whereby a handicapped pupil, in the normal school, is given assistance for its extra needs by specialists from a school for Special Education or a teacher from special class.

In art. 1 integrated education is defined as education of both persons with disabilities and persons who do not have disabilities, with the provision of special educational conditions for disabled persons.

## 3. GOAL OF SPECIAL NEEDS EDUCATION: SOCIAL INTEGRATION OF THE HANDICAPPED PERSON IN SOCIETY

Based on the Salamanca Statement on special needs education from UNESCO-E.C. programme Helios (Handicapped People in the European Community living independently in an Open Society) on European Education Resolutions signed by the Ministers of Education from the Community, and on personal experiences contributions in co-operation agreements and study visits in Spain, Denmark, Ireland, the Netherlands and Germany.

The trend in social policy during the past two decades has been to promote integration (see art. 14: I.E.D.) and participation and to combat exclusion. Inclusion and participation are essential to human dignity and to the enjoyment and exercise of human rights. Experience in many countries demonstrates that the integration of children and youth with special educational needs is best achieved within inclusive schools that serve all children within a community. It is within this context that those with special educational needs can achieve the fullest educational progress and social integration.

The fundamental principle of the inclusive school is that all children should learn together, wherever possible, regardless of any difficulties or differences they may have (see art. 13: where you mention the right of a disabled person to education in a normal school setting). Inclusive schools must recognise and respond to the diverse needs of their students, accommodating both different styles and rates of learning and ensuring quality education to all, through appropriate curricula, organizational arrangements, teaching strategies, resource use and partnerships with their communities.

Within inclusive schools, children with special educational needs should receive whatever extra support they may require to ensure their effective education. Inclusive schooling is the most effective means for building solidarity between children with special needs and their peers. Assignment of children to special schools, or special classes or sections within a school on a permanent basis, should be the exception, to be recommended only in those cases where it is clearly demonstrated that education in regular classrooms cannot meet a child's educational or social needs or when it is required for the welfare of the child or that of other children.

That assignment to special education is determined by the PMPAB (art. 22). The advisory board is the organ, which clearly demonstrates that a child really needs the segregated special guiding.

The situation regarding special needs education varies, as I said before, enormously from one country to another. There are, for example, countries that have well-established systems of special schools for those with specific impairments.

Such special schools can represent a valuable resource for the development of inclusive schools. The staff of these special institutions has the expertise needed for early screening and identification of children with disabilities.

Special schools can also serve as training and resource centres for staff in regular schools. Finally, special schools or units within inclusive schools may continue to provide the most suitable education for the relatively small number of children with disabilities who cannot be adequately served in regular classrooms or schools.

Investment in existing special schools should be geared to their new and expanded role of providing professional support to regular schools in meeting special educational needs.

Countries that have few or no special schools would, in general, be well advised to concentrate their efforts on the development of inclusive schools and the specialised services needed to enable them to serve the vast majority of children and youth, with especially the provision of teacher training in special needs education and with the establishment of suitably staffed and equipped resource centres to which schools could turn for support. Experience, especially in developing countries, indicates that the high cost of special schools means, in practice, that only a small minority of students, usually an urban elite, benefits from them.

The vast majority of students with specials needs, especially in rural areas, are as a consequence provided with no services whatsoever. Indeed, in many developing countries, it is estimated that less than 1% of children with special educational needs are in specialised schools.

Experience suggests that inclusive schools, serving all the children in a community, are most successful in eliciting community support and in finding imaginative and innovative ways of using the limited resources that are available.

Educational planning by governments should concentrate on education for all persons, in all regions of a country and in all economic conditions, through both public and private schools.

This point of view is intended as an overall guide to planning action in special needs education. It evidently cannot take into account the vast variety of situations encountered in the different regions and countries of the world and must, accordingly, be adapted to fit local requirements and circumstances. To be effective, it must be complemented by national, regional and local plans of action inspired by a political and popular will to achieve education for all. Thus the normal school may become more competent to give answers to children with special needs, in a system where there is room for adaptation of the learning process, for differentiation, individual guidance and adequate answers to the questions of children with pedagogical, didactic, psychological, social, mental and affective needs.

COR MEIJER[1]

# Overview of the Funding of Special Needs Education in Europe

The presentation examines a number of key factors in the relationship between financing and inclusive education. It elaborates on how the funding of special needs education is organised in the participating countries.

Different funding models are described on the basis of two main parameters: destination locus (who gets the funds?) and funding conditions (how are the funds allocated?). The advantages and disadvantages of these models and the ways in which they can be combined, are discussed.

## FINDINGS

It reveals that financing of special needs education is one of the most significant factors determining inclusion. If funds are not allocated in line with an explicit policy, inclusion is unlikely to be realised in practice. The mechanisms of financing may explain discrepancies between general policies and practical organisation and implementation. In fact, financing could be regarded as one of the most important factors that may contribute to the further development of inclusive practices.

In more detail, the study reveals:

- In countries where the financing system is characterised by a direct input-funding model for special schools (more pupils in special schools – more funds), the most criticism is raised. These countries point to the different forms of strategic behaviour within the educational field (by parents, teachers or other actors). These forms of strategic behaviour may result in less inclusion, more labelling and rising costs. A great deal of money is spent on non-educational matters such as litigation and diagnostic procedures. It is not surprising that these countries can be identified as having relatively higher percentages of pupils with special educational needs in separate settings.

[1] European Agency for Development in Special Needs Education.

*Jan De Groof and Gracienne Lauwers (eds.), Special Education*, 9–10.

- Countries with a strongly decentralised system – where the region or municipality has the main responsibility for the organisation of special education – generally report positive effects of their systems. These countries mention almost no negative side effects to their systems and are generally very satisfied with their financing systems. Systems where the municipalities make decisions on the basis of information from school support services or advisory centres and where the allocation of more funds to separate settings directly influences the amount of funds for mainstream schools, seem to be very effective in terms of achieving inclusion.
- Pupil-bound budgeting seems to have some clear disadvantages. At times mainstream schools are eager to have pupils with special needs (and their budgets) within their brief. However, it is likely that they prefer pupils (with budgets) who do not cause them too much additional work. In addition, parents will always attempt to get the best for their child and, as a result, will try to get the highest amounts of special needs funding. A pupil-bound budget system does not appear to be advisable for pupils with milder special needs. Criteria for learning disabilities are vague, ambiguous and change over time and this in itself may be a source of debate if budgets are linked to pupils. In practice, only clear-cut criteria are useful if funds are tied to pupils. If it is not possible to develop these, it seems that pupil-bound budgets should not be used. Generally, it appears desirable that funds are spent on special education itself (in an inclusive setting), instead of on bureaucratic procedures such as diagnosis, categorisation, appeals and litigation.

## Changing funding systems

The descriptions of financing of special needs education in the 17 countries reveal that funding models are currently in the process of being developed. In some countries, major changes are expected or have recently been implemented. A number of areas in which improvement of the financing of special needs education could be made are identified, not with a view to imposing certain funding models onto certain countries or regions but rather to stimulate a debate at various levels of policymaking concerning the question of how funding may enhance inclusive practices.

NEVILLE HARRIS

# Judging Special Educational Needs: The Contribution of the Courts to the Developing Law of Special Educational Needs in England and Wales

## INTRODUCTION

The law of Special Educational Needs (SEN) in England and Wales aims to ensure that children who have a 'learning difficulty' that gives rise to a need for special educational provision are identified and given appropriate support within the education system (or in some cases outside it). It is a complex and continually evolving field of law, recently amended further by the Special Educational Needs and Disability Act 2001 (the 2001 Act). The present law, contained in the Education Act 1996 and in regulations,[1] originates in legislation enacted 20 years ago – the Education Act 1981 – and retains many of its key elements.

The report upon which the 1981 Act was based, the Warnock Report,[2] estimated that as many as 20% of children of school age had special educational needs, a figure that also reflects the position today ('One in five children – a total of 1.9 million – in England and Wales are considered by their school to have special educational needs').[3] Warnock contemplated that very many of these children could be educated in mainstream settings, including some who have severe learning difficulties and associated disabilities. The law reflected this principle of integration or, as it is now generally described, inclusion. It is a concept which also chimes with the present government's broader policy of promoting inclusiveness in education; and the duty to educate children in mainstream setting has in fact been strengthened under

1 1996 Act Part IV and the Education (Special Educational Needs) (England) (Consolidation) Regulations 2001 (SI 2001/3455).

2 Warnock (Mary) Chair, Special Educational Needs Cmnd 7212 (London: HMSO, 1978).

3 Audit Commission, *Special Educational Needs – A Mainstream Issue* (London: Audit Commission 2002), p. 2.

*Jan De Groof and Gracienne Lauwers (eds.), Special Education*, 11–29.

the 2001 Act.[4] The law of SEN was updated by the Education Act 1993 (now consolidated into the 1996 Act), which introduced the SEN tribunal, extended appeal rights, and provided for a code of practice made by the government, to which all those with responsibilities under the legislation must have regard.[5] The code, a new version of which was introduced in January 2002,[6] provides for a staged process of assessment and provision, beginning (and in the majority of cases ending) with school-based assessment.

Over 80 per cent of pupils with SEN are assessed and provided for by the school (the code calls this 'School Action') or by the school with additional support ('School Action Plus'). Those with the most severe learning difficulties are likely to require a *formal* assessment, conducted by the local education authority (LEA) and based on a range of professional opinions.[7] Parental representations must be considered and the new code of practice stresses that LEAs should also seek the views of the child and should record them as part of the statutory assessment process. But it acknowledges that not all children will be able to contribute and recommends that in relation to those who cannot, an agent – parent, class teacher, educational psychologist or other adult who knows the child – should be approached to ascertain and communicate the child's views.[8] Formal assessment must (s 323 of the 1996 Act) be carried out where a child has SEN and the LEA is of the opinion that that it is 'necessary' for the authority to determine the special educational provision which his or her learning difficulty calls for. Alternatively, a formal assessment must be carried out at the request of the parent in some situations (s 329) or, under an amendment brought into effect in January 2002, at the request of the head teacher or proprietor of the school (s 329A). Again the test is one of necessity.

Following the formal assessment the authority must, if in its view it is necessary to 'determine' the special educational provision the child needs, make a statement of those needs (1996 Act, s 324). The code of practice stresses that the basis for this decision should be whether or not the provision that the child needs can be made from the school's own resources, either with or without intervention from

4 Introducing into the 1996 Act, new ss 316 and 316A and amending the Disability Discrimination Act 1995. As regards the general policy, see DfEE, *SEN and Disability Rights in Education Bill Consultation Document* (London: DfEE, 2000), Annex B, para 20. See also, Disability Rights Task Force, *From Exclusion to Inclusion* (London: DfEE/DRTF, 1999).

5 1996 Act, s 313(2).

6 Department for Education and Skills, *Special Educational Needs Code of Practice* (London: DfES, 2001).

7 This is separate from the new duty to carry out assessments of persons above compulsory school age who have a learning difficulty and who are in the last year of schooling, introduced by the Learning and Skills Act 2000, s 140.

8 *Special Educational Needs Code of Practice*, supra note 4, p. 85, para 7.

a professional service outside the school.[9] The statement would only be needed if the schools' own resources (supplemented, e.g. by a specialist employed by the LEA or health authority, such as a speech therapist) were inadequate. The code recommends that a 'note in lieu' should be recorded if a statement is not made. This note does not have the same legal status as a statement. For parents, and for schools, the attraction of a statement is that it translates a commitment to provide a particular level of support into a specific legal duty.

The proportion of pupils with statements in England has increased from 1.8% of children in 1989 to 3% of the child population of 9.5 million in 2002,[10] or in numerical terms from 140,000 to 275,000 children over this period. In 2000, the rate of increase was reported as slowing over the previous five years.[11] However, it was recently reported that overall expenditure on pupils with statements has increased in LEAs in England and Wales over the past three years by 10 times the rate at which expenditure for non-statemented pupils has increased over this period.[12] Variations in statementing rates across different LEAs are less marked than in the past, when there was less uniformity of approach to the exercise of quite a wide discretion,[13] but tend to reflect socio-economic factors: in London, for example, only 1.4% have statements in wealthy Kensington and Chelsea compared to 4.2% in Tower Hamlets, with its predominance of poorer families.[14] The Audit Commission has recently argued that the variations in statementing rates (including a five-fold variation between LEAs in England and Wales) 'call into question how far SEN reflects the real level of need among pupils, or rather different institutions' ability to respond'.[15] The way that SEN decision-making is resource-driven is reflected in many of the cases coming before the courts where parents have questioned a failure to make a statement or the provision proposed in one (see below).

The statement must be in the required form and contain various information, including the child's educational needs, the required educational and non-education provision and the type of school or other institution (i.e. the placement) that would be appropriate for the child.[16] Many of the disputes in the field of SEN centre on the making of statements and on the contents of statements. The contents are particularly

9 Ibid., p. 2, para 8

10 Audit Commission (2002), supra note 3, p. 6. DfEE, *Statistics of Education: Special Educational Needs in England: January 2000, Issue 09/00* (November 2000), p. 7.

11 DfEE supra note 10, p. 12.

12 Audit Commission, supra note 3, p. 13, para 38.

13 See Audit Commission/HMI, *Getting in on the Act – Provision for Pupils with Special Educational Needs – the National Picture* (London: HMSO, 1992).

14 Supra note 10.

15 Audit Commission (2002) supra note 3, p. 11, para 31.

16 See 1996 Act, s 324(2) and the Education (Special Educational Needs) (Consolidation) Regulations 2001 (SI 2001/3455).

important, for the 1996 Act (s 324) provides that where there is a statement in force then, unless the parents have, in relation to the child's education, made their own 'suitable arrangements' (a term whose meaning has also been in question) the LEA must arrange for the special educational provision specified in it to be made for the child and may arrange for any non-educational provision that is referred to. Moreover, if a particular school is specified in the statement as the appropriate placement, the child must be admitted to the school.[17] Once made the statement will continue until the child leaves school, but the authority may cease to maintain a statement if it considers that it is no longer necessary or may amend a statement. In either case there is a set procedure and a right of appeal.

The general principle of parental involvement was a theme of the Warnock report; and the theme of 'partnership' was carried through into the updated statutory scheme and the code of practice. One aspect of this is before the statement is finalized the parents must be consulted and must be given an opportunity to express a preference for a placement.[18] If the parent instead selects an independent school this duty does not apply but the general principle (in the Education Act 1996, s 9) that children are to be educated in accordance with the wishes of their parents provided that it would be 'compatible with the provision of efficient instruction and training and the avoidance of unreasonable public expenditure' will come into consideration.

As noted above, resources are, in fact, central to many of the disputes arising in this field. LEAs distribute resources to schools to meet the requirements of children with SEN as part of their general delegation of budgets to schools, with the exception of resources for statemented children, for which the authority ring-fences resources in order to meet its statutory requirements. This causes problems for LEAs who want to spend more on children at School Action or School Action Plus but lack the necessary resources because of the need to meet their obligations under statements.[19] One authority which tried to limit the allocation of resources towards the needs of statemented children in order to meet shortfalls across its budget as a whole was held by Collins J in the High Court to have acted unlawfully, because children's statemented needs would not be met.[20] The case illustrates the budgetary pressures faced by LEAs in respect of special educational provision, which involve 'the unenviable task of eking out resources inadequate to meet all the demands upon them'.[21]

17 1996 Act, s 324(5)(b).

18 Ibid., schedule 27: see below.

19 Audit Commission (2002) supra note 3, p. 13, para 38.

20 *R v London Borough of Hillingdon ex parte Governing Body of Queensmead School* [1997] ELR 331. See further H. Bines, 'Special educational needs in the market place', *Journal of Education Policy* (1995), 10(2), 157–171, 159.

21 *Richardson v Solihull Metropolitan Borough Council and the Special Educational Needs Tribunal; White and Another v London Borough of Ealing and the Special Educational Needs Tribunal; Hereford and Worcester County Council v Lane* [1998] E.L.R. 319 (C.A.), per Beldam LJ at 334H–335A.

Resources are also very important where a child's parents want him to be educated at an independent school. Many of these schools have excellent specialist facilities and are approved to take children with SEN. But they are expensive to run and often charge substantial fees which the LEA would have to meet if the school was named in a child's statement. Some parents identify such a school as offering the best hope for maximizing their child's educational attainment. However, LEAs will tend to resist naming them in a statement and argue that they can meet the child's needs in a maintained school. Many disputes revolve around this issue. In 2002, only 4% of pupils with statements in England (and 2% in Wales) were placed in independent schools; of the others, 61% (76% in Wales) were in mainstream schools and 35% (23% in Wales) in special schools or pupil referral units.[22] The proportion attending mainstream schools has increased from 54% in 1995[23] but it is Government policy to promote the inclusion of children with SEN in mainstream schools[24] and a recent Audit Commission report stresses that LEAs need to develop inclusion strategies that 'ensure that all children's needs may be met locally and, as far as possible, in the mainstream sector'.[25]

## THE ROLE OF THE TRIBUNAL AND COURTS

In England and Wales the courts have played a highly significant role in the development of the law relating to SEN and provision. As SEN is an area of considerable conflict, disputes are bound to arise over the meaning and scope of the elaborate legislative framework and the wide discretionary power. Moreover, wider legal principles have become increasingly relevant to disputes – in particular, human rights following incorporation of the European Convention on Human Rights into UK law and the duty of care in respect of negligence in the performance of professional duties in the field of education.[26]

The fact that there is a direct link from the SEN appeals process into the court system in England and Wales – the only area of education decision-making where there is a right of appeal from an appeal panel or tribunal to the court – obviously guarantees judicial involvement. In all other education cases, court action must be pursued via a separate process known as an application for judicial review. As judicial review involves the courts in assessing the legality of actions by government or public official at all conceivable levels – from those of Secretaries of State down to an individual

22 Audit Commission (2002) supra note 3, p. 16, Exhibit 2.

23 DfEE (2000) supra note 10, p. 3.

24 Department for Education and Employment, *Excellence for All Children: Meeting Special Educational Needs* (London: DfEE, 1997).

25 Audit Commission (2002), supra note 3, p. 21, para 55.

26 See N. Harris, 'Liability under education law in the UK – How much further can it go?', *European Journal for Education Law and Policy* (2001), 4, 131–140.

school's head teacher or governing body – the process is subject to conditions to limit access to it and thereby inhibit weakly-grounded claims and undue interference with public administration. These conditions emanate from the statutory rules of procedure (recently updated) mixed with the traditional practices and common law principles developed by the courts. The conditions include seeking and acquiring the court's permission to pursue the application (a filtering process to sift out weak or frivolous cases), a time limit of three months within which to make an application (with extensions rarely granted) and the prior exhaustion of alternative avenues of redress. In judicial review the court may quash a decision that it finds was made unlawfully but will not consider itself able to substitute a decision. Judicial review remains highly important in relation to such dispute areas as exclusion from school, school transport arrangements, local reorganisation of schools and questions of parental choice concerning admission to school, but also in some SEN disputes (see below).[27]

The process whereby special educational needs cases normally find their way into the courts is different, the time limit is less strict and leave is not required. It involves an appeal[28] against a decision of the special educational needs and disability tribunal (SENDIST) (renamed as such by the Special Educational Needs and Disability Act 2001).[29] The tribunal, which has a lawyer chair and two other members, was the subject of a paper given at the ELA conference in Dublin in 1996[30] and a book based on empirical research.[31] An appeal against the SENDIST's decision to the court can only be brought on a point of law. This might imply that the court's role would be limited to discussing the finer points of specific legislative requirements. Certainly that does occur; but often the courts are also concerned with the way that the various decision-makers took account, or failed to take account, of various pieces of factual evidence about a child's needs, including the wishes of parents and the cost of various alternative sets of educational arrangements, such as a school placement.

Either the LEA or the parent may appeal against the decision of the tribunal to the High Court. The case will normally be heard by a single judge. Unlike the tribunal, whose membership comprises two experts on special educational needs sitting with a lawyer as chairman/woman, the judge is unlikely to have any specific expertise in this area of the law, although many judges have acquired considerable

27 See generally, N. Harris, 'Judicial Review and Education', in T. Buck (ed) *Judicial Review and Social Welfare* (London: Pinter, 1998), 1–38; P. Meredith, 'Judicial review and education', in B. Hadfield (ed), *Judicial Review: A Thematic Approach* (Dublin, Gill & Macmillan, 1995), 67–98.

28 Provision for which is made by the Tribunals and Inquries Act 1992s 11, as amended by the Education Act 1993.

29 It was previously known as the Special Educational Needs Tribunal.

30 'Special Educational Needs and Access to Justice – the Role of the Special Educational Needs Tribunal in England and Wales', in J. de Groof (ed) *The Legal Status of Pupils* (Kluwer, 1998), 177–194.

31 N. Harris, *Special Educational Needs and Access to Justice* (Bristol: Jordans, 1997).

knowledge over the past seven years through their regular involvement in cases in this field. With leave, a further appeal may be brought to the Court of Appeal and from there, also with leave, which will only be granted if the case involves a point of wide importance, to the House of Lords. To date only one non-judicial review case on special educational needs has reached the highest court, the House of Lords, the case of *B v London Borough of Harrow and Others*, decided in January 2000.[32] I am excluding the two House of Lords decisions concerning negligence liability in the field of special educational needs, *X (Minors) v Bedfordshire County Council* etc in 1995[33] and *Phelps v London Borough of Hillingdon* etc in 2000[34] which are not relevant to the present discussion.[35] In addition, 10 cases have reached the Court of Appeal via the direct appeal route and around the same number, mostly earlier cases (predating the introduction of that route), via the judicial review.

The jurisdiction of the court is determined with reference to that of the tribunal. The parents of a child may appeal to the tribunal under the Education Act 1996, as amended, in respect of the following decisions:

**Decisions appealable to the SENDIST**

| |
|---|
| **A decision not to make a statement** (s 325) |
| **A decision to make, amend or not to amend a statement** (s 326) The appeal may be against the description of the assessment of SEN, the specified provision or the school, if specified. |
| **Refusal of parent's request for *statemented* child to be further assessed** (s 328) |
| **A refusal to comply with a request by a parent of a child for whom there is *no statement*, that the child's needs be formally assessed** (s 329) |
| **A refusal to comply with a request by the responsible body of a school that the needs of a child's (whether or not the subject of a statement) be formally assessed** (s 329A) |
| **A refusal not to comply with a request for the naming of a different school in a statement of special educational needs** (Schedule 27, para 8) |
| **A decision to cease to maintain a statement** (Schedule 27, para 11); LEA may not cease to maintain a statement until the determination of the appeal: para 11(5) (added by s 6 of 2001 Act) |

32 [2000] ELR 109.

33 [1995] ELR 404; 2 AC 633; [1995] 3 WLR 153; [1995] 3 All ER 353; [1995] 2 FLR 276, HL.

34 [2000] ELR 499; [2000] 3 WLR 776; [2000] 4 All ER 504, HL.

35 For discussion, see supra note 26.

*Table 1:* Number of appeals registered with the SENT, 1994–2001[36]

| *94–95* | *95–96* | *96–97* | *97–98* | *98–99* | *99–00* | *00–01* |
|---|---|---|---|---|---|---|
| Appeals registered | | | | | | |
| 1,170 | 1,622 | 2,051 | 2,191 | 2,412 | 2,463 | 2,728 |

*Table 2:* Appellant success rates for main appeal grounds (2000–01)[37]

| | |
|---|---|
| Refusal to statement | 70% |
| Statement contents | 88% |
| Refusal to assess | 67% |

*Table 3:* Appeals from SENT (SENDIST) to the High Court 1994–2001

| | |
|---|---|
| Appeals lodged | 258 |
| Appeals determined | 86 |
| Appeals in progress | 88 |
| Appeals withdrawn | 77 |

The fact that the number of appeals to the tribunal has increased each year since its inception (see Table 1) has in turn increased the potential involvement of the courts.

The 2001 Act imposes a new duty on LEAs to make and publicise arrangements for the avoidance or resolution of disputes between LEAs/governing bodies and parents.[38] The Government clearly hopes that there will be fewer SEN appeals. That would mean, in turn, a fall in the number of appeals from the SENDIST to the High Court each year. However, the fact that quite a high proportion of appeals to the tribunal are successful (see Table 2) already limits the potential pool of further appeal cases.

The cases which have reached the High Court are shown in Table 3. The figures relate to appeals only and exclude judicial review applications.

There have also been around 50 judicial review cases. Judicial review was used before the direct appeal route was opened up in 1994 and is still used to bring legal challenges in respect of matters not covered by a right of appeal, such as:

- Whether a local education authority was entitled, in order to meet budgetary pressures, to cut funding allocations to schools for non-statemented provision in order to subsidise statemented provision.[39]

36 *Special Educational Needs Tribunal Annual Report 2000–2001* (London: SENT, December 2001).

37 Section 3, inserting s 332B into the 1996 Act.

38 Ibid.

39 *Queensmead* case, supra note 20.

- Whether a local education authority's general policy, under which children with intelligence scores (development quotient) within a set range would not have statements but would instead have provision determined by their school, was unlawful because it limited its discretion in individual cases as to whether to make a statement.[40]
- Whether a district health authority acted lawfully in refusing (on economic grounds) a local education authority's request for assistance for a child requiring speech therapy and physiotherapy.[41]
- Whether a local education authority was obliged to meet the fees for a child to attend an independent school from the date that the statement was made (September 1996) or from the date the tribunal ordered that the statement be amended to name that school (May 1997).[42]
- Whether a local education authority was in breach of its statutory duty to implement a statement amended by order of the special educational needs tribunal to provide for the applicant to be taught by a teacher with experience of working with pupils with autism and communication disorders, the applicant contending that the teacher did not have the requisite experience.[43]

The last of these examples highlights a particularly problematic aspect of the special educational needs adjudication system: there is currently no method of enforcing the decision of the SENDIST other than by separate court action via judicial review procedure. Parliament has responded to the way that some LEAs delay implementation of a tribunal's decision by providing that if the tribunal makes an order the LEA must comply with it within a prescribed period, defined by regulations.[44]

The jurisdiction of the SENDIST now includes complaints of disability discrimination in schools brought under Part 4 of the Disability Discrimination Act 1995. The caseload of the SENDIST is fairly certain to increase as a result. There are separate regulations governing the procedure in such cases. The tribunal's constitution has been changed slightly so that it now comprises a lawyer chairman plus two members with knowledge and experience of SEN or disabilities or both;[45] the members

40 *R v Cumbria County Council ex p NB* [1996] ELR 65, QBD.

41 *R v Brent and Harrow Health Authority ex p London Borough of Harrow* [1997] ELR 187.

42 *R v London Borough of Barnet ex p G* [1998] ELR 281 QBD and CA. The court held that the tribunal's order applied from the latter date.

43 *R v Wandsworth London Borough Council ex p M* [1998] ELR 424, QBD. The court held that on the facts the LEA could not reasonably have concluded that the teacher they appointed had the necessary experience. See also *R v London Borough of Brent and Vassie ex p AF* [2000] ELR 550.

44 Section 336B, added by the 2001 Act. The prescribed period is to be prescribed in regulations. So far, only the Special Educational Needs Tribunal (Time Limits) (Wales) Regulations 2001 (SI 2001/3982) have been made.

45 Special Educational Needs and Disability Tribunal (General Provisions and Disability Claims Procedure) Regulations 2002 (SI 2002/1985), regs 3 and 5.

will be selected for the case in question by the President and disability expertise will clearly be needed in cases concerned wholly or partly with a claim under the 1995 Act. An appellant giving notice of a SEN appeal can request that the appeal be heard together with a disability discrimination claim.[46] Although one of the disjunctive definitions of SEN refers to disability,[47] it is as yet unclear whether discrimination claims are likely to be commonplace additions to SEN appeals or generally pursued as discrete actions.

## THE DEVELOPING CASE LAW

### *Discretion, policy, advocacy and judgment*

The Education Act 1996 provides a legal framework which aims to ensure that a child's SEN and parental aspirations with regard to provision are met, but leaves LEAs a degree of choice and discretion in deciding how this aim should be realized. As mentioned previously, LEAs face resource constraints which limit their capacity in responding to a child's SEN, thereby engendering conflict where parental wishes are not fully met.[48] LEA discretion in individual cases is often constrained by policy goals which demand the careful rationing of limited resources. There is an underlying assumption built into the law that a trade-off is necessary and that needs can only be met up to a particular finite point. On the whole the courts have accepted as a general principle that policy decisions can control the exercise of discretion in individual cases, not least where resources are concerned, unless perhaps the curbing of expenditure is the dominant policy consideration, as in *Queensmead* above (see also *ex p T*[49]).

The law fails to give absolute primacy to parental choice, because it would have a hugely de-stabilising effect on resource allocation. LEAs can deny parental wishes if, for example, they can show that granting them might prejudice 'the efficient use of resources'[50] or that there would be 'unreasonable public expenditure'.[51] Nonetheless, parental activism and advocacy can exercise a powerful influence over

46 Special Educational Needs Tribunal Regulations 2001 (SI 2001/600), reg 7(4) (as substituted by the Special Educational Needs Tribunal (Amendment) Regulations 2002 (SI 2002/2787) reg 5).

47 Educaiton Act 1996 s 312.

48 See further Ann Blair, 'Rights, duties and resources: the case of special educational needs' (2000) 12: 3 *Education & the Law* 177–193; S. Riddell *et al.*, *The Justice Inherent in the assessment of Special Educational Needs in England and Scotland* (Edinburgh: University of Edinburgh, 2001).

49 *R v East Sussex County Council ex p T* [1998] ELR 251; *ex p Tandy* [1998] EdCR 206, HL.

50 1996 Act, s 316 and Sched 27 para 3 (below).

51 1996 Act s 9 (general principle of adhrence to parental wishes as regards the education of their children) and UK reservation to Article 2 Protocol 1 ECHR.

the overall pattern of decision-making and provision in this field, leading to claims by some that it is middle class parents pushing for their children to be statemented that has skewed resource allocation by LEAs in their favour. One must be wary of such a generalization, although there is evidence giving some credence to it. Lange and Riddell[52] explain how research in Scotland revealed that a predominantly middle class group of parents of children with specific learning difficulties were much more likely than other parents to challenge professional judgment. The parents, however, 'felt short-changed by the system' and as though 'prisoners within an unwieldy bureaucratic system which went to great lengths to ignore their requests'.[53] To the education professionals however, this group of parents exerted a powerful, indeed an unhealthily powerful, grip on the system, 'extracting an unfairly large amount of financial support for their particular children to the disadvantage of other groups lacking powerful advocates'.[54]

The law does not make it easy to resolve such tensions between perceptions of needs and required provision to meet them, presenting tribunals and to a lesser extent the courts with a difficult task. The reason why the court's role is less difficult than the tribunal's is that the courts will tend to defer to the tribunal's judgment on such matters, preferring to concentrate on the way that decisions were reached (e.g. juridical questions relating to whether there was sufficient evidence for the approach adopted by the LEA or tribunals, or whether the statute was properly adhered to), rather than substantive issues based on educational and other matters that the court regards as outside its jurisdiction or provenance.

### *Special educational needs and provision*

The courts have been able to clarify the scope of the legislation. It has been held not to apply to higher education,[55] nor most probably to giftedness per se.[56] Over the years the courts have also had to decide whether each of the following factors falls

52 'Special educational needs policy and choice', in M.J. McLaughlin and M. Rouse (eds), *Special Education and School Reform in the United States and Britain* (London: Routledge, 2000), 126–146.

53 Ibid., p. 141.

54 Ibid.

55 *R v Portsmouth City Council ex parte Faludy* [1999] ELR 115, CA, which concerned an intellectually gifted child who, at the age of 15, won a place at Cambridge University; the Court of Appeal held that the LEA had no duty to support his education under the 1996 Act Part IV. The court held that because the Education Act 1996 states that 'nothing in this Act confers any functions with respect to higher education' (s 1(4)), Part IV of the Act (concerning special educational needs) could not apply in respect of a person's attendance at a university.

56 *R v Secretary of State for Education ex p C* [1996] ELR 93; *R v Portsmouth City Council ex p F* [1998] ELR 619.

within the definition of a special educational need: dyslexia (yes);[57] a need for speech therapy (generally yes);[58] a child's religion and culture (no);[59] and a child's difficult domestic circumstances (no, unless there was a direct relationship between the circumstances and the learning difficulty).[60] As the statutory definition of special educational needs refers to a need that requires 'special educational provision', the latter phrase has also received judicial consideration. Neither provision of a lift to provide access to a classroom or of a nurse to ensure proper medical supervision of a pupil amounted to special educational provision,[61] whereas a combination of occupational therapy, speech therapy and physiotherapy could be.[62]

The last of these cases, in the Court of Appeal, reveals much about the problems of trying to establish legal certainty in a field where there is still a diversity of approach and practice, despite an attempt to increase uniformity through a national code of practice, referred to earlier, where the nature and extent of educational needs is so wide and where provision may not necessarily be exclusively educational. The pupil concerned, aged 12, had multiple physical disabilities and could do nothing for himself, not even sitting up or standing. The parents disagreed with the LEA about placement. They considered that his special school, maintained by the LEA, was not meeting his needs. They preferred a specialist independent residential school, but that would have cost the LEA an extra £20,000 per year. The question was whether the boy's needs for physiotherapy, occupational therapy and speech therapy were educational needs and should be recorded as such in his statement. The tribunal found that a need for physiotherapy, occupational therapy and speech therapy might at least in part be an educational need. In the Court of Appeal, Sedley LJ said that Parliament had deliberately chosen to provide for flexibility as opposed to a rigid categorisation which might have been 'productive of far more doubt, dispute and litigation than what I would hold to be the method of Parliament's choice'.[63] He said that some provision was 'unequivocally educational' and some 'unequivocally non-educational', but in other cases provision could be classed as educational or non-educational and it was left to the LEA or the SENDIST 'to exercise a case-by-case judgment which no prescriptive legislation could ever hope to anticipate'.[64] Sedley LJ's reasoning is faultless but shows that it may be unrealistic to expect the courts to provide truly definitive

57 *R v Hampshire Education Authority ex p J* (1985) 84 LGR 547, QBD.

58 *R v Lancashire CC ex p CM (A Minor)* [1989] 2 FLR 279, CA.

59 *G v London Borough of Barnet and the SENT* [1998] ELR 480.

60 *G v Wakefield Metropolitan Borough Council*, 29 January, 1998 (unreported).

61 *R v London Borough of Lambeth ex p MBM* [1995] ELR 374; *City of Bradford Metropolitan Council v A* [1997] ELR 417, QBD.

62 *Bromley London Borough Council v Special Educational Needs Tribunal* [1999] ELR 260, CA.

63 Ibid., at 296E.

64 Ibid., at 295G–296A.

guidance on matters of substance. The code of practice, where one might expect to find more specific definitional guidance, adds little other than to confirm that speech therapy should normally be regarded as educational provision,[65] itself merely reflecting an earlier Court of Appeal decision to that effect.[66]

*Assessment and statements of special educational needs*

The above view is also manifested in the approach taken to the decisions on whether to carry out a formal assessment or on whether a statement of special educational needs should be made or ceased. In both cases the LEAs' duty to act is dependent on their opinion that it is 'necessary' to do so.[67] In *H v Kent County Council and the Special Educational Needs Tribunal*[68] Grigson J endorsed the conclusions of the European Commission of Human Rights in *Simpson v United Kingdom* in 1989,[69] where (in relation to a dispute over school placement) the Commission recognised that 'there must be a wide measure of discretion left to the appropriate authorities as to how to make the best use possible of the resources available to them in the interests of disabled children generally'. The Commission also noted that while weight should be placed by the authorities on parents' and pupils' views, Article 2 of Protocol 1 (which requires the state in exercising education functions to respect the right of parents to ensure education and teaching in conformity with their own religious and philosophical convictions) did not compel the state to support, by paying fees, the placing of a dyslexic child in a private specialized school when a suitable place was available in an ordinary school with special teaching facilities. The court in H accepted that the LEA had been entitled to refuse to conduct a statutory assessment of a 10-year-old girl with epilepsy, and the tribunal was entitled to uphold the decision on the basis 'appropriate special educational provision is made, and will continue to be made ... from within the resources available to her school'.

In another recent case[70] the parents appealed against the LEA's refusal to make a statement in respect of their 9-year-old child and the tribunal ordered the authority to reconsider. The authority did reconsider and still decided not to make a statement. The court held that there was no further right of appeal[71] in respect of that reconsideration. Maurice Kay J, adopting established judicial reasoning,[72] referred to the

65 Supra note 6, p. 49, para 8.

66 *R v Lancashire County Council ex p CM (A Minor)* [1989] 2 FLR 279, CA.

67 Education Act 1996 ss 323(1), (2) and 324(1).

68 [2000] ELR 660.

69 (1989) 64 DR 188.

70 *O v London Borough of Harrow and Another*, 12 July 2001 [2001] EWHC Admin 542.

71 Under s 325 of the 1996 Act.

72 Especially *R v Secretary of State for Education and Science ex p Lashford* [1988] 1 FLR 72, CA.

way that the necessity test permits the LEA or tribunal to avoid making a statement following an assessment and considered that there were no grounds for interfering with the authority's decision the child's needs could be met through the resources available to his school. The courts therefore continue to recognise the wide discretion resting with by LEAs (guided now by the code of practice, to which regard must be had) when it comes to judging whether the evidence produced by the assessment process, including any representations made by parents, fulfils the test of necessity (i.e. that it is necessary for special educational provision to be determined, requiring a statement).[73]

Generally, then, the courts have acknowledged that the statutory scheme for SEN must be operated by LEAs on the basis of flexibility and financial reality. Yet there must be limits to this flexibility, particularly in the case of statements of SEN. A statement must, inter alia, 'specify the special educational provision to be made for the purpose of meeting [the child's] needs'.[74] Specificity becomes a key issue as parents press for clearly specified provision in the statement, in order to benefit from the LEA's conditional duty[75] to 'arrange that the special educational provision specified in the statement is made for the child' unless the child's parent has made 'suitable arrangements'.[76] LEAs, on the other hand, prefer to keep the statement vague, ostensibly to leave more scope for flexibility in meeting needs, but equally to share more discretion over resource allocation. The regulations provide no real guidance on specificity, requiring the statement to 'specify (a) any appropriate facilities and equipment, staffing arrangements and curriculum ...',[77] while the code of practice states that 'Provision should normally be quantified (e.g. in terms of hours of provision, staffing arrangements) although there will be cases where some flexibility should be retained in order to meet the changing special educational needs of the child concerned'.[78]

The code therefore establishes a presumption as to a reasonably high degree of specificity, but permits a degree of flexibility if the circumstances warrant it. Arguably

73 *R v Secretary of State for Education and Science ex p L* [1988] 1 FLR 72 and *R v Isle of Wight County Council ex p RS* [1993] 1 FLR 634.

74 Education Act 1996, s 324(3)(b).

75 Education Act 1996, s 324(5).

76 On the meaning of 'suitable arrangements', see *R v Governors of Hasmonean High School ex p N and E* [1994] ELR 343, CA; *G v London Borough of Barnet and the Special Educational Needs Tribunal* [1998] ELR 480, QBD; *White and Another v London Borough of Ealing and the Special Educational Needs Tribunal; Richardson v Solihull Metropolitan Borough Council; Solihull Metropolitan Borough Council v Finn and the Special Educational Needs Tribunal* [1998] ELR 203, QBD; and *R v London Borough of Hackney ex p GC* [1995] ELR 144, QBD and [1996] ELR 142, CA.

77 Education (Special Educational Needs) (England) (Consolidation) Regulations 2001 (SI 2001/3455), Sched between Sched 2.

78 *Special Educational Needs Code of Practice* (2001), op. cit., p. 37, para 8.

this reflects the judicial guidance on this matter, which commenced with a decision 10 years ago by the Court of Appeal[79] to the effect that a statement would be deficient if the educational provision specified in one of its sections did not adequately address each one of the needs specified in another section. The courts subsequently refined that approach to stress that: line-by-line matching up was not required;[80] LEAs could compensate for any vagueness in the statement by furnishing further evidence as to what provision it proposed to make;[81] and it might be justifiable not to specify the hours of support (such as speech therapy) because children's needs could be met in a variety of ways.[82] The crucial test that has emerged is whether the statement 'is so specific and so clear as to leave no room for doubt as to what has been decided is necessary in the individual case', which may not be possible without specifying the number of hours of specialist support per week.[83] As Stanley Burnton J said in a recent decision,[84] 'Provision might be "specific" although unquantified'. What was sufficiently specific would depend upon the facts of each case, he said. In another recent case[85] the tribunal had approved provision stated as one hour of specialist support from the LEA's learning support service, with the teacher to be appropriately qualified for such support work, the input to be a structured apprenticeship or shared approach to develop the child's contextual reading strategies, and a variety of other specified support and learning methodologies. The court held that the provision was adequately specified in the statement and well understood by everyone and that it would have been bureaucratic to set it out in every detail.

On the face of it, LEAs also have quite a wide discretion when deciding on a placement for the child. But here it is subject to parental rights. Parental wishes are a factor to be considered, but are no more than that, when deciding on a mainstream placement for a statemented child.[86] They cannot override the duty to educate the child in a mainstream school if the LEA has decided that such a school will provide a suitable education. Nonetheless, there is a separate duty on the LEA, when it

79 [1992] 1 FLR 377.

80 *Re L* [1994] ELR 16 at 22, *per* Leggatt LJ, CA.

81 See *Joyce v Dorset County Council* [1997] ELR 26; *C v SENT* [1997] ELR 390 and *B v Isle of Wight* [1997] ELR 279, QBD.

82 *R v Cumbria County Council ex p P* [1995] 337 at 348D–E; *J v Devon County Council and Strowger* [2001] EWHV Admin 958.

83 *L v Clarke and Somerset CC* [1998] ELR 129, QBD, per Laws J at 136, applied in *H v Leicestershire County Council* [2000] ELR 471, QBD; *S v City and Council of Swansea* [2000] ELR 315, QBD; *R (on the application of W) v Bedfordshire County Council ex p B* [2001] ELR 645, QBD; *E v Rotherham Metropolitan Borough Council* [2002] ELR 266.

84 *E v LB Newham and SENT* [2002] ELR 453, QBD, at paras 36 and 37.

85 *E v Flintshire CC and the SENT* [2002] 378, QBD.

86 *L v Hereford and Worcester County Council and Hughes* [2000] ELR 375, QBD; *L v Worcestershire County Council and Hughes* [2000] ELR 674, CA. See also Education Act s 316 above.

makes or amends a statement, to include the name of the maintained school (but not an independent or private school) selected by the parents unless either (a) 'the school is unsuitable to the child's age, ability or aptitude or to his special educational needs', or (b) 'the attendance of the child at the school would be incompatible with the provision of efficient education for the children with whom he would be educated or with the efficient use of resources'.[87] Following amendments made by the 2001 Act, the LEA can seemingly ignore the duty to ensure a mainstream placement, if it accepts that it has a duty to meet parental choice. In other words, the LEA can agree to a non-mainstream school despite the inclusion duty. If, however, the LEA decides to deny parental choice under (a) or (b) above, it must nonetheless comply with the conditional duty (above) to ensure a mainstream placement.[88]

The House of Lords held that the 'resources' in question for the purposes of (b) are those of the LEA in which the child resides.[89] So if the parents select a school in a neighbouring LEA's area, the LEA of residence (which is the one responsible for the child under the legislation) may consider the impact on its own resources of meeting the additional cost of the child's attendance at another authority's school. In a separate judgment, the High Court held that a school named in a statement has a mandatory duty to admit a child irrespective of whether it is in the area of the LEA with responsibility for the child.[90]

The cost of a placement at an independent school will generally exceed that of a placement at a maintained school, whether a special school catering for pupils with SEN or a mainstream school. If the parents want their child to attend an independent school the parental choice provisions above do not apply. The only rights which may be invoked are contained in the Education Act 1996, s 9, which lays down a general principle, noted above, that 'children are to be educated in accordance with the wishes of their parents', provided the parent's wishes would be compatible with the provision of 'efficient instruction and training and the avoidance of unreasonable public expenditure'. In a series of judgments the courts have held that parental wishes must be taken into account but need not prevail if the independent school placement, which, like the mainstream placement, is adequate, involves significant additional expenditure[91] – perhaps a difference in annual costs[92] as small as £2,000. The same is true if, costs being equal, the school preferred by the LEA is clearly the more

87 1996 Act, Sched 27 para 3(3).

88 See ibid., s 316A(4).

89 *B v London Borough of Harrow* [2000] ELR 109.

90 *R v Chair of Governors and Head Teacher of A and S School ex p T* [2000] ELR 274.

91 *Surrey County Council v P and P* [1997] ELR 516, QBD, per Kay J at 523C.

92 Which means the cost for which the LEA itself would be responsible: *S v Somerset County Council*, 25 July 2002, Administrative Court (unreported).

suitable.[93] Latham J said in one case that if the tribunal found the placement proposed by the LEA to be more suitable, it was entitled to regard parental preference as 'of little significance'.[94] Parental preference is therefore only likely to sway the matter if both the costs and the quality of provision in the two schools are equal.[95] The courts have also held that if costs are unequal but so are the educational benefits of the respective placements, a balancing act will be necessary: the question will be whether expenditure on the additional cost of a particular placement is justified because of the relative educational advantages of that placement.[96]

### *The impact of human rights*

Human rights arguments have also been raised in connection with school placement, especially since the incorporation of the European Convention on Human Rights into UK law following the Human Rights Act 1998 (in force 2 October 2000), but the courts have been unsupportive. The Act requires the courts to act consistently with the Convention and to have regard to established Strasbourg jurisprudence. Arguments that Article 2 of Protocol 1 requires parental beliefs in the importance of inclusive (mainstream) education to be respected to the extent that they curtail the discretion of the state were rejected by the Commission of Human Rights,[97] despite the growing weight of opinion in favour of inclusive education. In a case before the English courts in October 1999[98] it was argued that the Article gave the parents a right to veto a mainstream placement where it conflicted with their religious and philosophical convictions. Carnwath J said that there were 'very sincere and practical reasons why [the mother] feels as strongly as she does, but they have nothing to do with a religious or philosophical opposition to mainstream schools. They are concerned, very properly and understandably, with practical concerns about the day to day needs and education of her child.'[99] Recently, in *T v Special Educational Needs Tribunal and Wiltshire County Council*,[100] Richards J refused to consider an argument, raised before the court but not previously, that the tribunal's decision breached

93 *S and S v Bracknell Forest Borough Council and the Special Educational Needs Tribunal* [1999] ELR 51, per Scott Baker J.

94 *W-R v Solihull Metropolitan Borough Council and Wall* [1999] ELR 528 at 543D–E.

95 *C v Buckinghamshire County Council and the Special Educational Needs Tribunal* [1999] ELR 179, CA, per Thorpe LJ at 189F–G.

96 *Oxfordshire County Council v GB and others* [2002] ELR 8, CA.

97 *PD and LD v United Kingdom* (1989) 62 D.R. 292; *Graeme v United Kingdom* (1990) 64. D.R. 158; *Klerks v Netherlands* (1995) 82 D.R. 41. See also *W and KL v Sweden* (1983) Application No 14688/83, *Simpson v United Kingdom* (1989) above; *Cohen v United Kingdom* (1996) 21 E.H.R.R. CD 104.

98 *L v Hereford and Worcester County Council and Hughes* [2000] ELR 375.

99 Ibid., at 384D–E.

100 [2002] ELR 704, QBD.

their Protocol 1 Art 2 right to have their philosophical convictions (supporting inclusive education) upheld. He said that even if he had been prepared to consider the matter, he did not accept that a commitment to mainstream, inclusive education amounted to such a conviction.

A further human rights argument which has been raised concerns Article 8 of the Convention, which provides for respect for privacy and family life, although (in Article 8(2)) permits interference with this right in so far as it is necessary in the interests of national security, public safety or the economic well-being of the country, the prevention of crime, the protection of health or morals or the protection of the rights and freedoms of others. In *CB v London Borough of Merton and Special Educational Needs Tribunal*[101] the parents invoked Article 8 in challenging the LEA's decision to place their child, who suffered from bilateral sensory hearing loss, in a boarding school, away from his family. The court held that such a placement was prime facie an interference with family life for the purposes of Article 8, but that it was justified (within the terms of Art 8(2)) if the tribunal considered that the school put forward by the LEA, and no other mentioned, would meet the child's needs.

## CONCLUSION

In the course of recent judgments on negligence in the context of professional duties concerning SEN, the courts have shown an acute awareness of the importance of an effective response to children's learning difficulties.[102] Yes their involvement in adjudicating disputes arising from decisions under the statutory framework has not resulted in any shift in the balance of rights and responsibilities among the relevant actors. LEAs' discretion continues to be significant, despite the additional regulation imposed by the 2001 Act. Human rights arguments advanced by parents have not prospered, while the legitimacy of cost and resource-based decision-making has met with little judicial interference.

The courts have nonetheless carefully picked over the complex minutiae of this area of the law, demonstrating, in the course of their clarification of provisions of often ambiguous or uncertain meaning, a laudable sensibility with regard to professional practice and educational theory, despite their deference to the specialist knowledge and expertise of the SENDIST, LEAs, and teachers. Not all the judicial interpretations have met with approval from practitioners or academics, but they nonetheless demand the attention of decision-makers. On the whole, they have brought about greater certainty, but there are some parts of the statutory framework that have been stubbornly resistant to attempts at judicial clarification, notably the

[101] [2002] ELR 441, QBD.

[102] See for example Lords Slynn and Clyde in *Phelps v London Borough of Hillingdon* [2000] ELR 499 at 514D and 533D–E, respectively.

question of the specificity of statements of SEN and the pivotal educational/non-educational distinction.

The benefits of this degree of judicial involvement, and one should include the tribunal (which has 'proved its worth'[103]) as well as the court here, also include the subjection of LEAs' decision-making in individual cases to external, legal accountability in a way that is unequalled in any other area of educational practice in the UK. Although effective utilisation of redress mechanisms is not equally distributed across the social spectrum, the courts and tribunals are guaranteeing a degree of procedural justice, promoting or ensuring a degree of 'fair play' in the context of the increasingly numerous disputes in this important field of education law, policy and practice.

[103] *O v London Borough of Harrow and Sherwin* [2002] ELR 195, CA, per Sedley LJ at para 30.

ANN BLAIR[1]

# Special Educational Needs and Disability Discrimination: New Departures in Education Law in England and Wales: Rights of Children with Disabilities in the UK

## 1. Introduction

The current approach to meeting Special Educational Needs (SEN) in England and Wales was inspired by the Warnock Report of 1979 and introduced by the *Education Act 1981*.[2] The legislation provided a framework for the identification and assessment of SEN and gave pupils with serious or complex needs the right to resources necessary to address their learning difficulties. Subject to important qualifications, it also introduced a presumption in favour of the education of pupils with special needs being in mainstream schools.

Whatever rights pupils with SEN have had under the regime introduced by the *1981 Act*, these have fell short of a right of pupils not to be discriminated against because of any disability they might suffer. For many years, this lack of protection for disabled people was replicated across most areas of life. Between 1979 and 1995 there were 14 separate attempts to introduce effective disability discrimination provisions, but it was only in 1994, with a shrinking majority, that the government of the day relented. When it had begun to look as though a private members Bill the *Civil Rights (Disabled Persons) Bill* would succeed, the government were unable to ignore the demand for reform and agreed to introduce a government sponsored Bill in return for its withdrawal.[3] This was enacted as the *Disability Discrimination Act*

1 Department of Law, University of Leeds, LS2 9JT.

2 This was updated by the *Education Act 1993* and consolidated in *the Education Act 1996* which is itself updated by *SENDA* and remains the source of the primary legislation.

3 Gooding, C (1996) *Blackstones Guide to the Disability Discrimination Act 1995* Oxford: Blackstone Press. A House of Lords Bill, sponsored by Lord Ashley of Stoke, which aimed to update the *DDA* in 2002, has suffered the same fate as the pre 1995 attempts to get reforms through Parliament using private members Bills.

*Jan De Groof and Gracienne Lauwers (eds.), Special Education*, 31–50.

*1995* (*DDA*), but unlike the sex and race discrimination provisions of domestic legislation, the Act did not include individual rights to complain of disability discrimination in education. Monitoring and reporting requirements were included, but it seems to have been assumed the needs of disabled pupils would be met adequately through the SEN provisions of education law.

This paper assesses the extent to which the provisions of the *Special Educational Needs and Disability Act 2001 (SENDA)* have addressed the limitations of the law it amends.[4] In order to assess the impact of the new legislation this paper adopts an analysis based on a number of deficits identified within the system for meeting the needs of disabled pupils and those with SEN before *SENDA* came into force. These are (a) an inclusion deficit, (b) a participation deficit, (c) a consistency deficit, and (d) an enforcement deficit. It considers the extent to which the new legislation, new codes of practice and other measures have addressed these deficits and considers some issues that remain outstanding.[5] Before it does this, we need a brief explanation of how the system works.

## 2. THE SYSTEM OF SEN PROVISION

*The SEN legislation is found in* Part IV *of the* Education Act 1996 (*hereafter the* 1996 Act). *This provides that where children have learning difficulties*[6] *they are owed a series of duties by the Local Education Authority (LEA), the school, headteacher, teachers and the governing body. Together these duties should ensure that needs are identified and addressed within the school at the early stages and that where needs are serious or complex the needs are made subject to formal assessment by the LEA. Formal assessment may be requested by the school or the child's parent. Parents have various rights of appeal against decisions the LEA makes as part of the statementing procedure.*[7] *Where the assessment identifies the need for a formal statement of these needs the statement should specify in some detail what the needs are and what resources, above those normally provided for a child of this age, are necessary to meet them. Once a statement has been produced, LEAs are under a duty to fulfill the terms of the statement.*[8] *Schools are under a less onerous obligation to use their best endeavours to ensure that any child attending the school*

4 Brief accounts of the effect of *SENDA* can be found in Hay, D. The Special Educational Needs and Disability Act 2001 [2001] ELJ 72 and Linden, T. "Disability Discrimination in Education: The New Law" [2002] ELJ 82.

5 *SENDA* also extends the provisions of the *DDA* to post-16 education as *ss 28R* to *28Q DDA*. Consideration of this is outside the scope of this paper.

6 Defined below.

7 Discussed below.

8 *Section 324(5)(a)(i)*.

*receives the special educational provision that their learning difficulty calls for.*[9] *A child with a formal statement has a right to the resources specified in the statement, which can be enforced by judicial review if necessary.*[10]

The statutory duties are supplemented by regulation, and since 1994 the duties have been filled out by a statutory Code of Practice, which the LEA and the governing body must have regard to. The 1994 Code of Practice[11] set out five stages for assessment, 3 school-based and 2 involving the LEA in the formal assessment of needs.

There are strict time limits for the statutory assessment and statementing procedure. These are designed to ensure that once the need to consider formal assessment is identified the child does not have to wait indefinitely to receive the provision that their learning difficulty calls for.[12]

The revised SEN provisions of *SENDA* came into force in January 2002. At the same time new regulations[13] and a new Code of Practice on SEN were also introduced.[14] This was necessary for two reasons, first to ensure that the new law was adequately reflected in the guidance, but also to address concerns that the system as applied until then concentrated too many resources on meeting needs as compared with resources devoted to preventing SEN arising in the first place.

## 3. Deficits within the pre–2001 system for meeting special educational needs

What then were the problems within the SEN system that called for the radical overhaul that is found in *SENDA* and its associated regulations and codes?

### *(a) The inclusion deficit*

The *1996 Act*, which contains the SEN, continues to provide in *s316* that, subject to certain conditions the child

> is to be educated in a school which is not a special school unless that is compatible with the wishes of his parent.

9 *Section 317(1).*

10 *R v Hillingdon London Borough Council ex parte Queensmead School* (The Times 9 January 1997), *Bromley London Borough Council* v *SENT* [1999] 3 All ER 587.

11 DfE (1994) *Code of Practice on the Identification and Assessment of Special Educational Needs.*

12 *The Education (Special Educational Needs) Regulations 1994* SI 1994/1047.

13 *Education (Special Educational Needs) (Consolidation) Regulations 2001* SI 2001/3455.

14 DfES (2001) *Special Educational Needs Code of Practice 2001* available at http://www.dfes.gov.uk/sen/viewDocument.cfm?dID=260.

Prior to 2001 this was subject to certain conditions: that this was compatible with the child receiving the special education which his or her learning difficulty calls for[15] and that inclusion was compatible with the efficient use of resources and the efficient education of other pupils.[16] Following the decision in *Burridge v Harrow LBC*,[17] the resources in question are those of the LEA itself, placing pupils with SEN at a disadvantage with other pupils who are in a better position to obtain a place at a school maintained by another LEA. However, where the preferred school is over-subscribed, the provisions that guarantee parents a place for their child at the school named in the statement place the parents of pupils with SEN at an advantage over parents of pupils who are not "statemented".[18]

Nevertheless, under this system parental wishes could override a pupil's right to inclusion in the mainstream.[19] Parents could not insist on a place at a special school paid for by the LEA where this was not necessary to address the child's learning difficulties.[20] Nevertheless, if parents' wish for their child to attend a special school, the LEA had no power to prevent this where they believed the child's best interests would be served by a mainstream place.[21] In this way parental choice has taken precedence over the child's right to inclusion and to professional assessment of the welfare of the child.

### *(b) The participation deficit*

If any right of the child to inclusion cannot in any real sense be said to belong to the pupil because it is contingent up on their parents' preferences, prior to 2001 the legal rights of pupils to participate in SEN decisions that affected them were also very limited. Nothing in legislation before 2001 required the child's view to be obtained as part of the statementing process. Only a single paragraph in the 1994 Code refers to securing the child's views and appending these to the draft statement where they had been obtained. This came nowhere close to suggesting that a child of sufficient maturity should have his or her views taken into consideration as a matter of course.

This deficit also extends to the child's ability to participate in the appeal process. Under the pre-*SENDA* system appeals could be made to the Special Education Needs

15 *Section 316(2)(a).*

16 *Sections 316(2)(b)* and *312(2)(c).*

17 [2000] 1 WLR 223.

18 *Schedule 27, para 3* provides that the statement shall name the parents preferred school unless the school is unsuitable for the child or incompatible with the proven efficient education of other children, and *section 324(5)(b)* states that if the school is named in the statement the child shall be admitted.

19 *Section 316(1) EA 1996.*

20 *Richardson v Solihull MBC* [1998] ELR 319.

21 Ibid.

Tribunal (SENT) in a variety of circumstances, but the child had no appeal rights independent of his or her parents, and under the 1994 regulations governing the procedure to be followed at appeal the child had little in the way of rights to appear before the SENT either.[22]

### *(c) Consistency deficits*

There are many areas where the rights of the child in the SEN system are inconsistent with rights in the *DDA*. Three areas are explored here: inconsistency in definitions and the coverage of rights; inconsistency in approaches to justification between the two systems and inconsistency in duties to take positive steps to address SEN and disability.

First consistency in definitions. Since 1995 disabled persons[23] have been protected from discrimination in employment and in the provision of goods and services. However, paradoxically those with disability were not entitled to protection from discrimination in the education system that will give access to the knowledge, experience, skills and qualifications that will enable them to compete with others in the jobs market and through this give access to many goods and services. Thus prior to *SENDA* a school or LEA might be under a duty to make adjustments to accommodate the needs of a disabled teacher or ancillary worker, or to provide auxiliary aids or services for a person attending a leisure class in the school but would not be required to make the same adjustment for a disabled pupil.[24] This fundamental point more than any other made the case for extending the provisions of the *DDA* to education unanswerable. This can be characterised as a deficit in consistency of treatment.

In leaving education outside the scope of the *DDA* it seems to have been assumed that most needs would be met through SEN provisions. However there are further inconsistencies in the differences between the scope of the two sets of provisions that mean this is not guaranteed to be the case. First, it is certainly not true that all needs of disabled pupils could be met by the SEN system because the definitions of who falls within the scope of the protection of the provisions are different.

*Section 1(1) DDA*, which has applied to all parts of the Act as it was originally brought into force, defines disability as:

> a physical or mental impairment, which has a substantial and long term effect on his or her ability to carry out normal day-to-day activities

22 A recent discussion can be found in Monk, D. (2002) "Children's Rights in Education – making sense of contradictions." *Child and Family Law Quarterly* 14: 45–56. A detailed account is available in Harris, N. (1997) *Special Educational Needs and Access to Justice*. Jordans: Bristol.

23 Within the meaning of the *DDA*.

24 Part II of the *DDA* relates to employment, Part III to goods and services.

A disabled person is defined as a person who has such a disability, s. 1(2). This definition will include most of the conditions that will commonly be recognised as disabling learning difficulties, psychiatric and psychological disorders as well as physical impairments. Blindness, partial sightedness and deafness will always be covered where the cause is organic.[25] Chronic fatigue syndrome (ME or post-viral syndrome)[26] has been recognised as falling within the scope of the *DDA*. The definition is modified in that the Act adds some conditions to the scope of the definition that would not be caught by the basic definition.[27] Regulations and the schedules to the Act exclude other conditions that might otherwise be caught by the basic definition.[28] Mental impairment that is the result of mental illness is only recognised if it is a "clinically well-recognised illness". Tendency to set fires, tendency to steal, tendency to physical and sexual abuse of others, exhibitionism and voyeurism are all excluded.[29] The impairment must have an effect on "normal day-to-day" activities.[30] The impairment must also have "substantial and long-term effects". This has been said to require something more than trivial, but does not mean very large.[31] The effect must also be "long term". This means something lasting for 12 months or more, or likely to last for at least 12 months, or for the remainder of the life of the person affected.[32]

25 Following *Staffordshire University v Morgan* [2002] IRLR 190 where a disability has a psychological cause it must result from a "clinically well-recognised" condition. See also *Goodwin v The Patent Office* [1999] IRLR 4.

26 *O'Neill v Symm & Co.* [1998] IRLR 233.

27 This includes severe facial disfigurement and conditions that have been corrected (except for sight defects that are corrected by spectacles or contact lenses), *schedule 1*, and certain past disabilities, *s 2* and *schedule 2*. See *Greenwood v BA* [1999] IRLR 600.

28 *Schedule 1*.

29 As is any form of addiction **except** where it is the result of administering medically prescribed drugs or other medical treatment.

30 *Goodwin v The Patent Office* It has been recognised that just because a person can carry out activities it does not mean that the ability to do so has not been impaired *Goodwin v The Patent* Office. However a man who could not lift heavy weights at work following heart surgery did not come within the definition because he was capable of lifting everyday objects. *Quinlan v B&Q* (1999). (Lawtel)

31 *Goodwin v The Patent* Office.

32 The *DDA* also covers progressive conditions, but only from the point where the condition has some effect. In cases such as Cancer, Muscular Dystrophy, Multiple Sclerosis or AIDS, protection of the Act is available as soon as any symptoms appear. It does not matter if the effects are not yet substantial. Nevertheless this does not protect sufferers while symptom free. Conditions such as HIV infection are likely to attract discrimination even though the sufferer may be symptom free for a long period or even indefinitely, this is not covered. Equally the Act is incapable of addressing discrimination against those with a genetic pre-disposition to a condition.

By way of contrast the definitions of disability and learning difficulty in the *1996 Act* are much less detailed. A child is defined as having SEN if he or she has a learning difficulty that calls for special educational provision to be made for him or her. A child has this learning difficulty if he or she;

(a) has a significantly greater difficulty in learning than the majority of children of the same age; or
(b) has a disability, which either prevents or hinders the child from making use of educational facilities of a kind provided for children of the same age in schools within the area of the LEA.[33]

*Section 312(2) Education Act 1996*
The definition of SEN does refer to disability, but this relates to disability that impedes access to educational facilities not in carrying out day-to-day activities. Given this, and the detailed scope of the *DDA* definition, there is little doubt that many individuals that are covered by that legislation will fall outside the scope of the SEN provisions. Equally the artificial exclusions of some disability (particularly the anti-social disorders) from the *DDA* would be unlikely to prevent a child being seen as having SEN if they arise in that context. SEN clearly covers not just physical and mental impairments but also specific learning difficulties, some of which might not be covered under the *DDA*,[34] and behavioural disorders which might not be seen as a consequence of physical or mental impairment. This lack of coherence between the provisions creates difficulties in ensuring a seamless fit between the provisions of the *DDA* and those of the SEN system.

The second area of inconsistency concerns approaches to justification. A justification defence is available in all claims of disability discrimination. How does this compare with the contingencies which apply to inclusion in education through the SEN provisions?

The *DDA* provides that there is no discrimination although the disabled person has been treated less favourably,

> if and only if the reason for it is both material to the circumstances of the particular case and substantial.[35]

Thus an employer can refuse an otherwise well-qualified applicant a post, or promotion etc. for reasons such as health and safety, attendance at work or the ability to carry out the work in question. If the reason is to be material to the circumstances it

[33] Plus certain children under the age of 5 and under the age of 2. Difficulties based solely on differences between the home language and the language the child is taught in are not to be regarded as learning difficulties.

[34] For example, the highly intelligent pupil with dyslexia who is not significantly disabled by the impairment.

[35] *Sections 5(1)(b), 5(2) and 5(3).*

must be based on the circumstances of the particular case, which means that there should be an individual assessment based on sound evidence. Substantial evidence suggests a high threshold. It has been suggested that this must relate to something important to the employer's needs, but in fact has been interpreted as meaning something less than minor or trivial.[36] In goods and services provisions less favourable treatment can be justified where the provider holds a reasonable opinion that one of a variety of circumstances applies.[37] Where the discrimination arises from a failure to adjust policies, practice or procedures; to alter a physical feature of property; or to provide auxiliary goods and services as required by *s 21* (discussed below) this is justified only where failure to take such steps is reasonable.

There is no directly analogous parallel to this approach to justification in SEN provision. However, clearly the assessments of SEN are contingent on two things, the professional judgments about the degree of need and the provision necessary to meet it. Not all interventions that might be possible must be put in place. It is submitted that in the course of the professional assessments that are made about whether needs are established and what resources are necessary to meet them, questions of justification are relevant, even where not articulated consciously. Inclusion rights are also contingent on the factors discussed at (a) above. Questions of efficiency and impact on other pupils will justify differential treatment of pupils with SEN, so clearly questions of justification do infect the system even if not spelled out explicitly. The question is whether, given that the point is not made explicit, resources are withheld only if the reason for withholding them is "both material to the circumstances of the particular case and substantial" and whether reasonableness within the meaning of the *DDA* is to be understood in the same way that unreasonable withholding of resources would be understood within the SEN system. In fact as we have seen the threshold of materiality in the justification defence has been set quite low. In addition it has been held in employment cases that the question of reasonableness in employment is to be assessed according to the knowledge of the employer. As long as the employer has sufficient basis on which to make a judgment the tribunal is not free to substitute its own opinion.[38] By way of contrast, one can deduce from general principles of public law that SEN resources may only be withheld where this is reasonable, but the standard by which this is judged is not the same as materiality and substantiality and would be more difficult to challenge.[39]

The final area where questions of consistency arise is in the context of duties to take positive steps to address disability discrimination and in relation to the provision

[36] Doyle, B. (1996) *Disability Discrimination Law and Practice 2nd. ed.* Jordans: Bristol *c.f. Heinz v Kenrick* [2000] IRLR 144. See Linden, T. *op. cit.*

[37] Found in *s 20(4)*.

[38] *Jones v Post Office* [2001] IRLR 384. According to Linden *op. cit* the same principle should apply in education cases.

[39] Reasonableness in this context would be *Wednesbury* unreasonableness. Decisions that are so unreasonable that no reasonable authority would make them. See footnote 62, *supra*.

of resources to meet SEN. The justification defence in the *DDA* has to be read in the context of a parallel duty on the employer or provider of goods and services to make reasonable adjustments. In employment cases the tribunal should first determine whether the employer is under such a duty and decide whether the employer has complied with it before going on to decide whether the employer is justified in treating the disabled person less favourably.[40]

In employment the duty is to take such steps as is reasonable in all the circumstances of the case in order to prevent arrangements or physical features of the premises placing the disabled person at substantial disadvantage as compared with persons who are not disabled.[41] This requires a balancing exercise between the interests of the disabled employee and the interests of the employer.[42] However in employment the duty applies only in respect of job-related arrangements not arrangements for personal care.[43]

The *DDA* provides a list of examples that an employer might reasonably be required to make.[44] These are: adjustment to premises; re-allocation of duties; transfer to vacant post; change in working hours; change in place of work; allowing time for rehabilitation, assessment or treatment; arranging time off for training; acquiring or modifying equipment; modifying instruction or reference manuals; providing a reader or interpreter; or providing supervision.

The *DDA* does not specify what steps are reasonable, but identifies what considerations should be taken into account in deciding what is reasonable.[45] These are: the extent to which taking the step would prevent the effect; the extent to which it is practicable to take the step; financial or other costs in taking the step and the extent to which it will disrupt the employer's activities; extent of resources; and the availability of financial or other assistance in taking the step.

The duty is owed to a person who has notified the employer that he or she may be an applicant for employment or an employee. The duty is therefore not imposed

40 *Morse v Wiltshire CC* [1998] IRLR 352.

41 *Section 6(1)(b)*, The duty to adjust arrangements refers only to arrangements for determining whom employment is offered to, or any term condition or arrangement relating to promotion, transfer, training or any other benefits offered or afforded, see *sections 6(2)* and *6(1)(a)*. However, the duty has been interpreted as including a duty to make arrangements that will allow a disabled employee to remain in employment *Morse v Wiltshire op. cit.* The following count as physical features: any feature arising from the design or construction of a building or premises; approach to or exit from or access to such premises; fixtures, fittings, furnishings, equipment and materials in or on the premises; and any other physical element or quality of any land comprised in the premises, *Disability Discrimination (Employment) Regulations 1996*, SI 96/1456.

42 *Baynton v Saurus General Engineers Ltd.* [1999] IRLR 604.

43 In *Kenny v Hampshire Constabulary* [1999] IRLR 76.

44 *Section 6(3).*

45 *Section 6(4).*

unless the employer knows of the affected person.[46] The Act specifies that subject to the provisions of *Section 6*, nothing in this part of the Act is to be taken to require an employer to treat a disabled person more favourably than he treats or would treat others.[47] The provisions have been interpreted as creating a free-standing action for breach of the duty to make reasonable requirements rather than as was initially thought the duty only being relevant in establishing whether there had been disability discrimination under *Section 5*.

In goods and services, where the discrimination arises from a failure to alter a practice, policy or procedure which makes it impossible or unreasonably difficult for disabled persons to make use of a service; where the provision of an auxiliary aid or service would enable or facilitate the use of a service; or, where a feature of property makes it impossible or unreasonably difficult for disabled persons to make use of a service the service provider is required to take reasonable steps to prevent the discriminatory effect of this, a failure to take such steps is a free-standing cause of discrimination.[48] As noted above such adaptations can only be withheld where this is reasonable.

How does this compare with the right to resources to meet need under the SEN provisions? In many of these cases the needs that arise from the disability will properly be classed as educational needs that can be met through the statementing process. However, not all disability covered by the *DDA* will be covered by the SEN provisions, and not all needs of disabled pupils will be educational needs. Non-educational needs can be specified in the statement, but the LEA is only under a duty to specify non-educational needs which they propose to meet or are satisfied will be met by another body such as health and social services. This is not a duty to make non-educational provision, but a power to do so.[49] If such need is specified the statement has to go on to specify the objectives of such provisions and the arrangements that have been made to ensure its delivery. However, there is no general requirement to assess such need or to ensure its provision. In any event the LEA is only responsible for meeting educational provision not non-educational provision[50] and if this provision is not met parents will have little in the way of effective remedy even by way of judicial review except in the most extreme cases. Such non-educational needs cannot be required of the SEN system although schools might be able to provide them perfectly easily. When it might be relatively simple to make adjustments that would address barriers to inclusion, it is doubtful whether as a matter of logic or as a matter of social justice this distinction between educational and non-educational

46 *Section 6(5)* and see *Rideout v TC Group* IRLR [1998] 628.

47 *Section 6(7).*

48 *Section 20(2).*

49 *Section 324(5)(a).*

50 There is merely discretion to meet non-educational provision, *section 324(5)*. See *Bromley London Borough Council* v *SENT* op. cit. See also Harris, N. (2002) *op. cit.*

needs is justifiable following the extending of the *DDA* to education. The only possible justification would be to ensure that such provision does not have to be made from LEA resources if more appropriately provided by another authority.

### *(d) The enforcement deficit*

Given that parents have long had an appeal to the SENT who can substitute their own assessments of need for those made by the LEA, this appears to be a robust rights-based system.[51] Rights to the resources specified in the statement can be enforced through judicial review where LEAs have failed to meet them, however judicial review is a complex and expensive process and is significantly less accessible than the remedies that are available in the SENT.[52]

Matters under the control of the SENT are not unproblematic however. Reports of the Local Government Ombudsman (LGO) regularly disclose failures to meet the statutory timetable for assessment. The LGO has challenged these vigorously but they recur with alarming regularity.[53] In addition, LGO reports have increasingly concerned delays in making the provision specified in the statement. Here the LGO has been less inclined to intervene except where the delays have been clearly attributable to a lack of willingness to make progress. It has been noted elsewhere[54] that this approach seems unnecessarily timid. It is submitted that great many of these cases if taken to judicial review might well have succeeded in a finding of illegality. At times it seems that the delay in the assessment procedure that the 1994 regulations sought to address has simply been shifted to the implementation phase. Many pupils have been left unconscionably long in having their educational needs met; and this delay will usually be capable of having an adverse impact on the success of the child's education.

This is not to dismiss the frustration that LEAs must feel at what may often seem to them to be flawed assessments by the SENT. It seems clear that LEAs sometimes feel that the SEN of an individual child is inappropriately expensive and that funds would be better spent on either preventing such need arising in the first place or in meeting collective rather than individual needs. These difficulties can often be attributed to the mismatch between the level of assessed need and the resources available to meet it.[55] However, this is not a defence for failing to meet a statutory duty.

51 Recent discussion of the role of the courts in SEN can be found in Harris, N. (2002) "Special Educational Needs – the Role of the Courts." *Child and Family Law Quarterly*, 137–156.

52 Harris, N. (1997) *op. cit.* note 21.

53 Brief examples can be gleaned from report summaries in the LGO website; full reports are also published on a regular basis. http://www.lgo.org.uk/report.htm

54 Blair, A. Ombudsman Reports, [2001] ELJ 164, and [2000] ELJ 107.

55 Blair, A. "Rights, Duties and Resources: The Case of Special Educational Needs." [2000] *Education and the Law* 19.

The failure to provide an accessible remedy in cases of failure to meet the terms of the statement does not compare well with the remedies for failing to make reasonable adjustments under the *DDA* that are found in the Employment Tribunal or with the goods and services provisions that are enforced in the County Court.

## 4. Addressing the Deficits

### *(a) Addressing the inclusion deficit*

Inclusion in terms of the limits on children's access to and exclusion from school on grounds of disability is significantly improved by *SENDA*.[56] Now that the SEN provisions of *SENDA* have been brought into force the right to a place in a mainstream school is conditional only on the wishes of the parent and the provision of efficient education for other pupils.[57] The restrictions based on the child receiving the educational provision that the learning difficulty calls for have gone, as have the provisions that relate to the efficient use of resources. In this way the right to inclusion is strengthened considerably. *SENDA* narrows the deficit further by reducing the scope of the justification in *s 316(3)(b)* where the provision of efficient education for other pupils is affected. In relation to their mainstream schools taken as a whole, LEAs may rely on the exception in *s 316(3)(b)* (as amended) only if they can show that there are no reasonable steps that they could take to prevent the incompatibility.[58] In relation to a particular mainstream school the LEA may rely on the exception only if there are no reasonable steps that it or another authority could take in relation to the school to prevent the incompatibility.[59]

Another thrust to increase inclusion is found in the increased emphasis in the 2001 Code of Practice on addressing the needs of all pupils with SEN, not just on those who are likely to require statemented provision. The 5-stage procedure has been abandoned and the emphasis in the new code is away from a process that seems to lead inexorably to the top level and the resources that go with it. The 2001 Code emphasises instead the responsibility of schools to address learning difficulty early within their own (but enhanced) resources. The new Code reduces the stages to three. The first two stages are school-based and referred to as "school action" and "school action plus".[60] The final stage in the new code is simply referred to as statutory assessment. Overall the major shift in emphasis is the importance the new

56 The details of this are discussed at (c) below.

57 *Section 316(3)* as amended by *SENDA*.

58 *Section 316A(5)* as amended by *SENDA*.

59 *Section 316A(6)* as amended by *SENDA*.

60 For children under 5 years of age this is referred to as Early Years Action and Early Years Action Plus.

Code places on ensuring that schools work with pupils to prevent the need for formal assessment arising wherever this is possible.

The deficit remains insofar as these provisions do not guarantee the child a right to a place in the mainstream school of its parents' choice. The naming of the school in the statement is still contingent. This depends on the school being suitable to the child's age, ability or aptitude and to meeting his special educational needs. It is also still contingent on the attendance of the child at the school being compatible with the provision of efficient education for the children with whom he or she is to be educated with and with the efficient use of resources. The primacy of parental wishes remains intact.

The extension of the *DDA* to school admissions and exclusions is an important step towards increasing inclusion in its own right. A right to claim disability discrimination in Admission Appeals and in Exclusion Appeals will strengthen the right to inclusion further. Overall these changes represent a great step forward.

### *(b) Addressing the participation deficit*

The participation deficit remains in the legislation and the right to inclusion is still the right of the parent not the child given that parental wishes can override it, but this deficit has been addressed, at least in part, in other ways.

The 1994 regulations[61] did not provide for the child to be consulted during the assessment and statementing process. The latest version of the regulations does not alter this, but there are[62] changes addressing the participation deficit in the 2001 Code of Practice. As well as updating guidance to account for the additions to the legal framework, this also emphasises an extra-statutory duty on the part of LEAs and schools to involve pupils in decisions about their own education and statementing.

Whereas previously a single paragraph referred to appending the child's views to the draft statement where they had been obtained, now the child's views infect every part of the process of identifying, assessing and meeting needs both at the formal stages which may lead to statementing and at the school-based stages. Given that the doctrine of relevant considerations will apply to the statutory guidance,[63] LEAs and schools will be under an indirect obligation to consult the child itself where the child is of sufficient maturity to participate meaningfully. This is a great departure and will address some of the deficiencies that education law in England and Wales has been subject to criticism over. It results in a situation where in most cases the LEA will

61 *Education (Special Educational Needs) Regulations 1994,* SI 1994/1910

62 *Education (Special Educational Needs) (England) (Consolidation) Regulations 2001,* SI 2001/3455.

63 *APP v Wednesbury Corporation* [1948] 1KB 223 and *Gillick v West Norfolk and Wisbech Health Authority* [1986] AC 112.

no longer be able to make a reasonable decision on SEN without considering the child's views.

One area where the views of the child are recognised in the new primary legislation relates to a child's wish to have the existence of their disability to be treated as confidential. If a pupil of sufficient understanding or a pupil's parent asks for the existence of the disability to be treated as confidential, the responsible body can take this into account in determining whether it is reasonable to take a particular step to accommodate the child's disability.[64]

On participation in appeals it is still the parent not the child that exercises the right to appeal. The implementation of *SENDA* has, however, highlighted the lack of child rights in education generally because claims under the *Sex Discrimination Act 1975* (*SDA*) and the *Race Relations Act 1976* (*RRA*) may be brought by the child.[65] It seems that this discrepancy is a function of having chosen the education appeals system as the site for enforcing the new education provisions of the *DDA*. As the *SDA* and the *RRA* have functioned without any observable problems brought about by the dangerous possibility of the child having its own rights in education for over 25 years this suggests that recognition of the child's independent rights and status might have been addressed in education more generally without significant problems.

If SENDA itself does little to address the lack of participation rights, the *Special Educational Needs Tribunal Regulations 2001*[66] introduce two welcome changes.[67] First a new right for the child to attend the tribunal. Second, a new duty on the part of the LEA to show that the child's views on the issues raised by an appeal have been ascertained and if not there is a requirement that the LEA state the reasons for this. A significant omission however is the fact that the procedure in disability cases introduced by the *Special Educational Needs and Disability (General Provision and Disability Claims Procedure) Regulations 2001*[68] contains no equivalent to the duty to ascertain views. This may simply recognise that there is no certainty that a LEA will be involved in these processes as is inevitably the case with SEN.[69] Whatever the reason it leaves children with disability claims less well placed to have their views taken into account than in SEN claims.

[64] New *section 28C(6).*

[65] The landmark race discrimination case *Mandla v Dowell Lee* [1983] 1 All ER 1062 was brought against a school in the names of the child and his parent.

[66] SI 2001/600 Regulation 13(2) and 30(2).

[67] The effect of the new procedures in the regulations is discussed by Aldridge, T. "Special Educational Needs Tribunal: New Procedure." [2001] ELJ 131.

[68] SI 2001/1985.

[69] This point was raised in the committee stages of the Bill's passage through Parliament. Margaret Hodge refused to concede a right of the child to bring a claim in his or her own name. She suggested that the disability procedure regulations would contain the equivalent of regulations 13 and 30 but in the event these participation rights are absent. Standing Committee B 3 April 2001.

Of course since the ratification of the UN Convention on the Rights of the Child and its implementation into most of UK child law in the *Children Act 1989* the absence of a voice for the mature child in education law has been much remarked upon and much criticised.[70] There are signs of changes here though. In Scotland children have recently been guaranteed a voice. *Section 2(2) of the Standards in Scotland's Schools etc. Act 2000* provides that:

> in carrying out their duty [to secure that the education is directed to the development of the personality, talents and mental and physical abilities of the child or young person to their fullest potential], an education authority shall have due regard, so far as is reasonably practicable, to the views (if there is a wish to express them) of the child or young person in decisions that significantly affect that child or young person, taking account of the child or young person's age and maturity. [71]

South of the border very recent steps have also been taken but these are much more tentative. *Section 176* of the *Education Act 2002* creates a new duty (yet to be brought into force) for LEAs and governing bodies to "have regard to any guidance given from time to time by the Secretary of State [...] about consultation with pupils in connection with the taking of decisions affecting them". This commitment is not a duty to ascertain the child's wishes, but to have regard to guidance. It is not yet clear how dramatic the effect of this will be. In SEN we must await the guidance itself and wait to see how strong an emphasis the courts are prepared to put on it before we can be sure that participation rights will be strengthened substantially by this innovation.

### *(c) Addressing consistency deficits*

*Sections 11–25* of *SENDA* extend the scope of the *DDA* to schools.[72] It does this by inserting a new chapter 1 of *Part IV* of the *DDA* (*sections 28A–28Q*).[73] This extends

70 Eekelaar, J. (1986) "The Eclipse of Parental Rights." 102 *Law Quarterly Review* 4; Furniss, C. and Blair, A. (1997) "Sex Wars: Conflict in, and Reform of, Sex Education in Maintained Secondary Schools." 19 *Journal of Social Welfare and Family Law* 189–202; Harris, N. (2000) "Education law: excluding the child." 12 *Education and the Law* 31–46; Meredith, P. (2001) "Editorial Comment: the child's right to education." 13 *Education* and *the Law* 5–8; Monk, D. (2002) "Children's Rights in Education – making sense of contradictions." 14 *Child and Family Law Quarterly* 45–56.

71 Harris, N. (2000) "Education law: excluding the child." 12 *Education and the Law* 31–46; Meredith, P. (2001) *Ibid.*; Monk, D. (2002) "Children's Rights in Education – making sense of contradictions." 14 *Child and Family Law Quarterly* 45–56.

72 Other parts of *SENDA* extend the *DDA* to Further and Higher Education.

73 New Chapter 2 of part 4 applies to further and higher education and includes new *ss 28R–28X*. New chapter 3 has miscellaneous provisions new *ss 31B* and *31C* and various amendments to other sections of the Act.

protections against discrimination to discrimination in: admission arrangements, the terms on which the school[74] offers to admit the pupil to the school, refusing or deliberately omitting to accept the pupil, and applications for admission; education or in associated services provided for or offered to the pupils as the school;[75] exclusion; and victimisation.[76]

The meaning of discrimination in this part of the *DDA* is found in *s 28B*:

> (1) For the purposes of section 28A a responsible body discriminates against a disabled person if
> (a) for a reason which relates to his disability, it treats him less favourably than it treats or would treat others to whom that reason does not or would not apply; and
> (b) it cannot show that the treatment in question is justified.
> (2) For the purposes of section 28A, a responsible body also discriminates against a disabled person if
> (a) it fails, to his detriment, to comply with section 28C; and
> (b) it cannot show that its failure to comply is justified.

*S. 28B*

This has obvious and intentional parallels with the provisions in the existing parts of the *DDA*. Less favourable treatment is justified if it is a permitted form of selection,[77] otherwise less favourable treatment, or a failure to comply with *s. 28C*, is justified only if the reasons for it is both material to the circumstances of the case and substantial.[78]

*Section 28C* though not identical, seems to mirror the *section 6* duty in the employment provisions to make reasonable adjustments, rather than the *section 21* duty that applies to the goods and services provisions, and is phrased in terms of a duty not to place disabled persons at “a substantial disadvantage” compared with persons who are not disabled. It reads:

> The responsible body for a school must take such steps as it is reasonable to have to take to ensure that
> (a) in relation to the arrangements it makes for determining the admission of pupils to the school, disabled persons are not placed at a substantial disadvantage compared with persons who are not disabled; and

[74] Or other responsible body.

[75] The Secretary of State is given a power to specify any services that are to be regarded as such services, or to specify services that are not to be regarded as such services.

[76] In general claims may only be brought by those who fall within the definition of disability in the Act but victimisation claims may be brought by those who are not disabled.

[77] Section 28B(6).

[78] Section 28B(7).

(b) in relation to education and associated services provided for, or offered to, pupils at the school by it, disabled pupils are not placed at a substantial disadvantage compared with pupils who are not disabled.

*Section 28C(1)*
However, significantly it goes on to state that:

That does not require the responsible body to
(a) remove or alter a physical feature (for example, one arising from the design or construction of the school premises or the location of resources); or
(b) provide auxiliary aids or services.

*Section 28C(2)*[79]
A rule-making power is attached to clarify what steps it is always reasonable for the responsible body to have to take. It also provides for rules to specify what steps it is never reasonable for the responsible body to have to take, and as to circumstances in which it is reasonable (or not reasonable) for a responsible body to have to take steps of a prescribed description. The responsible body must have regard to the statutory Code of Practice produced by the Disability Rights Commission. This code fleshes out the obligations that the *DDA* imposes on schools.[80] This includes guidance on determining whether it is reasonable to take a particular step in order to comply with the duty in *28C(1)*.

The lack of a duty to alter features of the premises or to provide auxiliary aids and services appears to be highly deficient. To offset this, all LEAs must have an accessibility strategy and all maintained schools, independent schools and special schools which are not maintained but are approved under *s 342* of the *1996 Act* must have an accessibility plan. The purposes of accessibility strategies and accessibility plans are: to increase the extent to which disabled pupils can participate in the curriculum; improve the physical environment so that disabled pupils can take advantage of education and services provided or offered by the schools; and to improve the delivery of information which is provided in writing for pupils that are not disabled in terms of the time and the manner in which the information is provided. This last requirement is to enable schools to take into account the pupils' disabilities and preferences expressed by pupils and their parents. Depending on how responsible bodies embrace this last factor this could be used to address the participation deficit.

[79] Curiously these are 2 of the 3 varieties of "reasonable adjustment" required in the goods and services provisions. The term reasonable adjustment is not actually used in either the goods and services or the new education provisions of the *DDA* but the term is used in the DRC codes of practice and the description is a convenient one.

[80] Disability Rights Commission (2002) Code of Practice for Schools, http://www.drc-gb.org/drc/documents/SchoolsCoP2.doc

Accessibility strategies and plans must provide for making these improvements over a prescribed period. LEAs are under a duty to implement the strategy and the responsible body is under a duty to implement the plan (in the case of maintained schools this is the governing body). However in spite of these welcome innovations it is not difficult to imagine situations where LEAs will not be required to make quite simple adjustments that would be reasonable in the case of employees or in the provision of goods and services because they are not specified in the accessibility strategy.

Despite the fact that the DRC Code of Practice talks about the aim of the legislation being to "dovetail" the SEN and the *DDA* provisions, the fact that definitions of disability in the *1996 Act* and in the *DDA* may be non-commensurable has not been addressed. The definition of disability is still likely to cover pupils who have no right to access resources through SEN yet may have significant needs that would be appropriate to be met by reasonable adjustments if they were disabilities of a teacher not a pupil. Consistency deficits still give cause for concern.

### *(d) Addressing the enforcement deficit*

The role of enforcing the new provisions of the *DDA* will fall principally to a newly constituted Special Education Needs and Disability Tribunal (SENDT). Complaints regarding discrimination in admissions and exclusions will fall to the appropriate body for hearing such appeals.

*Section 4* of *SENDA* introduces for the first time prescribed periods for meeting the terms of an order of SENDT. *The Education (Special Educational Needs) (Consolidation) Regulations 2001*[81] implement this by providing a series of time-limits in respect of a number of different orders that the tribunal is empowered to make. These do not extend to any circumstances concerning delay in meeting the provision specified in the statement. This is perhaps not surprising, as one would have expected such a fundamental change to be highlighted more prominently, however it is disappointing.[82] Nevertheless if the orders address delays in the assessment procedure they are to be welcomed.

An innovation is the requirement for LEAs to make provision for parents to receive independent advice and in addition there is a new requirement to establish dispute procedures.[83] Perhaps this is the last chance for the LEA that drags its heels. If the enforcement deficit is not addressed effectively by these informal procedures it is submitted that it will be time to refer questions of enforcement to the SENDT.

The ultimate enforcement deficit however has been introduced by *SENDA* rather than resolved by it. This is the decision that the SENDT should have no jurisdiction

81 SI 2001/3455.

82 *C.f.* Hay, D. The Special Educational Needs and Disability Act 2001 [2001] ELJ 72.

83 New *ss. 332A* and *332B 1996 Act.*

to award compensation for disability discrimination. It is hard to see how this can be justified. Damages can be awarded to a child complaining about race or sex discrimination in education in a claim brought in the County Court. Equally, disabled adults who bring goods and services or employment claims, or indeed students over the age of 16 who bring claims under the post 16 provisions introduced by *SENDA* can also seek compensation, including damages for injury to feelings. This point was argued in the House of Lords and in the Committee stages of the Bill but amendments to the Bill failed.[84] When one adds to this the point already made about children being unable to bring a claim in their own right (where no such restriction applies in the case of claims under the *SDA* or the *RRA*), this diminishes the satisfaction that can be taken in having seen disability discrimination in schools addressed by *SENDA*.

## 5. Conclusions

Many of the deficits in the pre-existing provisions of the law of special educational needs and of the law of disability discrimination as they apply to pupils in the school system of England and Wales are addressed by the changes being brought in by *SENDA*. Even where not all of the deficiencies are addressed by *SENDA*, changes in the secondary legislation and the statutory Codes of Practice, particularly the SEN Code, look set to prove highly significant. The agenda for inclusion is strengthened considerably and a great deal of inconsistency is removed from the law.

Nevertheless, as one might expect, inconsistency remains. In the provision of resources the changes introduced by extending the *DDA* to education are clearly not as favourable as in the other parts of the Act. *SENDA* has tried to square the eternal problem of how to match need to resources through the development of accessibility strategies and plans rather than accepting that a minority of disabled pupils should be able to call for a reasonable adjustment because they have needs that cannot be met through the SEN system. Fears of cost are legitimate, but the idea of planned improvements rather than individual rights seems to be at cross-purposes with much of the rest of the *DDA*. The whole ethos of the employment provisions of the *DDA* is that adjustments are targeted on individual needs. Accessibility strategies are important but so are rights for individuals. If the desire is to avoid having to make expensive adjustments to meet individual need for this very reason it is not clear that the exclusion is necessary. The rest of the *DDA* requires only *reasonable* adjustments to be made, and the expense and availability of financial resources to meet this expense are explicit considerations in determining what exactly is reasonable. If the purpose is to have collective rights met by these anticipatory duties it is not clear that this could not have gone hand in hand with a more robust approach to protecting the

[84] Lord Ashley of Stoke. House of Lords debates 19 December 2000 col. 655.

individual rights of disabled children in education. If the purpose is to prevent duplication, this could have been achieved through a better-targeted proviso that an adjustment would not be necessary under the Act if it is to meet an educational need that could be met through the SEN system. Similarly the availability of support from other sources could also be an explicit consideration in determining the question of what is required by way of reasonable adjustment, as is the case in other parts of the *DDA*.

The SEN provisions have improved rights to education in the mainstream. Nevertheless there are no guarantees of the resources that will allow this to be in the mainstream school of choice. The reasoning behind this is, presumably, also to ensure affordability. However, there is a danger that this could develop into a contingent right of inclusion where LEAs could make improvements to a particular mainstream school and channel all of the pupils with the relevant needs into that school. This would run counter to inclusion as an ideal. It is by no means clear that special units in mainstream schools are intrinsically more inclusive than provision in special schools.

As ever in the education law of England and Wales the balance between the rights and welfare of the child and the rights of the parent continues to come down very firmly on the parent's side. However, in the tribunal regulations and in the SEN Code the child's independent voice is being heard. In the end inclusion is always going to be an ideal to be pursued rather than a goal to be achieved, but overall potential cost and concerns about the fears of the educational establishment have left the provisions less effective than they might otherwise have been.

Finally, the requirement to implement Directive 78/2000/EC establishing a framework for equality in employment in Europe will mean disability discrimination rights being established in all EU Member States. The UK has perhaps been ahead of the game in many ways, but here is an opportunity for other EU countries to avoid some of the inconsistency and complexity that has arisen due to the lack of coherence between the UK's SEN and disability provisions. The directive applies only to employment but if careful thought is not given to implementation, disparities between the treatment of the disabled teacher and the disabled pupil will become a Europe-wide phenomenon. In the UK the Government have chosen to implement the changes that are necessary as a result of the directive only in the field of employment. The author of this paper hopes to be forgiven for deciding that the scope of the proposed changes is beyond the scope of this work.[85] The changes will introduce further layers of complexity and further significant inconsistencies between the employment and the non-employment provisions of the *DDA*. That however will be another story.

[85] Regulations updating the *DDA* to conform to Directive 78/2000 are currently found in draft form on the DTI website as *The Disability Discrimination Act 1995 (Amendment) Regulations 2003*. Due to come into force in the UK on 1 October 2004. See http://www.dti.gov.uk/er/equality/index.htm

CHARLES J. RUSSO AND RALPH D. MAWDSLEY[1]

# Special Education Law in the United States

## INTRODUCTION

American children with disabilities benefit from broad-based statutory protections most notably under the Individuals with Disabilities Act (IDEA)[2] and Section 504 of the Rehabilitation Act of 1973.[3] In light of developments protecting children with disabilities, this section of the article reviews legal developments in the United States with regard to their educational rights.

## EARLY HISTORY

The impetus for ensuring equal educational opportunities for all American children can be traced to *Brown v Board of Education, Topeka*.[4] Although decided in the context of school desegregation, in *Brown* the Supreme Court set the tone for later developments in its assertion that "[e]ducation is perhaps the most important function of state and local governments."[5]

1 Charles J. Russo, J.D., Ed.D., Panzer Chair of Education, University of Dayton, Dayton, OH, USA and Ralph D. Mawdsley, J.D., Ph.D., Cleveland State University, Cleveland, OH, USA.

2 1400 U.S.C. §§ 1400 et seq. The IDEA was initially enacted in 1975 as the Education for All Handicapped Children Act. In order to avoid inconsistency, unless otherwise noted, this article uses the current title and/ or acronym throughout.

3 29 U.S.C. § 794. A third statute, the Americans with Disabilities Act (ADA), although similar to Section n. 504, is beyond the scope of this article. The ADA, 42 U.S.C. § 12101 et seq., was passed in 1990 to provide "a comprehensive national mandate for the elimination of discrimination against individuals with disabilities." 42 U.S.C. § 12101(b)(2). The ADA effectively extends the protections of section 504 to the private sector but has implications for public entities such as schools.

4 3 U.S. 483 (1954).

5 *Id.* at 493.

*Jan De Groof and Gracienne Lauwers (eds.), Special Education*, 51–68.

Following *Brown*, an attitude of neglect remained in effect with regard to the disabled. In fact, throughout the 1950s, twenty-eight states had laws requiring the sterilisation of individuals with disabilities while others limited such basic rights as voting, marrying, and obtaining a drivers' license.[6] By the1960s, the percentages of children who were served in public schools began to rise; the 12% of children in schools in 1948 increased to 21% in 1963 and 38% in 1968.[7] As of July 1, 1974, the Bureau for the Education of the Handicapped reported that about 78.5% of the Nation's 8,150,000 eligible children with disabilities received some form of public education. Of these children, 47.8% received special education and related services, 30.7% did not receive related services, and the remaining 21.5% did not receive educational services at all.[8]

The data notwithstanding, the major push for the development of special education came in two federal cases. In *Pennsylvania Association for Retarded Children* v *Pennsylvania (PARC)*,[9] a federal trial court, in a consent decree, established the bases for what developed into the IDEA. In *PARC* the parties agreed that children with disabilities could neither be denied admission to a public school nor be subjected to a change in educational placement unless their parents received procedural due process and that a placement in a regular school classroom was preferable to one in a more restrictive setting. Similarly, in *Mills v Board of Education of the District of Columbia*,[10] another federal trial court ruled that despite the school system's claims that it lacked the resources for all of its students, it could not deny services to children with disabilities and that they could not be excluded from public schools without receiving due process. Insofar as *Mills* originated in Washington, D.C., it was probably among the more significant influences moving federal law makers to act to ensure adequate protection for children with disabilities when they adopted Section 504 and the IDEA.

In light of legal developments following *PARC* and *Mills*, this section of the article reviews major statutory developments, under Section 504 of the Rehabilitation Act and the IDEA, in safeguarding the educational rights of American children with disabilities. Further, in the wake of the literally thousands of lawsuits that have been filed in federal and state courts, rather than address cases in separate headings, they are generally incorporated by references.

6 S.B. Thomas & C.J. Russo, Special Education: Issues & Implications for the '90s (NOLPE 1995) at 4–5.

7 J. Ballard, B.A. Ramirez, & F.J. Weintraub, F.J. (1982) Special education in America: Its legal and governmental foundations. Reston, VA: Council for Exceptional Children at 2.

8 House Report No. 332, 94th Congress (1975) at 11.

9 334 F. Supp. 1257 (E.D. Pa. 1971), 343 F. Supp. 279 (E.D. Pa. 1972).

10 348 F. Supp. 866 (D.D.C. 1972).

## Section 504

The Rehabilitation Act of 1973 was the first federal civil rights law protecting the rights of the disabled. Among its provisions, Section 504 declares that "[n]o otherwise qualified individual with a disability in the United States ... shall, solely by reason of her or his disability, be excluded from the participation in, be denied the benefits of, or be subjected to discrimination under any program or activity receiving [f]ederal financial assistance ...."[11]

According to Section 504, recipients of federal financial aid must file an assurance of compliance; engage in remedial actions where violations are proven; take voluntary steps to overcome the effects of conditions that resulted in limiting the participation of students with disabilities in their programmes; conduct a self evaluation; designate a staff member, typically at the central office level, as compliance co-ordinator; adopt grievance procedures; and provide notice to students and their parents that their programmes are non-discriminatory.[12]

Section 504 offers broad-based protection to individuals with disabilities. It is important to note that while Section 504 covers both students and employees, this article focuses on the rights of children. The Act defines an individual with a disability as one "who (i) has a physical or mental impairment which substantially limits one or more of such person's major life activities, (ii) has a record of such an impairment, or (iii) is regarded as having such an impairment."[13]

In order to have a record of impairment, an individual must have a history of, or been identified as having, a mental or physical impairment that substantially limits one or more major life activities,[14] including schooling. Once a student is identified as having a disability, the next step is to determine whether he or she is "otherwise

[11] 29 U.S.C. § 794(a).

[12] 34 C.F.R. § 104.

[13] 29 U.S.C. § 706(7)(B). The regulations further define physical or mental impairments as including:

(A) any physiological disorder or condition, cosmetic disfigurement, or anatomical loss affecting one or more of the following body systems: neurological; musculoskeletal; special sense organs; respiratory, including speech organs; cardiovascular; reproductive, digestive, genito-urinary; hemic and lymphatic; skin; and endocrine; or

(B) any mental or psychological disorder, such as mental retardation, organic brain syndrome, emotional or mental illness, and specific learning disorders. 45 C.F.R. § 84.3(j)(2)(i), 34 C.F.R. § 104(j)(2)(i). Further, a note accompanying this list indicates that it merely provides examples of the types of impairments that are covered; it is not meant to be exhaustive.

[14] An individual who is regarded as having an impairment has:

(A) a physical or mental impairment that does not substantially limit major life activities but that is treated by a recipient as constituting such a limitation; (B) a physical or mental impairment that substantially limits major life activities only as a result of the attitudes of others toward such impairment; or (C) none of the impairments ... but is

qualified." In order to be qualified, as the term is applied to pre-school, elementary, and secondary school students, a child must be "(i) of an age during which no handicapped persons are provided such services, (ii) of any age during which it is mandatory under state law to provide such services to handicapped persons, or (iii) [a student] to whom a state is required to provide a free appropriate public education [under the IDEA]."[15] An individual who is "otherwise qualified," meaning that he or she is eligible to participate in a programme or activity despite the existence of an impairment, must be permitted to participate in the programme or activity as long as it is possible to do so by means of a "reasonable accommodation."

Reasonable accommodations may involve modest adjustments such as permitting a child to be accompanied by a service dog[16] or providing basic health services to allow a student with a physical impairment to be present in a classroom.[17] Further, in making a modification, officials do not have to make every classroom and/ or area of a building available; it may be enough to bring services to a child such as offering a keyboard for musical instruction rather than revamping an entire music room for a student who wishes to take piano classes.[18]

Even if a child appears to be otherwise qualified, schools can rely on one of three defenses to avoid being charged with non-compliance. First, schools can be excused from making accommodations that would result either in "a fundamental alteration in the nature of [a] program."[19] This defense illustrates a major difference between Section 504 and the IDEA. A second defense permits school officials to avoid compliance if a modification imposes an "undue financial burden[s]."[20] This is a second major difference between Section 504 and the IDEA since the latter requires school systems to provide programmes regardless of their cost.

The third defense available under Section 504 is that an otherwise qualified student with a disability can be excluded from a programme if his or her presence creates a substantial risk of injury to himself or to others. For example, a child with a spastic condition may be excluded from a chemistry laboratory due to fear of exposure to the flames of a Bunsen Burner. In order to comply with Section 504, a school may have to offer the reasonable accommodation of providing a computer assisted program to accomplish a goal similar to that of the laboratory class.

---

treated by a recipient as having such an impairment. 45 C.F.R. § 84.3(j)(2)(iv), 34 C.F.R. § 104.3(j)(2)(iv).

15 45 C.F.R. § 84.3(k)(2).

16 Sullivan v Vallejo City Unified Sch. Dist., 731 F. Supp. 947 (E.D. Cal 1990).

17 Irving Indep. Sch. Dist. v Tatro, 468 U.S. 883 (1984); Cedar Rapids Community Sch. Dist. v Garrett F., 526 U.S. 66 (1999).

18 At the same time, at least one court has held that Section 504 does not require affirmative efforts to overcome a student's disability but only prohibits discrimination on the basis of the disability. *See* Lyons v Smith, 829 F. Supp. 414 D.D.C. (1993).

19 Southeastern Community College v Davis, 442 U.S. 397, 410 (1979).

20 *Id.* at 412.

Section 504 also prohibits discrimination by requiring educators to make individualised modifications for otherwise qualified students with disabilities. This means that schools must provide aid, benefits, and/or services that are comparable to those available to students who are not disabled. As such, children with disabilities must receive comparable materials, teacher quality, length of school term, and daily hours of instruction. These programmes should not be separate from those available to those who are not disabled, unless such segregation is necessary for the programme to be effective. If programmes are separate, facilities must be comparable.

After being identified, each qualified student with a disability is entitled to an appropriate public education, regardless of the nature or severity of his or her disability. In order to guarantee that an appropriate education is made available, Section 504's regulations include due process requirements for evaluation and placement similar to those under the IDEA.[21]

## IDEA

Unlike Section 504, which has fairly broad standards, in order to qualify under the IDEA, a child with a disability must meet three statutory requirements. First, the child must be between the ages of three and twenty-one.[22] Second, the child must have a specifically identified disability. [23] Third, the child must be in need of

[21] 34 C.F.R. § 104.36.

[22] 20 U.S.C. § 1400.

[23] 20 U.S.C. § 1401(3) offers the following definition:

(3) Child with a disability

(A) In general

The term "child with a disability" means a child

(i) with mental retardation, hearing impairments (including deafness), speech or language impairments, visual impairments (including blindness), serious emotional disturbance (hereinafter referred to as "emotional disturbance"), orthopedic impairments, autism, traumatic brain injury, other health impairments, or specific learning disabilities; and

(ii) who, by reason thereof, needs special education and related services.

(B) Child aged 3 through 9

The term "child with a disability" for a child aged 3 through 9 may, at the discretion of the State and the local educational agency, include a child –

(i) experiencing developmental delays, as defined by the State and as measured by appropriate diagnostic instruments and procedures, in one or more of the following areas: physical development, cognitive development, communication development, social or emotional development, or adaptive development; and

(ii) who, by reason thereof, needs special education and related services.

special education,[24] meaning that he or she must receive a free appropriate education (FAPE)[25] in the least restrictive environment (LRE) that conforms to an individualised education program (IEP).[26] Further, if necessary, each child with a disability is entitled to needed related services to assist him or her in benefiting from the IEP.[27]

## APPROPRIATE PLACEMENT

Although the IDEA requires school districts to provide each student with a disability with a FAPE, the statute offers little guidance in defining what may be considered appropriate. The IDEA's regulations indicate that an appropriate education consists of special education and related services that is provided in conformance with an IEP.[28] Even so, a precise definition of the term appropriate cannot be found in either the statute or its regulations. As such, it is necessary to turn to judicial interpretation for further guidance on the meaning of FAPE.

In *Board of Education of the Hendrick Hudson Central School District* v *Rowley*,[29] the Supreme Court offered a minimal definition of a FAPE. *Rowley* arose when the parents of a kindergarten student who was hearing impaired protested their school district's refusal to provide their daughter with a sign-language interpreter. Lower courts ordered the district to provide the interpreter on the basis that an appropriate education was one that would have allowed the child to achieve at a level commensurate with that of her peers who were not disabled. The Court, in noting that the child was achieving passing marks and advancing from grade to grade without the sign-language interpreter, reversed. The Court held that an appropriate education was one that was formulated in accordance with all of the IDEA's procedures and is "sufficient to confer some educational benefit"[30] upon a child with a disability. Since

[24] *Id.* § 1401 (3)(A)(ii).

[25] 20 U.S.C. § 1401(8) Free appropriate public education [reads]:

> The term "free appropriate public education" means special education and related services that
>
> (A) have been provided at public expense, under public supervision and direction, and without charge;
> (B) meet the standards of the State educational agency;
> (C) include an appropriate pre-school, elementary, or secondary school education in the State involved; and
> (D) are provided in conformity with the individualised education programme required under section 1414(d) of this title.

[26] 20 U.S.C. §§ 1401(11), 1414(d).

[27] *Id.* § 1401 (3)(A)(ii).

[28] 34 C.F.R. § 300.8.

[29] 458 U.S. 176 (1982).

[30] *Id.* at 200.

the student in *Rowley* received some educational benefit without the sign-language interpreter, the Court ruled that educators were not required to provide one even though she might have achieved at a higher level with the services.

*Rowley* establishes a minimum standard of what constitutes a FAPE under federal law. Yet, individual states, such as North Carolina,[31] New Jersey,[32] Massachusetts,[33] Michigan,[34] and California[35] upheld higher standards of appropriateness. In some of these cases, courts have specifically ruled that the higher state standards replaced the federal requirements since one of the essential elements of the IDEA is that special education programmes must meet "the standards of the state educational agency."[36]

The *Rowley* standard has been further refined as courts have indicated that the "some educational benefit" criteria requires more than just minimal or trivial benefits.[37] Other courts have expanded the criteria by declaring that the educational benefit must be meaningful[38] or appreciable.[39] One court went so far as to maintain that the gains made by a student must be measurable to meet the *Rowley* criteria.[40]

## LEAST RESTRICTIVE ENVIRONMENT

According to the IDEA, each student with a disability must be educated in the least restrictive environment.[41] In two cases, federal appellate courts in New Jersey and California ordered school districts to place students with disabilities in regular settings as opposed to segregated special education classrooms.[42] In these cases, the

31 Harrell v Wilson County Sch., 293 S.E.2d 687 (N.C. Ct. App. 1982); Burke County Bd. of Educ. v Denton, 895 F.2d 973 (4th Cir. 1990).

32 Geis v. Bd. of Educ. of Parsippany-Troy Hills, 774 F.2d 575 (3d Cir. 1985).

33 David D. v. Dartmouth Sch. Comm., 775 F.2d 411 (1st Cir. 1985); Roland M. v. Concord Sch. Comm., 910 F.2d 983 (1st Cir. 1990).

34 Nelson v. Southfield Pub. Sch., 384 N.W.2d 423 (Mich. Ct. App. 1986); Barwacz v. Michigan Dep't of Educ., 681 F. Supp. 427 (W.D. Mich. 1988).

35 Pink v. Mt. Diablo Unified Sch. Dist., 738 F. Supp. 345 (N.D. Cal. 1990).

36 20 U.S.C. § 1401(a)(18)(B).

37 Hall v. Vance County Bd. of Educ., 774 F.2d 629 (4th Cir. 1985); Carter v. Florence County Sch. Dist. Four, 950 F.2d 156 (4th Cir. 1991), *aff'd on other grounds sub nom.* Florence County Sch. Dist. Four v. Carter, 510 U.S. 7 (1993).

38 Board of Educ. of East Windsor Reg. Sch. Dist. v. Diamond, 808 F.2d 987 (3d Cir. 1986); Polk v. Susquehanna Intermediate Unit 16, 853 F.2d 171 (3d Cir. 1988).

39 Chris C. v. Gwinnett County Sch. Dist., 780 F. Supp. 804 (N.D. Ga. 1991).

40 J.S.K. v. Hendry County Sch. Bd., 941 F.2d 1563 (11th Cir. 1991).

41 20 U.S.C. § 1412(5)(A).

42 Oberti v. Board of Educ. of the Borough of Clementon Sch. Dist., 995 F.2d 1204 (3d Cir. 1993); Sacramento City Unified Sch. Dist. Bd. of Educ. v. Rachel H., 14 F.3d 1398 (9th Cir. 1994).

courts held that educators must consider a variety of factors when determining the LRE for a student. As summarised by the Ninth Circuit, the four factors that must be addressed in making a placement are the educational benefits of placing a child with a disability in a regular classroom; the non-academic benefits of such a placement; the effect that the student's presence would have on the teacher and other children in the class; and the costs of an inclusionary placement.[43] Inherent in these decisions is the principle that educators must make reasonable efforts to place students with disabilities in mainstream settings by providing them with supplementary aids and services to ensure success.

Even with the focus on inclusion, not all students with disabilities must be placed in regular education classes. Courts have approved segregated settings where educators showed that students could not function in regular classrooms or would not benefit in such settings, even with supplementary aids and services.[44] The bottom line is that an inclusionary placement should be the setting of choice and a segregated setting should be contemplated only if an inclusionary placement has failed despite the best efforts of educators or there is overwhelming evidence that it is not feasible.

## PRIVATE AND RESIDENTIAL SCHOOL PLACEMENTS

Insofar as the IDEA's preference for placing students in the mainstream is not feasible for all students, the law requires school officials to offer a continuum of placement alternatives to meet the educational needs of children with disabilities.[45] In this regard, a private school setting may be required when a district lacks an appropriate placement such as when a student has a low incidence of disability and there are not enough children with the same type of disability within the system to warrant the development of a programme .[46] Courts have recognized that since smaller districts cannot afford to develop specialised programmes for small numbers of students, they must look elsewhere for placements.

A court may order a residential placement for a student with severe, profound, or multiple disabilities[47] if the child needs twenty-four hour per day programming or consistency between the school and home environments. Residential placements may also be necessary for a student with significant behavioral disorders[48] or who requires total immersion in an educational environment in order to progress.[49]

[43] *Id.* Rachel H.

[44] *See, e.g.*, Clyde K. v. Puyallup Sch. Dist. No. 3, 35 F.3d 1396 (9th Cir. 1994); Capistrano Unified Sch. Dist. v. Wartenberg, 59 F.3d 884 (9th Cir. 1995).

[45] 34 C.F.R. § 300.551(a).

[46] *See, e.g.*, Colin K. v. Schmidt, 715 F.2d 1 (1st Cir. 1983).

[47] Gladys J. v. Pearland Indep. Sch. Dist., 520 F. Supp. 869 (S.D. Tex. 1981).

[48] Chris D. v. Montgomery County Bd. of Educ., 743 F. Supp. 1524 (M.D. Ala. 1990).

[49] Abrahamson v. Hershman, 701 F.2d 223 (1st Cir. 1983).

If a residential placement is required for purely educational reasons, its cost must be fully borne by a school district which cannot require parents to contribute toward the cost of a residential placement.[50] However, if a placement is made for other than educational reasons, for example, for medical or social purposes, then a school system is only required to pay for the educational component of the residential setting[51] and may enter into a cost-share agreement with other agencies.

## Extended school year programs

If a student with a disability requires an educational programme that extends beyond the regular school year, it must be provided. An extended school year programme is generally required when a student regresses and the time it takes to recoup lost skills interferes with overall progress toward the attainment of the goals and objectives of the child's IEP.[52] Any regression that a student suffers must be greater than the regression that normally occurs during a school vacation. If a regression is minimal, an extended school year programme is not required.[53]

## Related services

School districts must provide related, or supportive, services to a child with a disability if they are necessary to help the student to benefit from special education.[54] The only limit on what can be a related service is that medical services are exempted unless they are specifically for diagnostic or evaluative purposes.

One of the most controversial topics under the rubric of related services involves the distinction between medical and school health services. In 1984 the Supreme Court held that a service such as catheterisation that can be performed by a school nurse or trained layperson is a required related service under the IDEA.[55] Procedures

50 Parks v. Pavkovic, 753 F.2d 1397 (7th Cir.1985).

51 McKenzie v. Jefferson, EHLR 554:338 (D.D.C. 1983).

52 Armstrong v. Kline, 476 F. Supp. 583 (E.D. Pa. 1979), *rem'd sub nom.* Battle v. Commonwealth of Pa., 629 F.2d 269 (3d Cir. 1980), *on rem'd* 513 F. Supp. 425 (E.D. Pa. 1981).

53 Anderson v. Thompson, 658 F.2d 1205 (7th Cir. 1981).

54 20 U.S.C. § 1401(a)(22) The IDEA specifically lists developmental, supportive, or corrective services such as transportation, speech pathology, audiology, psychological services, physical therapy, occupational therapy, recreation (including therapeutic recreation), social work services, counselling services (including rehabilitation counselling), medical services (for diagnostic or evaluative purposes only), and early identification and assessment as related services.

55 Irving Indep. Sch. Dist. v. Tatro, 468 U.S. 883 (1984).

that must, by law, be performed by a licensed physician would be exempted from medical services. Thus, psychiatric therapy would not be a related service since a psychiatrist is a licensed physician. Many students with significant medical needs require round-the-clock nursing services. This type of service falls somewhere on the continuum between school health services and medical services. In *Cedar Rapids Community School District v Garret F.*,[56] the Supreme Court recently ruled that school districts are required to provide, and pay for, a full-time nurse while a student is in school if the child's medical condition requires constant nursing services.

Another potentially costly related service is assistive technology devices[57] or services.[58] An assistive technology device is an item or piece of equipment that is used to increase, maintain, or improve the functional capabilities of individuals with disabilities. These devices may include commercially available, modified, or customised equipment. An assistive technology service is designed to assist an individual in the selection, acquisition, or use of an assistive technology device.[59] The IDEA includes the need to evaluate a child's needs, provision of the assistive technology device, training in its use, co-ordination of other services with assistive technology, and maintenance and repair of the device. These services are required when it is necessary for a child to receive an appropriate education under the *Rowley* standard and may also allow a student with disabilities to benefit from education in a less restrictive setting.

## REMEDIES

When a school district fails to provide a student with disabilities with a FAPE, the IDEA authorises the courts to grant appropriate relief.[60] Frequently, the relief orders district officials to provide specified special education and related services. However, if parents have unilaterally obtained the necessary services at their own expense, the courts may order educators to reimburse them for all legitimate expenses.

## DAMAGES

Courts generally have not imposed punitive damages on school authorities for failing to provide a FAPE to a child with a disability.[61] Similarly, general damages

[56] 526 U.S. 66 (1999).
[57] 20 U.S.C. § 1401(a)(1).
[58] 20 U.S.C. § 1401(a)(2).
[59] 20 U.S.C. § 1401(a)(2).
[60] 20 U.S.C. § 1415(e)(2).
[61] *See, e.g.*, Marvin H. v. Austin Indep. Sch. Dist., 714 F.2d 1348 (5th Cir. 1983).

awards for "pain and suffering" have not been prevalent.[62] Yet, recent litigation indicates that this may be changing.[63] Courts have indicated that monetary damages may be available under other statutes, such as section 504, if the parents can show that school officials intentionally discriminated against the student or egregiously disregarded the student's rights.[64] The operative word here is intentional. If school officials act in good faith but their efforts fall short of meeting statutory requirements, they should be immune from damages.

## TUITION REIMBURSEMENT

Sometimes parents who are dissatisfied with their child's placement unilaterally enrol the youngster in a private school and seek to recover tuition expenses. The Supreme Court has held that parents are entitled to tuition reimbursement if they can show that a school official failed to offer a FAPE and that their chosen placement is appropriate.[65] The Court reasoned that awarding reimbursement simply requires a school district to pay retroactively the costs it should have been paying all along. The Court later held that parents are also entitled to reimbursement even if their chosen placement is not in a state-approved facility as long as it provided an otherwise appropriate education.[66] Even so, when parents unilaterally place their children, they do so at their own financial risk because they are not entitled to reimbursement if school officials can show that they offered, and could provide, an appropriate educational placement. Parents are also entitled to reimbursement for unilaterally obtained related services if they can demonstrate that a school district failed to provide the needed services.[67]

62 *See, e.g.*, Ft. Zumwalt Sch. Dist. v. Missouri State Bd. of Educ., 865 F. Supp. 604 (E.D. Mo. 1994).

63 For a discussion of this topic, *see* C.J. Russo & A.G. Osborne (2000). "Recent Developments in the USA: Damages in Special Education," *Education and the Law,* Vol. 12, No. 4, 297–302.

64 *See, e.g.*, W.B. v. Matula, 67 F.3d 484 (3d Cir. 1995); Whitehead v. School Dist. for Hillsborough County, 918 F. Supp. 1515 (M.D. Fla. 1996).

65 Burlington Sch. Comm. v. Department of Educ., Commonwealth of Mass., 471 U.S. 359 (1985).

66 Florence County Sch. Dist. Four v. Carter, 510 U.S. 7 (1993).

67 Courts have ordered districts to reimburse parents for the costs of counselling or psychotherapy where they succeeded in proving that the services were necessary for their children to benefit from special education. *See, e.g.*, Gary A. v. New Trier High Sch. Dist. No. 203, 796 F.2d 940 (7th Cir. 1986); Straube v. Florida Union Free Sch. Dist., 801 F. Supp. 1164 (S.D.N.Y. 1992).

## Compensatory services

Tuition reimbursement is likely to be of little use to parents who are unable to make a unilateral placement in a private school because they cannot afford to pay for tuition. When parents cannot afford to make a unilateral placement, their child may remain in an inappropriate setting while the dispute winds its way through due process hearings and judicial proceedings. In such a situation, a court may award additional educational services and prospective relief to compensate the parents, and child, for the loss of appropriate educational services.

The courts have ruled that compensatory services, like reimbursement, compensate a student for a district's failure to provide a FAPE. The reasoning behind a compensatory services award is that an appropriate remedy should not be available only to students whose parents can afford to provide them with an alternate educational placement while litigation is pending.[68] Generally, compensatory services are provided for a period of time equal to that for which the child was denied services[69] and may be granted even after a student has passed the ceiling age for eligibility under the IDEA.[70] As with tuition reimbursement, awards of compensatory educational services are granted only when a hearing officer or court has determined that a district failed to provide an appropriate placement.

## Attorney fees

Litigation can cost a great deal. Many parents, after prevailing in court against a school district believe that they should be reimbursed for their expenses. These parents argued that they achieved hollow victories when they prevailed but were left with burdensome legal bills. In 1984 the Supreme Court held that recovery of legal expenses was not available under the IDEA.[71] However, two years later Congress responded by amending the IDEA with the passage of the Handicapped Children's Protection Act (HCPA).[72] The HCPA gave courts the power to award reasonable attorney fees to parents who prevailed against school districts in actions or proceedings brought pursuant to the IDEA. An award must be based on the prevailing rates

68 *See, e.g.*, Lester H. v. Gilhool, 916 F.2d 865 (3d Cir. 1990); Todd D. v. Andrews, 933 F.2d 1576 (11th Cir. 1991); Manchester Sch. Dist. v. Christopher B., 807 F. Supp. 860 (D.N.H. 1992).

69 *See, e.g.*, Valerie J. v. Derry Cooperative Sch. Dist., 771 F. Supp. 483 (D.N.H. 1991); Big Beaver Falls Area Sch. Dist. v. Jackson, 624 A.2d 806 [861] (Pa. Commw. Ct. 1993).

70 *See, e.g.*, Pihl v. Massachusetts Dep't of Educ., 9 F.3d 184 (1st Cir. 1993); Jones v. Schneider, 896 F. Supp. 488 (D.V.I. 1995).

71 Smith v. Robinson, 468 U.S. 992 (1984).

72 20 U.S.C. § 1415(e)(4)(B).

in the community in which the case arose. Under the HCPA, courts may determine what is a reasonable amount of time spent preparing and arguing a case. An award may be limited if a school system made a settlement offer more than ten days before the proceedings began that was equal to or more favourable than the final relief obtained.[73] Further, a court may reduce an award if it finds that parents unreasonably protracted the dispute,[74] an attorney's hourly rate was excessive,[75] or the time spent and legal services furnished were excessive in light of the issues.[76] The HCPA was made retroactive to July 4, 1984, the day before the Supreme Court declared that attorney fees were unavailable under the IDEA.

## DISCIPLINE

Perhaps the most controversial legal issue in special education concerns disciplinary sanctions and students with disabilities. In fact, until its 1997 Amendments were adopted, the IDEA did not make a direct reference to discipline. Discipline of students with disabilities is a sensitive issue since it pits the duty of administrators to maintain order, discipline, and a safe environment against the rights of each child to receive a FAPE in the LRE. Even though most will agree that the power of school officials to maintain discipline should not be frustrated, it must be understood that a student should not be denied the rights accorded by the IDEA if misconduct is caused by the child's disability.

School officials may impose disciplinary sanctions on special education of a child as long as they follow procedures that do not deprive the student of his or her rights. As such, educators may use normal disciplinary sanctions, including suspensions, with special education students by following usual procedures and providing customary due process.[77] Administrators face some restrictions when they intend to impose more drastic punishments such as an expulsion or wish to change a student's placement for disciplinary reasons. Basically, in these situations, the due process procedures in the IDEA replace the normal due process protections.

A long line of case law holds that although students with disabilities cannot be expelled for misconduct that is related to their disabilities, they can be excluded if there was no relationship between their misconduct and disability.[78] While the

[73] *See, e.g.*, Verginia M.C. v. Corrigan-Camden Indep. Sch. Dist., 909 F. Supp. 1023 (E.D. Tex. 1995).

[74] Howie v. Tippecanoe Sch. Corp.,734 F. Supp. 1485 (N.D. Ind. 1990).

[75] Beard v. Teska, 31 F.3d 942 (10th Cir. 1994).

[76] Mr. D. v. Glocester Sch. Comm., 711 F. Supp. 66 (D.R.I. 1989); Hall v. Detroit Pub. Sch., 823 F. Supp. 1377 (E.D. Mich. 1993).

[77] Those procedures were spelled out in the Goss v. Lopez, 419 U.S. 565 (1975).

[78] *See, e.g.*, S-1 v. Turlington, 635 F.2d 342 (5th Cir. 1981).

Supreme Court's landmark decision in *Honig v Doe*,[79] supported the prohibition of expelling students for disability-related misconduct, this ruling did permit special education students to be suspended for up to ten days. During that cooling off period, school personnel may attempt to negotiate an alternative placement with a student's parents. If they are unsuccessful, and can show that the student is truly dangerous, educators may obtain an injunction or order allowing them to exclude the student from school.

The 1997 Amendments, which codified case law since *Honig*, while clarifying many of the gaps in the statute, implemented the most far-reaching changes to the IDEA since it was enacted. The IDEA now contains specific requirements and provisions for disciplining students with disabilities. Further, regulations promulgated by the United States Department of Education explicitly state that the removal of a student with a disability from the child's current educational placement for more than ten consecutive school days constitutes a change of placement.[80] The regulations add that a series of shorter removals accumulating to more than ten days may be considered a change in placement depending on the length of each exclusion, the cumulative days that the child is out of school, and the proximity of the removals to one another.[81] Earlier, the ten day rule was interpreted strictly; now if a student receives a series of short term, two or three day, suspensions spread out over the school year that exceeds the ten day rule by a few days, and it is late in the school year, it is less certain that this will be interpreted as an impermissible change of placement.

In another major change, the IDEA increases the authority of educators to deal with students with disabilities who possess weapons or drugs.[82] Under these provisions, educators may transfer a student with a disability to an interim alternative placement for up to 45 days for possession of a weapon or possession, use, sale, or solicitation of drugs on school property or at a school function.[83] School officials may also order a change in placement to an interim alternative setting if this sanction is used for students who are not disabled under similar circumstances.[84]

When a student with a disability is moved to an alternative placement, educators must conduct a functional behavioural assessment and implement a behavioural intervention plan for the child if one is not already in place.[85] If a behavioural intervention plan was in place when the child misbehaved, the IEP team must review the plan and

79 484 U.S. 305 (1988).
80 34 C.F.R. § 300.519(a).
81 34 C.F.R. § 300.519(b).
82 34 C.F.R. § 300.520(a)(2).
83 20 U.S.C. § 1415(k)(1); 34 C.F.R. § 300.520.
84 34 C.F.R. § 300.520(a)(2).
85 34 C.F.R. § 300.520(b)(1)(I).

its implementation in order to make any necessary modifications.[86] Should a parent disagree with the alternative placement and request a hearing, consistent with the so-called stay-put provision, the student must remain in the alternative setting.[87] Once the 45 day period expires, educators must return the student to his or her prior educational placement[88] unless they can demonstrate that it is dangerous to do so.[89]

The amended IDEA has expanded the authority of hearing officers to order interim alternative placements of up to 45 days after expedited due process hearings.[90] Previously, under *Honig*, educators could not impose such a change unless they had a court order. Even with this change, educators bear the burden of proving that keeping a student in the then current placement is substantially likely to result in injury to the child or others.[91] Still, school officials must show that they took reasonable measures to minimise that risk in the student's current placement.[92]

The IDEA also requires an interim alternative placement to permit a student to continue to progress in the general education curriculum where he or she will still receive necessary services as outlined in his or her IEP.[93] Additionally, educators must include services and modifications designed to prevent the misbehaviour from recurring in the student's programme.[94]

For the first time, the amended IDEA establishes procedures required to evaluate whether misconduct is related to a student's disability.[95] The IDEA calls for this judgment to be made by the team that developed the student's IEP[96] within ten school days of when it chose to take disciplinary action.[97] At the so-called manifestation determination, the team must consider evaluative and diagnostic information, observations of the student, and the child's IEP and placement.[98] In evaluating whether misconduct is a manifestation of a disability, a team should examine whether a child's disability impaired his or her ability to understand the impact and consequences of the misbehaviour along with whether the disability impaired the student's ability to control the behaviour.[99] If, in making the determination, an IEP

86 34 C.F.R. § 300.520(b)(1)(ii).
87 34 C.F.R. § 300.526(a).
88 34 C.F.R. § 300.526(b).
89 34 C.F.R. § 300.526(c).
90 20 U.S.C. § 1415(k)(2); 34 C.F.R. § 300.521; 34 C.F.R. § 300.528.
91 34 C.F.R. §v 300.521(a).
92 34 C.F.R. § 300.521(c).
93 34 C.F.R. § 300.522(b)(1).
94 34 C.F.R. § 300.522(b)(2).
95 20 U.S.C. § 1415(k)(4).
96 34 C.F.R. § 300.523(b).
97 34 C.F.R. § 300.523(a)(2).
98 34 C.F.R. § 300.523(c)(1).
99 34 C.F.R. § 300.523(c)(2).

team is convinced that there were deficiencies in the student's IEP, its implementation, or the child's placement, it must order immediate steps to be taken to remedy those shortcomings.[100]

If an IEP team is convinced that a student's misbehaviour is not a manifestation of the disability, then the child may be disciplined in the same manner as any child who is not disabled.[101] The disciplinary options available to educators include expulsion if it is the usual sanction for the misbehaviour in question. A parent may challenge the result of a manifestation determination by requesting an expedited due process hearing.[102]

Another important change clarifies whether school officials can discontinue educational services for a student who is properly expelled for misconduct that is not disability-related. This provision codified existing policy from the United States Department of Education which ordered that delivery of educational services in this situation and effectively reversed a controversial decision of the Fourth Circuit which held that no such requirement existed under the IDEA.[103] The revised IDEA makes it clear that a FAPE must be made available to all students with disabilities including those who have been expelled from school.[104] In other words, even if a student with a disability has been expelled in accord with the IDEA's provisions, the child must be provided with services that will allow him or her to progress in the general education curriculum and achieve the goals of the student's IEP.[105] The regulations do not require officials to provide services to a child who has been suspended for ten days or less.[106] It is important to note that a student with a disability can still be suspended for up to ten school days as long as this penalty can be imposed on a child who is not disabled.[107] Even so, under such a circumstance, school officials must conduct a functional behaviour, if they have not already done so, and must address the student's misbehaviour.[108]

The courts have disagreed over the treatment of a student who has yet to be determined to be disabled but claims to be covered by the IDEA. School officials must now provide the IDEA's protections to a student if they knew that the child was disabled before the misbehaviour occurred.[109] School officials are considered to have

[100] 34 C.F.R. § 300.523(f).

[101] 20 U.S.C. § 1415(k)(5); 34 C.F.R. § 300.524.

[102] 34 C.F.R. § 300.525.

[103] Commonwealth of Virginia Dep't of Educ. v. Riley, 106 F.3d 559 (4th Cir. 1997).

[104] 20 U.S.C. § 1412(a)(1)(A).

[105] 34 C.F.R. § 300.121(d)(2)(i).

[106] 34 C.F.R. § 300.121(d).

[107] 34 C.F.R. § 300.121(d)(1).

[108] 20 U.S.C. § 1415(k)(1)(B).

[109] 20 U.S.C. § 1415(k)(8).

this knowledge if a parent expresses concern that his or her child may need special education or a makes a request for an evaluation. Educators may also be considered to be on notice of a child's disability based on a student's prior behavioural and academic history and/or concerns expressed by teachers.[110] An exception exists if educators already conducted an evaluation and determined that the student was not disabled.[111] If a parent requests an evaluation during the time when a student is subject to disciplinary sanctions, it must be conducted in an expedited manner.[112] Consistent with the IDEA's stay-put provision, until an expedited evaluation is completed, the student remains in the placement deemed appropriate by educators.[113] If the evaluation team decides that the child is disabled, school officials must provide the student with special education services.[114]

A final change in the law and regulations indicates that the IDEA cannot be interpreted as prohibiting school officials from reporting a crime committed by a student with a disability to the proper authorities or impeding law enforcement and judicial authorities from carrying out their responsibilities.[115] When school officials do report a crime, they must furnish a student's special education and disciplinary records to the appropriate authorities[116] to the extent that this is permitted under the Family Educational Rights and Privacy Act.[117]

## CONCLUSION

Special education in the United States is governed primarily by two major statutes: Section 504 of the Rehabilitation Act and the IDEA. Section 504 is an anti-discrimination law rather than an affirmative action statute. Put another way, pursuant to Section 504, an individual must be otherwise qualified despite his or her disability before being afforded statutory protection. On the other hand, the IDEA requires school systems to take affirmative steps to provide each student with a disability with a FAPE. In addition to providing students with disabilities with a basic floor of opportunity, the IDEA contains an elaborate due process mechanism spelling out how children are to be identified and evaluated.

[110] 34 C.F.R. § 300.527(b).
[111] 34 C.F.R. § 300.527(d).
[112] 34 C.F.R. § 300.527(d)(2)(i).
[113] 34 C.F.R. § 300.527(d)(2)(ii).
[114] 34 C.F.R. § 300.527(d)(2)(iii).
[115] 20 U.S.C. § 1415(k)(9); 34 C.F.R. § 300.529.
[116] 34 C.F.R. § 300.529(b)(1).
[117] 20 U.S.C. § 1232g.

As educational leaders, law makers, and policy makers seek to enhance the development of legal mechanisms to protect the educational rights of children with disabilities, they may wish to review the status in American law and borrow those elements that are most useful while avoiding those practices, perhaps such as the growing rate of litigation, that can bog matters down. By doing so, these interested parties will be working to ensure a more equitable future for all children.

GRACIENNE LAUWERS

# The Rights of Children with Special Needs in the Russian Federation

Despite the scepticism about the concrete legal protection of children with disabilities in Russia, this article shows that there is a rise to prominence in thinking about their rights. However, it makes also clear that it will be a long time before the government fully implements the measures called for in the laws and regulations.

First, a general overview of the actual situation and some initiatives is provided. Secondly, current Russian legislation is examined. Finally, the actual system of educational establishments is described.

## INTRODUCTION[1]

Disabled persons in Russia still face lots of problems (of a physical, psychological and social nature) relating to their treatment and assimilation into society. The architectural style of most government buildings, both in Moscow and in the regions, stand as an unchanging symbol of the government's indifference to senior and disabled citizens.[2] Medical facilities, retail establishments and cultural attractions are not much different from government buildings. Most theaters, concert halls and museums are not accessible.[3] Russian Orthodox churches are usually built on high ground and only rarely are the steep steps leading up to the church built with handrails.

[1] Based upon the review of Lev N. Indolev, "Accessibility in Russia, or the Lack of It", *Bimonthly web-zine of international disability news and views*, Issue no. 8 May–June 2001.

[2] An exception is the city council of St. Petersburg, located in the Marininsky palace which was built for Emperor Nicholas I, whose daughter, the princess Maria, was disabled and used a wheelchair.

[3] Including the Bolshoi Theater, the Pushkin Fine Arts Museum in Moscow, the Russian Museum, the Hermitage Museum in St. Petersburg.

*Jan De Groof and Gracienne Lauwers (eds.), Special Education*, 69–78.

Throughout Russia, public transportation, railways and air travel remain almost entirely inaccessible to disabled people. Experimental train cars equipped with one large, two-bed cabin designed for disabled people and their travelling companions now run on some lines. However, the train stations themselves are difficult to navigate. The high steps and narrow doors make buses and trolleys impossible for wheelchair users and those with difficulty walking. In Moscow only the elevator in the Altufievska metro station[4] makes it easy for a wheelchair user to get down to this station, but there are no other wheelchair-accessible stations.

The majority of the Russian population live in four- or five-story apartment buildings without elevators or nine-story buildings, which have only small elevators. Spacious freight elevators are found only in 16- and 22-story buildings which however, have narrow entranceways with a few steps and no railings. The government of Moscow is planning to build several dozen apartment buildings in the newer neighbourhoods that will be accessible to wheelchair users. In other large cities, such as Nizhny Novgorod and Samara, older apartments are being reconstructed to make them accessible. In Ulan-Ude, city officials are planning the construction of an apartment complex for wheelchair users.[5]

Neither individuals nor organizations of disabled people take local authorities to court with any frequency for failing to provide an accessible environment for disabled people. Non-governmental organizations have undertaken action to improve the accessibility in some cities.[6]

The situation for people with vision impairments is in general better than for people with mobility impairments, thanks to the efforts of the All-Russian Society of the Blind (ARSB), which provide many services to make society more accessible to blind people. Sidewalks and special pedestrian roads for visually impaired people are common in areas where businesses, health and recreation resorts, belonging to the ARSB, are located. At some Metro stations in Moscow, the flooring on the very edge of the platform has a unique texture. Some buses and trolleys are equipped with sound systems to announce not only the names of stops but also the route number and the direction in which the route is running. These and other conveniences, however, are characteristic only in Moscow and in specific neighbourhoods of a few other cities (Samara, Saratov, Bataisk), near enterprises that employ blind workers and where visually impaired people traditionally live in high concentrations. Because of financial reasons, the use of guide dogs has not caught on in Russia. There are, however, two schools in Russia where guide dogs are trained.

4 The metro station is close to a school for disabled children.

5 In conjunction with local disabled people's organizations through the Achievement Foundation.

6 For example, Novgorod-the-Great (joint project between the Novgorod Society of Disabled People and the non-profit organization Perspektiva), Ulan-Ude (project between the Foundation for the Builders of Housing for Disabled People), and Tver (project of Taniusha, an NGO of disabled people).

The situation for mentally disabled is the worst. Thirty-thousand mentally disabled children[7] stay in Russia's state institutions, where Russian laws have proved ineffective for over 10 years. According to Professor N. Dementyeva of the Central Institute of Disability Expertise, up to 40% of children kept in orphanages are declared *untrainable*.[8] The so-called "*untrainable*" children receive no upbringing, education or rehabilitation services. Most of the work is performed by nurses' aids, who have no professional training and are badly paid.

> "... certain categories of children declared untrainable are often placed in institutions regulated by the Ministry of Labour of the Russian Federation where they have no opportunity to develop since they find themselves outside of the educational environment.[9] (...) ... ensuring a medical and social rehabilitation of children with developmental disturbances is hampered in institutions of the Ministry of Labour of the Russian Federation.[10]

Around 25% of children are put into these institutions due to a wrong diagnosis of "deep mental disturbance". Other children (about 30%) suffer from moderate mental ineptitude and are taught nothing but elementary self-service skills.

> ... current regulatory documents (standard organizational and personnel structure, sanitary norms, personnel functions and standard provisions) have not been updated for decades ...[11]

## Legislation

The USSR ratified in 1990 the *UN Convention on the Rights of the Child*. The law on *Basic Principles for Social Protection in the USSR* was enacted in 1990, pursuant to which children in orphanages are guaranteed "uninterrupted care and education combined with social adaptation". For the purpose of the realisation of the rights and freedoms, which are recognised and guaranteed by the universally accepted principles and norms of international law, the following laws were adopted in 1993–1998, which were extremely significant for determining the legal status of disabled children: "The Family Code of the Russian Federation"; "Fundamental Provisions of the RF Legislation on Citizens' Health Protection"; the federal laws "On the

7 Sergey Koloskov, "The Desperate Situation of Children with Disabilities in Russian Institutions", in *International Children's Rights Monitor, Volume 14 No 2; May 2001*.

8 Report "On the Position of Children in the Russian Federation in 2000".

9 Report "On the Position of Children in the Russian Federation in 1998", December 1999, p. 26.

10 Report 1998, p. 47.

11 State Report "On the Position of Children in the Russian Federation in 1998".

Main Guarantees of Children's Rights", "On Social Protection of Disabled in the Russian Federation", "Fundamental Provisions of Social Services for the Citizens of the Russian Federation", "On Social Services for Elderly Citizens and Disabled Persons". The laws ensure living in a specialised nursing home, the protection of his/her life and health, the care, upbringing, education and rehabilitation of disabled children.

In 1992 Russia enacted the Law on Education. Its preamble states: "The right to education is one of the fundamental and inalienable constitutional rights of citizens of the Russian Federation." Furthermore, the law mentions "the opportunity to receive education regardless of (…) state of health, social (…) status." (Article 5.1). The principles of state policy with respect to education are: " the general accessibility of education, the adaptability of the educational system to the level and specificity of students' and pupils' development and training (Article 2(3)). For citizens with a developmental deficiency the state creates conditions for education, correction of the developmental deficiency, and social adaptation by means of special pedagogical methods (Article 5.6). For children and students with deficiencies in their development, agencies of educational administration set up special (corrective in nature) educational institutions (classrooms, groups), assuring the treatment, education and instruction of these students as well as their social adaptation and integration in society. The norms for financing such educational institutions are higher than the average ones. The Government of the Russian Federation determines the types of students and pupils that are assigned to the aforesaid educational institutions and the students who are fully state-supported. Children and juveniles with deficiencies in their development may only be assigned to the aforesaid institutions by the agencies of educational administration, with the consent of the parents (or their legal representatives) and following the results of a psychological, medical-pedagogical commission (Article 50.10).[12]

In 1993 a new *Russian Constitution* was enacted, which states that in the Russian Federation recognition and guarantees shall be provided for the rights and freedoms of man and citizen according to the universally recognised principles and norms of international law and according to the present Constitution (Article 17.1). Under Article 1 of the Constitution, the Russian Federation is a democratic federal law-bound State. The fundamental values of a democratic state are human life and human rights and freedoms. These provisions are enacted in Article 2, which also establishes that acknowledgement, observation and protection of human rights and freedoms constitute a duty of the State. It is securing human rights and freedoms, which constitutes the main objective of a democratic, lawful state. These values are of extreme importance for each member of society, especially when they are threatened with extinction. Developmental delays, whether physical or psychological, are

[12] Jan De Groof, Gracienne Lauwers, Vladimir Filippov, *Adequate Education Law for the Russian Federation*, Garant, 2001, 273–301.

indeed factors "of increased risk" which not uncommonly lead to infringement of the rights and freedoms of those who suffer from them.[13]

The *federal law "On Main Guarantees of Children's Rights"* states that "the goals of public policy in ensuring the rights of children are: to give full effect to the rights of children, ... and redress grievances whenever children's rights are violated ..." (Article 4.1). Further on, the law highlights that: "Public policy in ensuring the rights of children is a priority for the Russian Federation authorities ..." (Article 4.2). The law stresses that disabled children "are entitled to special care and protection of federal authorities, legislative and executive bodies of the subject of the Federation, as well as local authorities" (Article 15.1).

The *preamble of the "Law on the Social Protection of Disabled Persons in the Russian Federation"* provides that: "The goal of public policy in regard to the disabled is to ensure that citizens with disabilities have equal opportunities to exercise their civil, economic, political and other rights and freedoms guaranteed by the Constitution and universally recognised principles and norms of international law and international treaties of the Russian Federation." Article 2 of the Law says that the state guarantees social protection to people with disabilities as: "... a set of economic, social and legal measures facilitating rehabilitation and making up for the limitations in their lives due to their handicaps, and aimed at creating equal opportunities with other citizens to participate in the life of the society." Articles 9–12 of the Law provide that the state guarantees the rehabilitation of disabled persons through a set of "medical, psychological, pedagogical, social and economic measures ... rehabilitation is aimed at restoring the social status of the disabled, his/her material independence and social adaptation". Rehabilitation should be carried out in accordance with a "rehabilitation programme individually developed" for every disabled person, "the implementation of which is binding on respective federal and local authorities and organisations, regardless of their legal status and the form of ownership". Articles 18–19 of the Law provide that the state guarantees "education for the disabled children", "in accordance with their individual rehabilitation programme", as well as "appropriate rehabilitation measures" and creates "appropriate conditions" for their integration in general-type pre-school childcare facilities and for educating them in general-type educational establishments, equipped, where necessary, with specialised technical facilities." Only those children who have proved that "the condition of their health ... excludes the possibility of attending the general-type pre-school childcare facilities, specialised pre-school facilities shall be established."

The above-listed laws establish responsibility for their violation and oblige the Government of the Russian Federation (ministries and agencies) to bring all their

[13] Comments on the Russian Constitution by the Institute of Legislation and Comparative Legal Studies under the Russian Government; Comments on Russian Legislation in the Sphere of Psychiatry by the Institute of State and Law at the Russian Academy of Sciences.

normative documents in conformity with these laws. The Civil Code and the Criminal Code also provide for the responsibility of the violators of some provisions of these laws.

To implement these laws, in 1993–2000, the Government of the Russian Federation, its ministries and agencies adopted a number of regulatory documents.

## Establishments for special education[14]

Several ministries are responsible for the establishments for children with special needs. The lack of co-ordination between the different ministries involved causes a lot of difficulties. Children from birth to 3 are brought up in establishments of the Ministry of Public Health (pre-school kindergarden, children homes). The children's homes which look after children up to the age of 4–5, come under the auspices of the Ministry of Health.

Once the children reach this age, they are transferred to school establishments of the Ministry of Education. Children who are classified as mentally handicapped, are transferred to orphanages under the Ministry of Labour and Social Affairs, where they remain until the age of 18. At that age they are sent to psycho-neurological nursing homes for adults under the same ministry, where they remain until death.

### *(1) The system of Special Education in Russia*[15]

*Vertical structure*

The vertical structure is based on developmental features of students and on the levels of regular educational programmes.

The vertical structure consists of 5 levels:

- period of early childhood (from 0 to 3 years old);
- pre-school period (from 3 to 7);
- period of compulsory education (from 7 to 16);
- period of comprehensive education and vocational training (from 15 to 18 and down to 21 for the blind, deaf and physically handicapped);
- period of adult training.

At the period of early childhood (from birth to 3) children are trained and brought up at home, in babies' establishments and in children-orphans-homes.

[14] Jan de Groof and Gracienne Lauwers (Eds.) , *A New Framework of Special Education in the Russian Federation*, 2000, Garant, 242 p.

[15] Sjipitsina L., *Spetsialnoe obutsenie v Rossii u Flandrii: schodstva i razlitsija*, Mezjdunarodnij universitet deti i rebenka im. R. Vallenberga, Sankt-Peterburg, 1998.

For children of pre-school age there are the following types of establishments:

- special kindergartens with day and day-night stay;
- remedial children homes;
- special groups in regular kindergartens;
- special rehabilitation centres;
- pre-school groups in special schools (for children with visual, hearing, motion, mental disorders).

Special (remedial) educational establishments for children with developmental problems carry out the programmes of elementary education, general education and general comprehensive education. These establishments are a component of the system of education. They give an opportunity to have an education in the process of reception of development, within the frameworks of special state educational standards. They simultaneously solve also some special remedial problems, provide education, treatment, social adaptation and integration into society.

The forms of schooling are:

- special (remedial) school (daily or evening);
- special (remedial) boarding school;
- rehabilitation centres;
- remedial class at a regular educational establishment;
- individually in a regular educational establishment;
- home education;
- external education;
- education in conditions of a stationary medical establishment;
- centres for preventive care.

Persons with developmental problems have a possibility to get a regular education and vocational training in the following establishments:

- special average schools;
- special industrial workshops;
- centres of social-labour rehabilitation;
- special vocational schools.

For adults with special needs there are the following establishments:

- evening schools;
- special technical schools;
- special groups in technical schools and high-schools;
- rehabilitation centres;
- educational and industrial workshops of the societies of the blind, the deaf and disabled;
- special high-school for disabled persons in Moscow.

*Horizontal structure*
The horizontal structure takes into account a child's psycho-physical development, his/her comprehensive activities and the type of disorder.

The horizontal structure of Special Education in Russia has eight types of special establishments for children with developmental problems:

I. for the deaf (with classes for mentally retarded children);
II. for the hard of hearing (with classes for mentally retarded children);
III. for the blind (with classes for mentally retarded children);
IV. for visually impaired (with classes for mentally retarded children);
V. with hard speech and language disorders;
VI. with motion disabilities (with classes for mentally retarded children);
VII. with learning disabilities;
VIII. for mentally retarded (special classes for severely mentally retarded children, classes for children with multiple and complex disorders).

### *(2) Types of establishments for children with disabilities*

*I. Special (remedial) educational establishments for students with developmental disorders*;

*II. Special educational establishments for children and teenagers with deviant behaviour*;

For children and teenagers with deviant behaviour there exist three kinds of special educational establishments in Russia:

- special education school;
- special technical school;
- special (remedial) comprehensive school and special (remedial) vocational technical school for children and teenagers with developmental problems (learning disabilities, psychological deviations, slight mental retardation) and for children who committed socially dangerous acts.

Special educational establishments are of an open and closed type. The establishments of an open type carry out the functions of preventive institutions and are set up for children and teenagers with a steady illegal behaviour, those who were subjected to any form of psychological abuse, who refuse to visit regular educational establishments, who appear to have difficulties in communication with parents. The establishment of a closed type is set up for children who committed socially dangerous acts which are stipulated by the Criminal Code of the Russian Federation, those who require special conditions of education and who need a special pedagogical approach.

The special (remedial) establishment for children with deviant behaviour is also a closed type institution.

*III. Boarding schools and children's homes for children-orphans and children without parental care.*

A network of boarding establishments takes care of disabled children.

For frequently and chronically ill children there are educational establishments of the system of education of a sanatorium type, depending on the various types of diseases (for example, for children with tuberculosis, scoliosis, broncho-pulmonary, psychoneurological, gastro-enterological, heart-vascular pathology).

There are also schools at childrens' hospitals.

*IV. Rehabilitation centres*

Besides these traditional types of special educational institutions, new types of special establishments are created: rehabilitation centres, diagnostic classes, school-centres for diagnostics and integrated education.[16] For an admission to a special establishment, a decision is not made on the basis of a single assessment, but of an individual assessment during the educational process of each child.

These establishments, as a rule, are multifunctional. They include diagnosis, development, remediation and improvement of health. They also provide workshops to develop the abilities of "children with special needs" in crafts, arts, music and environment. They aim at the development of a child's personality, understanding of the environment and of the world. The establishments try to help a child to find his or her place in the new society.

The main goal of the rehabilitation centres' activities is not only and not primarily the reconstruction of the form and contents of work, but the desire to break and to rebuild as a whole the attitudes towards children with special needs with consideration for their needs and problems. This is achieved by the following:

- co-ordinate the efforts of various experts dealing with the children with disabilities;
- provide early diagnostics of developmental disorders;
- investigate a child's personality, reveal his/her abilities, optimise the choice of the adaptation and educational programme;
- elaborate a programme for the raising of children with different levels of disabilities in mental, intellectual and speech development according to special programmes and curriculum;
- remedy the lack of development during special lessons;
- elaborate preventive measures;

[16] For example, school N34 in St. Petersburg.

– prepare students for education in special classes at regular schools and through professional assimilation.

### *(3) The financing of Special Education in Russia*

The Russian Federation has today a huge network of 162,600 educational establishments (6.8% state educational establishments, 147.3% municipal educational establishments, 8.5% non-state educational establishments). As the financing of education and public health services and other branches is carried out mainly at the expense of local budgets, there are huge regional differences in life conditions of children with disabilities in Russia.

Many non-state educational institutions are being established. Already in 1993 there existed 368 non-state regular schools (with 33,000 students).

## CONCLUSION

Experience shows that disabled people should themselves be involved in monitoring social programmes designed for their benefit and insist that these programmes are carried out. Unfortunately, disabled communities still receive little support from the state and the major problem is still to change the social attitude. However, NGO's are starting to influence the policy makers for improving the education of children with special needs. More than 100 public organizations are dealing with the problems of disabled children, representing the interests of these families, raising disabled children, participating in the development of legislative and regulatory documents, ensuring compliance with new and earlier adopted legislative and regulatory documents and evaluating efficiency of current laws and regulatory documents. After several years of action, specialised classes for children with psychological and verbal deviations were finally granted the official status of a school and provide now specialised education in close co-operation with highly trained specialists and medical pedagogues that have had internships in Europe.[17]

[17] The question still to be solved is what happens when the children reach the age of 18.

VIKI VANDENBUSSCHE[†] Updated by JAN DE GROOF

# Integration of Disabled Children in Compulsory Education in Russia[1]

## 1. THE SYSTEM OF SPECIAL EDUCATION DURING THE SOVIET PERIOD

The system of special education during the Soviet period was a textbook example of segregation.

Until the end of the 1960s in Russia, the education and upbringing of children with serious mental disorders was carried out in institutions of the special education system (boarding schools) and of the education system (special classes for "imbeciles" in "support schools"[2]).

At boarding schools, most of the attention was geared to acquiring elementary skills for one-sided forms of labour. The educational-instructional work and social adaptation of the adults were inadequately brought into question.

In the so-called "imbecile classes" of a support school, the teachers' full attention was geared to their assignment which was to provide "imbeciles" with a minimum of general knowledge: reading, writing, arithmetic and job training, whereas the social adaptation of these children was neglected. The basic assignment of a special class was to detect children who would be able to receive education in regular classes of a support school and to prepare them for that.

In accordance with this objective, an educational plan for such classes was also drawn up. In this way, 14 hours per week were spent studying the Russian language, six hours were devoted to mathematics, two hours to gymnastics and rhythmics together, while a total of one hour was devoted to manual labour, handiwork, drawing and singing put together. Minimal attention was given to developing motor skills, manual skills, skills needed to live independently, life orientation and employment training.

[1] Reprint. de Groof J., Lauwers Gr., *A New Framework of Special Education in the Russian Federation*, Garant, 2000, 145–155.

[2] In Russian "vspomogatel'nye skoly", a type of special school.

*Jan De Groof and Gracienne Lauwers (eds.), Special Education*, 79–90.

The tendency of education of this target group to lean sharply toward reading, writing and arithmetic ultimately rendered the efficacy of the education very low and led to unsuitability of these children for independent living.

The low results of education in special classes at support schools led to their closing and only until very recently, the boarding schools of the social protection system were the only establishments for severely mentally disabled children (who make up approximately 15% of all cases of mental delay) where a complex of measures exists for their education and upbringing.

In 1996, there were 151 such establishments throughout all of Russia where in 1992, there were 32,359 children in the age group of 4 to 18.[3]

## 2. Groups that can benefit from integrated education

Since 1994, Integrated Education in Flanders has been accessible for children from all kinds of Special Education.

According to L.M. Sipicyna, Rector of the Wallenberg University in St Petersburg, Integrated Education in Russia primarily focuses on the following target groups:

- On the one hand, there are children without family, whose parents are deceased or missing. However, there are also a great number of children whose parents had their parental rights taken away because they are imprisoned or because they are not deemed fit to fulfill their parental duties due to the nature of their social behaviour.

  These "social" orphans make up an ever-growing group and the number of children from problem families and families with inadequate economic resources is increasing steadily as well.
- Children with special needs, that is to say with disorders in their psychological and/or physical development, who cannot be corrected or balanced within the framework of their own family.

  What is extremely alarming is the speed at which the number of children with psycho-physical disorders in Russia is growing. There is talk of a serious change in the genetic make-up, an increase in the number of children with hereditary disorders and also of children affected by catastrophes caused by man (wars, atomic disasters, such as Chernobyl).
- Children with behavioural disorders, due to which they all too quickly become mixed up in criminal surroundings or present a danger to themselves. These children show disorders to the extent that the family is not able to correct them adequately. These are not necessarily "difficult" children or children from "problem families". This type of situation can also arise in a normal family and

3 Sipicyna L.M., Ivanov E.C., Asikritov V.N., *Social'no-trudovaja reabilitacija i adaptacija detej s glubokim naruseniem intellekta*, Sankt Peterburg, 1996, 3–4.

not every family is able to deal with it. A phenomenon which is becoming more and more alarming in Russian society is the criminal and delinquent behavioural disorders in children and adolescents, the abuse of alcohol, tobacco and narcotic substances. The number of suicides and suicide attempts is on the rise, as is the number of children with severe forms of social alienation (marginalisation).[4]

## 3. Number of children who receive special education

According to Goskomstat[5] data of the Russian Federation, there were 342,700 registered disabled children aged up to 16 years at the beginning of 1994: this is almost four times as many as there were in 1985 (90,600). According to the latest data that date from 1 April 1998, this figure has already risen in the meantime to 481,021 children who receive special education.[6]

This figure increases considerably when taking into account children with disorders in intellectual and physical development who do not fall under the denomination "disabled" but who require upbringing and education under special conditions.[7]

Today, it is clear to everyone that the special education system in Russia needs change. In this way, it is hoped that a new attitude toward children with developmental disorders can be promoted. In connection to this, one must gradually resolve the issues surrounding their integration into society and integrated education.[8]

The development of the child's personality now all too often takes place in circumstances of psychological deprivation which prevail in various types of institutions, in children's homes, hospitals and in society in general.

The problem of psychological deprivation is very real in broken families and again those children with developmental problems are the victims thereof.

The change in the system of special education in Russia is inextricably linked to a whole series of facts:

- a considerable increase in the number of children with developmental problems and disabled children, partly related to ecologically unfavourable circumstances (such as the Chernobyl disaster and the events in Celjabinsk), the incidence of

4 Sipicyna L.M., Ivanov E.C., Danilova L.A., Smironova I.A., *Reabilitacija detej s problemami v intelektual'nom i fiziceskom razvitii,* Sankt Peterburg, 1995.

5 Gosudarstvennyj Komitet po Statistike: staatscomité voor de statistiek.

6 Data from the Obscij Nausno-Metodiceskij centr "Razvitie Korrekcija".

7 Sipicyna L.M., Ivanov E.C., Asikritov V.N., *Social'no-trudovaja reabilitacija i adaptacija detej s glubokim naruseniem intellekta*, Sankt Peterburg, 1996, 3.

8 X, *Korrekcija i reabilitacija detej s problemami v razvitii v uslovijach integrirovannogo obucenija*, Sankt Peterburg, 1994, 3.

children with complete disabilities, various forms of delays in the psychological development, autism, disorders of the motor system and others.
- the need to develop a system of psychodiagnostics and prophylactics of developmental disorders beginning from the earliest childhood years but also the need for early admittance to the process of education and upbringing in a family, and of integration of the problem child into society.
- the emergence of new rehabilitative establishments (the regular functioning of psychological-medical-pedagogical committees, the functioning of medical-pedagogical centres and social-employment rehabilitation and so on) for which training is required not only for special pedagogues but also for practical psychologists and social rehabilitators.
- the change of the socio-economic conditions in the country, the perestroika of education in general, the development of the government statements of the intentions, principles and organisation of a school, the on-going training of specialists at many levels, including university and post-university education levels.
- the change in the social life of society and the increase in self-determination of the parents, which leads to an increase in the number of children with a range of problems in regular schools. These are children with problems in education, behaviour, and social interaction (Table 1).

*Table 1:* The number of special schools and special classes for disabled children in general formative schools in the Russian Federation and their student numbers as of 1 April 1998[9]

| | *Number* | *Number of students* |
|---|---|---|
| Schools for the mentally handicapped | 1,424 | 208,326 |
| Schools for the blind | 22 | 3,785 |
| Schools for the partially sighted | 63 | 8,262 |
| Schools for the deaf | 83 | 10,876 |
| Schools for the hard of hearing | 81 | 11,214 |
| Schools for children with spina bifida | 51 | 6,570 |
| Schools for children with speech disorders | 61 | 11,556 |
| ZPR[10] schools (children with learning difficulties) | 82 | 14,495 |
| Schools for children with multiple (complex) disabilities | 18 | 2,489 |
| Remedial classes (for children with ZPR/learning difficulties) | 13,000 | 184,274 |
| Classes for the mentally disabled in regular schools | 1,750 | 16,624 |
| Classes for children with physical disabilities | 255 | 2,550 |
| Total number of classes | 15,005 | 203,448 |
| End total | 16,890 | 481,021 |

[9] Data from the Obscij Nausno-Metodiceskij centr "Razvitie Korrekcija".

[10] Zaderzka Psichiceskogo Razvitija: delay in psychological development.

In Russia, special education is developing along two lines: the differentiation line and the integration line. The differentiation line takes shape via the development of 8 types of special education and through the foundation of new forms of special education such as schools for autistic children and schools for children with deviant behaviour.

The integration line includes both the social integration of disabled children and integrated education. At this time, the development of special education is still taking place primarily by means of forming separate schools. That is the most adequate path for the time being, not only in connection to the existing system for training specialists but also due to the attitudes toward disabled children which exist in Russian society. In addition, the fact that the conditions set by integrated education are not yet being satisfied plays a role. This has bearing on the creativity, experience and skills of teachers, amongst other things.[11]

Nowadays, differentiation by means of separate schools is considered to be just about the only way to be able to offer Russian children adapted education. The introduction of integrated education still often encounters a lack of the necessary academic, organisational, personnel and methodical conditions. Russia finds itself as it were in a transitional phase between segregation and interschool differentiation on the one hand and integrated education on the other. From that perspective, experiences of other countries and the assessments thereof are extremely important for Russia.

In addition, the regular schools lack a number of important conditions which are necessary for integrated education: there are no teachers with special training, no psychologists, no social workers, no special programmes and no educational resources for remedial education.

## 4. Children with Developmental Disorders Integrated in Regular Schools

Integration is not a new problem for the Russian Federation. In regular kindergartens and schools in Russia, especially in small towns and in agricultural areas, there are many children with developmental disorders. This category of children is very much heterogeneous and "integrated" amongst their peers with normal development because of a variety of reasons. By approximation, one can discern four groups of such children:

- Undiagnosed children: their "integration" was due to the fact that their developmental disorder had not yet manifested itself.
- Children whose parents have been informed of their child's developmental disorders yet still insist on education in a regular kindergarten or school for a variety

[11] Sipicyna L.M., *The development of special education in regular schools*, Sankt Peterburg, 1998, 32–33.

of reasons (such as a great travel distance between their residence and the nearest special school). In this case, when the integrated education takes place solely on the basis of the parents' wishes, without taking into account expert opinion, this appears to be beneficial for only an insignificant number of children.

The majority, however, after several years of "integrated education" that was not adapted to their level of development, ends up in special development establishments or falls completely outside the education system.

- Pupils in special pre-school groups and classes in regular kindergartens and schools. The education and upbringing of such children occur while taking into account their developmental disorders but the special groups and classes often remain isolated.
- Children, who as a result of long term remedial efforts, provided with the help of teachers, defectologists and parents, are prepared for education in an environment with healthy peers, which allows specialists to recommend them for integrated education. As a rule, however, those children are denied the systematic remedial help which for them is absolutely necessary, and this reduces the effectiveness of the integrated education.[12]

In the development of integrated education, financial aspects are also of great importance. The costs of special education in boarding schools amount to approximately 5 times as much as the costs for one student in a regular school.

In addition to the disadvantage of the social isolation of education in separate schools for children with a disability, there are a variety of other objections:

- not all children with physical limitations require special education in a separate school (approximately 25% of them can be accommodated at regular schools);
- the lack of contact with peers with normal development;
- the need to place children in care (more than 80% of special education is coupled with boarding schools) and;
- the inadequate preparation for learning to deal with the problems of daily life due to the protected situation in which children at boarding schools reside.[13]

In past years, the integration issue has been brought up primarily by schools for special education. The schools for regular education still have little involvement in the discussion. It happens regularly that a regular school is not prepared to accept a child with developmental problems even if the child is ready for integration. Refusal of such a child sometimes takes place on the basis of educational principles

[12] Smatko M.D., *Dlia kogo mozet byt' effektivnym integrirovannoe obucenie*, Moskva, 1997, 2–3.

[13] Sipicyna L.M., *The development of social education in regular schools in Russia in again together to school in Amsterdam and St. Petersburg: similarities and differences*, 1998, 32–33.

but usually on the grounds of the fact that the teachers in a regular school are not able to work with children with specific educational needs.

At many Russian schools for regular education there is an active selection process with very competitive elements. This will occasionally lead to schools refusing to place children with developmental problems.

Such a decision is generally justified by stating that this is in the interest of the child. Regular schools, after all, cannot provide special help.

An important problem in realising integrated education is that regular education has insufficient knowledge of the diagnosis of and approach to developmental problems. This makes it desirable for both regular and special education to be involved in the integration process. The special school will not only have to prepare its students for the transition to a school for regular education but it will also have to assist the regular school in resolving the problems that the transition from a school for special education to a school for regular education entails.

## 5. Special classes in regular schools

In modern-day Russia, special classes in regular schools are the most popular form of integrated education. These special classes exist for:

- children with mental disabilities (especially in situations where there is no special school for these children);
- children with learning difficulties;
- children who belong to a so-called risk group (children with learning difficulties based on under-motivation, children with behavioural problems and children with poor health).

It occasionally happens that there are classes in regular schools for children with auditory and visual disabilities or for children with serious speech impediments. This actually only applies when the nearest special school is a great distance away and in situations where parents do not want to let their children attend boarding school.

One of the most difficult issues of the present Russian education is the problem that a large number of children does not succeed in mastering the normal subject matters in the time allotted. Various authors have stated that this is the case for 20–30% of students. There have been attempts to resolve this issue by means of differentiated education that takes into account differences in school readiness, health, psychological and physical development and interest.

This differentiation is usually given shape in the form of special classes for children with learning difficulties and special compensation classes for children who belong to the so-called risk group.

At this time, there is still no common terminology for describing children with learning difficulties, their school problems and the pedagogic-didactic methods developed for these children.

It is therefore very difficult for teachers to further educate themselves through the study of literature. This is because there are always different descriptions used in this literature, such as "children with limited progress", "slow learners", "children with learning difficulties", "children with delays in psychological development", "risk children", "pedagogically and didactically neglected children", "children of poor health", "nervous children" and so forth.

It is therefore also impossible to get a clear picture of the children who attend these special classes, all the more so because the names of such classes also differ at times. So there are "adaptation classes", "recreation classes", "classes for intensive development", "classes for compensative education", "classes with pedagogic-didactic support", "remedial classes", and "make-up classes".

The Ministry of Education of the Russian Federation officially distinguishes two types of classes:

- classes for children with learning difficulties (make-up classes), which are mentioned in an official decree of the Ministry of Education in 1981;
- compensation classes, which are mentioned in a provisional measure of the Ministry of Education in 1992.

## 6. Integrated education in regular classes

Within Russian education, the integration of children with auditory problems in a regular class of a regular school is a fairly new phenomenon. Until recently, it was a rare occurrence for children with auditory disabilities to attend a regular class in a regular school. When this did occur, it was for children in thinly populated areas (where there were no schools for special education and where the diagnostics were rather poor as well) or for very gifted children with auditory disabilities. The latter then often received additional support from their parents or from particular teachers. Now, placing children with auditory disabilities in regular classes does occur. However, this still happens on a very limited scale.

When parents of children who are deaf or hard of hearing opt for a regular school, various motivations play a role:

- inadequate information about the options for special education;
- the status-increasing effect of attending a regular school;
- the objective fact that the child is ready to attend a regular school;
- the parents' refusal to send their child to a boarding school. Russian special education makes a great deal of use of boarding schools. These serve very large areas. Some of these areas cover a greater surface than that of many a European country. Due to the great distances, students can only go home during school holidays but the rest of the year they stay at the boarding school.

Although the parents' choice regarding placement of a child in a regular class, regardless of motive, must be respected, it still appears that only a limited number of children with auditory disabilities benefits from integration in a regular class within a regular school. This is with regard to children who, due to early diagnosis and treatment qua speech-language development, function at a level which closely corresponds to their age group.

Children who are deaf or hard of hearing and who attend a regular school must receive special guidance from an "orthopaedagogic" centre. This centre must provide the child with special support in areas such as improving pronunciation, developing auditory perception and developing receptive and expressive language. This support can be a more or less constant need. In that case, it has the nature of regular remedial help.

This support can also be temporary. In that case, the parents or older fellow students are often called in. A number of things are largely dependent on the needs of the child in question. One thing is clear: with a lack of specific help, the student in question will not realise his or her potential.

From data gathered by Smatco, it appears that during the past year in Moscow and its surroundings, 48 children were integrated in regular education following training in experimental kindergartens and in classes associated with the Institute for Special Education of the Russian Academy for Pedagogical Sciences. In St Petersburg, there are currently approximately 50 students with auditory disorders who attend schools for regular education. All of these students were prepared for this at kindergarten.

In modern day Russia, the integration of children with visual impairments in regular education is also a rare occurrence. Regular education is not yet able to adequately accommodate these children. With the integration of visually disabled children in regular education, economic, organisational and educational problems play an important role.

Despite all the problems that go along with the integration of students with sensory disabilities into regular education, their integration will be realised in some way or another in the future.

The success of this integration will largely depend upon the opportunities for scientific research, legislation, financial resources and for the special training of teachers of regular education.

In Russia, the changing ideological basic principles regarding special education are strongly bound to the desire for integration. Realising this desire, however, requires major adaptations on the part of education. In addition, analysis of almost 30 years experience abroad teaches that integration is successful only when a number of conditions are satisfied:

- a democratic society that guarantees the individual rights of its citizens;
- the financial security that children with developmental problems receive the help they require also within regular education;
- the opportunity for freedom of choice, within objective limits, between integrated education and education in separate schools;

- a certain "readiness" of the civilisation and the individuals within it regarding the idea of "coexistence" of "normal" and "handicapped" people.

It is important to raise the new generation (probably even more than one) from very early on in such a way that integration of disabled children and adults becomes a part of their world-view. This involves people learning to take into account the specific difficulties and capabilities of the disabled. With all of this, it must not be forgotten that integrated education is not a goal in itself: ultimately what matters is the well-being of children with developmental problems.

## 7. Combined integration

In Russia, the most adequate circumstances for realising goal-oriented work for the integration of children with developmental disorders occur in the educational establishments of the combined sort, which include both special and regular pre-school groups and classes. Under those circumstances, one can effectively realise the integration of children with problems, taking into account the developmental level of each child and the selected beneficial, and for that child possible, "part" of integration, that is one of the following models:

- combined integration, geared toward children with a level of psychological and speech development which corresponds with or is close to the average for their age. One or two such individuals at the same level are taught in regular groups and classes whereby they receive on-going remedial help from a teacher-defectologist of a special group.
- partial integration, whereby children with developmental problems who have not yet achieved a level equal to that of their healthy peers attend regular groups or classes for only a part of the day (for example, the second half, for certain classes), alone or in pairs.
- temporary integration, whereby all pupils of a special group, independent of their psychophysical and speech development, join healthy children (not less than once or twice per month) in attending a variety of events of an instructive nature, such as celebrations, competitions, specific lessons,[14] etc.

The realisation of these models presumes absolute guidance in the process of integration by a teacher-defectologist who helps the regular teachers with organising the upbringing and education of the child with developmental disorders within the group of healthy peers.

Full integration may be recommended for children who, at the level of psychophysical and speech development, meet the standards of their contemporaries and are psychologically prepared for education together with their healthy peers.

[14] X, *Rossijssko-Flamandskii proekt "Special'noe obrazovanie" – proekt "Integracija"*, Moskva, 1995, 19–20.

Such children are accommodated, individually or in pairs, in regular kindergarten groups or in regular classes at the school located nearest to their home.

Over and above that, they must absolutely receive remedial help, either at the place of education (e.g. for children with speech disorders, at the speech therapy office of the educational establishment), either in a part-time department of a special kindergarten or school, or in various centres (e.g. for children with hearing impairments, in surdoaudiological speech rooms of the public health system).

For cities and other places where there are no special institutes, a model of combined integration may be recommended whereby children with certain disorders but with a high level of psycho-physical and speech development attend regular kindergarten or school, individually or in pairs.

A teacher-defectologist is assigned to the team of staff responsible for the group and is responsible for both formal lecturing and individual lessons with problem children as well as for group lessons. The teachers work with all young children. This model allows for the creation of possibilities, for early integration of a considerable number of children with developmental disorders on the one hand and for special pedagogical support for children without developmental disorders but with great difficulties in education due to other causes on the other hand (such as hearing children of deaf parents, bilingual children, children from families of refugees and forced immigrants and so forth).

## 8. Regulation of the Process of Integrated Education

A legal guarantee of the process of integrated education for children with special educational needs is as yet lacking in Russia. There are only documents of a general nature which reflect the belief that is supposed to be the position of persons with special needs in society and the state.

These are the declarations ratified by the Russian Federation: Declaration of the Rights of the Child" (1959); the "Declaration of the Rights of the Mentally Disabled" (1971), the "Declaration of the Rights of the Invalids" (1975) and the "Convention for the Rights of the Child" (1975).

The Russian Federation's Law on "Education of Persons with Limited Opportunities", which is currently still in a draft stage, is meant to become the basic rights document for the realisation of the programme for integrated education. But passing this law does not entirely do away with the problem of regulating the process of integrated education. The need for the development of additional legal actions remains.

These must be aimed at the following:

- determining the status of the integrating child and of the general formative establishments that accommodate such children;
- implementing a change in status of special establishments as a result of the expansion of their function in providing remedial help to integrating children;

- implementing changes in normative documents that regulate the material-technical guarantee of regular general formative establishments with the aim of creating therein the conditions for the upbringing and education of disabled children and children with developmental disorders.

Through aesthetic upbringing, one can guarantee the promotion of all potential social-adaptive capabilities of children with disabilities.

One way to achieve optimal conditions for uncovering creative talents and their use as a means to fully fledged participation in society may be the Russian Arts Festival for Children with Disabilities, which took place for the first time in the autumn of 1997. Dance, song, the literary genre, circus arts as well as decorative art forms are all on offer.

Finally, we would like to cite Malofeev[15] who has succeeded in making such clear comparisons of the situations in Russia and in Western Europe.

1. Russia arrived at integration 20 years after Western Europe. In addition, the trend toward integration in Russia comes into existence under principally different circumstances. Europe made the transition to the integrative period on the basis of far-reaching development of already established norms of democracy and in a period of economic bloom. Russia, on the other hand, began in a situation of establishing democratic norms of their very first legislative formulation, of the most far-reaching, deep economic crisis as well as crises of all governmental institutions.
2. The discussion of the problems of special education and integration are carried out in the West in the framework of strict legislative acts that regulate the process of integration. In Russia, however, discussions of that nature are not supported on a legislative basis.
3. In the West, there are rich traditions of charity, an extensive network of non-governmental special institutions, tax benefits for philanthropists, a system of preparing and shaping public opinion by means of mass media. In Russia, however, the tradition of charity was cut short in 1917 and in present times this is still merely a moribund social movement, not promoted by any financial legislation. Only in recent years has the mass media brought the issue of disabled children to the forefront.
4. It is fundamentally important that in the 1970s in the West, the idea of integrating people with developmental disorders came into existence in a context of resistance to all forms of discrimination (on the basis of race, gender, nationality, political convictions, religion, ethnicity and other distinguishing features).

   However, in Russia integration is proclaimed to be an essential part of human behaviour with respect to the disabled in a situation of sharp decline in the standard of living of various layers and social groups in the population and of national conflicts.

[15] Malofeev N.N., *Sovremennyj etap v razvitii sistemy special'nogo obrazovanija v Rossii: Resul'taty issledovanija kak osnova dlja postroenija programmy razvitija*, Defektologija 4 (1987), 11.

CECILIA BOUWER AND ANNA-BARBARA DU PLESSIS[1]

# Legal Aspects Concerning the Accommodation of Learners with Special Educational Needs in the Systemic Evaluation Programme of the South African Department of Education

## 1. INTRODUCTION

As the proof of the pudding is in the eating, so the worth of policy is demonstrated in its implementation. One great challenge in policy implementation is to achieve congruency between the values ensconced in the policy and the effects of policy implementation. Another challenge in policy implementation is to achieve consistency and harmony in actions and strategies within and across all systems and departments concerned, including systems and departments where other legislation, such as the Bill of Rights in the South African Constitution, is also operant. Policy implementation is systemic by its very nature.

The Systemic Evaluation (SE) Programme of the Department of Education of South Africa was mandated by the government to assess, on an ongoing basis, the performance of the education system. SE is bound by the South African Constitution, the Education White Paper 6 (EWP 6) on Special Needs Education and various other policy documents to include learners with disabilities and other barriers to learning and development in its operations.

In this paper, some developments in the international thinking and research about inclusive education and participation and the EWP 6 will be briefly contemplated in order to calibrate specifications for the first SE Project of South Africa, in respect of learners with disabilities. Legal justification for accommodations that are required in assessing the performance of learners contending with disabilities and other barriers to learning and participation will be looked at. A brief overview will be given of the aims and *modus operandi* of the SE Programme in general, followed by some

[1] Cecilia Bouwer, Department of Educational Psychology, Faculty of Education, University of Pretoria & Anna-Barbara du Plessis, Educational psychologist.

*Jan De Groof and Gracienne Lauwers (eds.), Special Education,* 91–109.

discussion of the measure in which learners with disabilities have been included in the Project and the effect thereof on the results of this pilot run for the Systemic Evaluation 2001/2002 at the Grade 3 level.

## 2. Terminology

Some terminology used in the text warrants brief clarification as a first step in a discussion of legal aspects in the accommodation of learners with special educational needs.

Internationally, the term *special education(al) need*, as used in the title, chiefly signifies learners who have a disability that is an intrinsic deficiency of a sensory, neurological, mental, physical or developmental nature. However, for several reasons, not everyone in South Africa is in favour of the term *special educational need*. Firstly, the term implies that there are two categories of learners: those with ordinary needs and those with special needs. Unfortunately, the latter category resulted in a separate, often inadequate, system of education. Secondly, the adjective 'special' fails to denote exactly what is regarded as special and is often used sloppily as a catch-all phrase to categorise all learners who somehow do not 'fit into' the ordinary education system. Thirdly, one could even question to what needs *special* education should respond: the needs of the learner, or the needs of the education system, or both? (based on Persson, 1998: 109).

The terms *barrier to learning and development* and (*special*) learning *need*, found increasingly in more recent texts and also in the EWP 6, include disability with organic and/or medical causes, but also acknowledge that the school and education systems particularly, and the family, social, economic and political systems in general, frequently contribute to or cause the various forms of need and challenge experienced by learners (see 3.2 for examples of such barriers to learning and development). The term *barriers to learning and development* does not threaten to divide the education system into a special and an ordinary school system like the term *special educational needs* did. It gives a better description of needs to be addressed than the rather vague term 'special' (also see Booth, Ainscow, Black-Hawkins, Vaughan & Shaw, 2000: 13). *Barriers to learning and development* does not focus on the so-called deficits of the learners, as some advocates of inclusion understand the term *special educational need*,[2] but draws attention to the responsibility of the school to render appropriate and adequate learning support to learners to overcome, cope with and/or eliminate barriers to their learning and development, regardless of the origin of the barrier(s) (Department of Education – DoE, 1997: 11). Learner needs should be monitored and

[2] It remains important not to negate the particular needs for learning support that learners contending with barriers to their learning and development have, in favour of viewing only their assets.

met in an attempt to prevent the harmful effect of both permanent and temporary barriers to learning and development (based on DoE, 1997: 12).

Influenced by the initial steps to implement inclusive education and participation policy in South Africa, an evolution of the term *barriers to learning and development* appeared in the literature, namely *barriers to learning and participation* (Muthukrishna, 2000). *Participation* stresses the fact that inclusive education that provides access to schools without the opportunity to participate in the full range of school activities is not inclusive education at all, but education filled with obstacles (within the learner, the school, the education system and/or the broader family, social, economic or political systems) that may hinder the learner from accessing and participating in educational provision.

Despite the above contextualisation of the terminology, the internationally accepted term *learners with special educational need* will be used in the paper, even though the acronym LSEN (**L**earners with **S**pecial **E**ducational **N**eed) may perpetuate the use of a term despite reconceptualisation of the real problems at issue, especially as these should be addressed in a SE.

## 3. EDUCATION FOR LEARNERS WITH SPECIAL EDUCATIONAL NEEDS

### *(a) Inclusive education policy implementation: International perspective*

Looking at the issues and research findings which are currently challenging the model of inclusive education and participation, might help to clarify our thinking and direct us towards wholesome and enabling practices in SE.

Approaching a decade after the Salamanca Statement (UNESCO, 1994) which sanctioned inclusive education and participation, the initial spate of change-oriented, ideology-based writing is making way for research-based fact and direction, in response to the need for solutions to the real-life issues of including learners with special educational needs in real-life classrooms (Crockett & Kauffman, 1999).

Contemplating the theories and discourses in inclusive education, Dyson (1999) distinguishes discrete, although not necessarily competing discourses, through which different theoretical notions of inclusion are constructed. In respect of the rationale for inclusion, he identifies the discourses of rights and ethics and of efficacy; and in a second dimension, namely that of implementing inclusive education, a political and a pragmatic discourse are noted. The exercise of applying theory and policy in the practice of SE might indeed be found to share some vital questions. For example, non-discrimination is an important feature in both assessment theory and the Constitution (Burns, 1998: 3; RSA, 1996a: Section 9(3)). But how should assessment items be adapted to accommodate all learners without then discriminating against learners who do not require the specific accommodations?

A call for outcome-oriented research specifically to inform an inclusive practice of teaching and learning is increasingly perceived, which would include not only academic outcome data such as grades, grade retentions and dropout rates systematically collected in respect of learners with special educational needs, but also enabling outcome measures such as social acceptance in the regular class, satisfaction with class placement, attitude toward learning, self-concept and parental satisfaction (Crockett & Kauffman, 1999).

Issues grappled with by decision-makers, furthermore concern whether the same outcomes can be defined for all learners, regardless of level of functioning, and whether outcomes for special education rest on different assessment systems from ordinary education (Bruininks, Thurlow & Ysseldyke, 1992). A serious oversimplification to be avoided, is to report the results of any programme or systems research collectively for all learners rather than as the separate effects for learners of different ability levels or disability classifications (Hallahan, Kauffman & Lloyd, 1996).

Implementing a policy on special needs education, however, is not about classrooms and schools or, for that matter, ordinary and special schools alone. It is about richly inclusive, nuanced thinking and functioning in all government departments and at all levels of society. The acid test for policy must be feasibility, which superficially may be thought to translate into considerations of cost and expertise. From the psychological perspective, however, the implementation of new policy might rest more fundamentally on issues of attitude and value, which would affect practice by the degree, quality and content of motivation invested in engaging with the challenges of the required change. These dynamics also hold true for achieving the spirit of respect for the dignity, rights and interests of learners with disabilities or other barriers to learning and participation in the SE Programme of the South African Department of Education.

### *(b) Inclusive education for learners with special educational needs: South African policy*

The South African education policy development for learners with special educational needs has finally culminated in the long-awaited EWP 6 on Special Needs Education.

The EWP 6 (DoE, 2001b) appreciates the broad range of learning needs existing among the South African learner population. Identifying the learners who are most vulnerable to barriers to learning and development (and therefore more prone to exclusion) as those who historically were termed *learners with special educational needs* (that is those with severe disabilities), 'different learning needs' are also located in various systems and at various levels, such as socio-economic deprivation, particular life experiences, a negative attitude towards and the stereotyping of difference, an inflexible curriculum, differences between the language of learning and teaching and the learner's home language, inaccessible learning environments, the non-recognition and non-involvement of parents, inadequate support services and training of educators, and policies and legislation. To evaluate the inclusive quality of South African education over time, these extrinsic factors will certainly need to be addressed in the SE Programme, although for various reasons they do not merit accommodations in the assessment instruments themselves.

The EWP 6 further provides a framework for the establishment of an inclusive education and training system in South Africa, covering the next 20 years. The following key areas are identified:

- Special schools will be retained to service learners with severe disabilities, and will furthermore be developed into centres of excellence to function as resource centres to surrounding schools.
- District-based support teams will be established to provide a co-coordinated professional support service. Their primary function will be to build the capacity in schools by supporting teaching and performing an evaluative function.
- Beginning in the 30 school districts which are currently participating in the national district development programme, 30 ordinary schools as well as their district support teams will be converted to full-service institutions during 2001–2003 and will strive to address the special educational needs of all their learners within a model of inclusive education and participation. The orientation and introduction of management, governing bodies and professional staff to the inclusion model and the targeting of early identification and intervention in the Foundation Phase are viewed as crucial in this regard. After selecting and studying the most successful models and strategies of service delivery, the programme will be expanded to 500 full-service schools during 2009–2021.
- The promotion of inclusive education and participation will take the form of an information and advocacy campaign by the Ministry, to communicate the policy proposals contained in the EWP 6. Public awareness and acceptance of inclusive education and participation is viewed as essential for the establishment of an inclusive society. The rights, responsibilities and obligations of all role players will be focused upon.

## 4. Legal justification for accommodations in assessing learners with special educational needs

In order to distinguish the playing field within which accommodations for learners with special educational needs should be made, it is necessary to know the parameters that legislation sets.

The Constitution of the Republic of South Africa starts by presenting the values on which South Africa is built (RSA, 1996a: Section 1(a–d)): human dignity, the achievement of equality and the advancement of human rights and freedoms. The values are similar to values in most democratic countries and are elaborated in the Bill of Rights in the Constitution (RSA, 1996a: Section 7–Section 39). What are the implications of human dignity, human rights and freedoms, and equality for accommodations in assessing learners with disabilities?

### *(a) Human dignity*

According to the Bill of Rights, every learner has an inherent dignity (true worth), and the right to have his or her dignity respected and protected (RSA, 1996a: Section 10). In assessment, learners with disabilities will not be able to demonstrate their true worth regarding their mastery of the learning content if appropriate accommodations are not made. Translating text in Braille for a learner who is blind is a simple example of respecting and protecting dignity during assessment.

### *(b) Human rights and freedoms*

Section 12(1)e of the Constitution states that everyone has the right not to be treated or punished in a cruel, inhuman or degrading way (RSA, 1996a). Not making accommodations for learners with disability to access the assessment items, can be regarded as cruel, inhuman and degrading. For example, consider a learner who is blind being expected to understand the assessment procedure without verbal or Braille explanations.

Everyone's right to privacy (RSA, 1996a: Section 14) includes the right not to have the privacy of one's communications violated (Section 14(d)). The same as for learners without disability participating in the SE Programme, the constitutional rights of learners with disabilities as to the confidentiality of their individual assessment results and information on the barriers to learning and participation which each experiences must obviously be upheld. However, this must not be confused with the benefits of group reports made available to institutions, to suggest ideas and strategies for enhancing the learning support and accommodations.

The right to use the language of his/her choice (RSA, 1996a: Section 30) is extended by the South African Schools Act (SASA) to include a recognised Sign Language as an official language for learning purposes at a public school (RSA, 1996b: Section 6(4)). Therefore, learners who are deaf should by law be accommodated in assessment should they require Sign Language.

The legal propriety of accommodation of assessment for learners, who are deaf, becomes even more complicated when one bears in mind that written language is conceptually and structurally a second language for learners who are deaf. Given the possibility of unfair discrimination against learners, some being assessed in their second language and others in their first language, it is valid to ask whether learners who are deaf not only have the right to be accommodated with Sign Language when they require it, but whether they have the constitutional right to be assessed only in their first language, namely Sign Language.

### *(c) Equality*

Equality is a condition of two or more objects or people being the same (equal) or being treated the same (equally), regarding all comparable characteristics. According to the Bill of Rights, everyone is equal before the law, has the right to the same protection of the law, and has the right to the same benefit of the law (RSA, 1996a: Section 9(1)). It implies that the Department of Education must treat all learners equally in the SE Programme.

According to the Bill of Rights, "*equality includes the full and equal* [same] *enjoyment of all rights and freedoms*" (RSA, 1996a: Section 9(2)). Some learners with disabilities can only have full and equal enjoyment as other learners without disability if certain accommodations are made to the assessment situation. For example, some learners with visual impairments can only access written assessment if they are given text in large print. Without large print text, they cannot have full and equal enjoyment of their right to education as learners who do not need the large print text. This logically leads to the term *equity* which refers to treating learners fairly, rather than necessarily treating them the same. It is fair to give learners with visual impairments the same opportunity to access assessment items by allowing large print text and other assistive devices as needed. It is unfair to expect them to show mastery of the learning content if they are unable to read the assessment items.

Equitable treatment is a more accurate reflection of the spirit of the Bill of Rights than equal treatment. Equitable, accommodating assessment practice requires that learners be treated fairly, rather than treating them the same to the letter. In developing an accommodating assessment instrument or practice for learners with disabilities, the aim is to adapt the assessment task(s) to be non-discriminatory, fair and valid with regard to all learners, that is to make all items equally accessible to all, irrespective of the degree or category of disability which a learner might be contending with. Assessment is *non-discriminatory* if it assesses learners' abilities and skills rather than their disabilities and/or lack of skills, that is if the assessment does not present an obstacle to achievement on the grounds of a learner's disability (based on Burns, 1998: 3–9). Assessment is *fair and valid* if it measures what it was designed to measure with learners who are not disabled.

Achieving the aim of non-discriminatory, fair and valid assessment usually entails adapting the conditions of assessment, the format of the assessment items, and the interpretation of the assessment results. Alternative assessment instruments or items, such as ones using different content, procedures and norms, and thus ultimately amounting to curriculum adaptation, might even be indicated when an instrument or item is inappropriate for a particular category of disability.

In the SE, the ultimate concern in developing assessment accommodations for various categories of disability is to evaluate whether learners with such disabilities are performing as per expectations and whether the processes, systems and resources constituting the system could be better organised to improve their performance. In developing accommodations for learners with disabilities, the challenge is therefore

- to achieve the balance between meeting individual needs while maintaining assessment reliability and validity, that is to accommodate the disability, not to compensate for it (that is not to provide learning support);

- to avoid implying, establishing, confirming, or reinforcing difference (that is not to create an exclusive frame); and
- to cause the results of the learning assessment of learners with disabilities to reliably reveal the needs for learning support which may exist in the learning system(s) being evaluated.

## 5. The South African systemic evaluation programme[3]

### *(a) The brief*

In accordance with national and international appeal for a monitoring system to assess development and outcomes in education (National Education Policy Act, DoE, 1996; Assessment Policy for General Education and Training, DoE, 1998; Mardulier, 2001), the South African Department of Education initiated the SE Programme to assess, on an ongoing basis, the performance of the education system at three points in the general education band, namely Grades 3, 6 and 9, to ensure that learners derive maximum benefit from the education system. The Education Policy Act specifically requires the Minister to evaluate and monitor the standards of education provision, delivery and performance against the provisions of the Constitution regarding education provision. It is emphasised in the Assessment Policy that the main objective of systemic evaluation is to assess the effectiveness of the entire system and the extent to which the vision and the goals of the education transformation process are being achieved by it. A Consortium consisting of the Human Sciences Research Council, the Research Institute for Educational Planning, the Centre for Education Policy Development and the University of Pretoria, South Africa, set out to undertake the first SE of the Foundation Phase (Gr 1–3).

The Department of Education defines SE as *'an assessment of the education system, using all relevant information impacting on the system such as resources and facilities, management structures, curriculum, teacher characteristics and learner characteristics. Learner performance is a key indicator, amongst others.'*

The Framework on Systemic Evaluation (DoE, 2001c) defines the purpose of SE as gaining an impression of learner attainment of key skills in a generalisable sample against the backdrop of contextual factors and the new curriculum for purposes of:

- measuring the performance of the system
- obtaining information on learner achievement
- aiding the assessment of district and school level performance and impact

[3] In the interest of accuracy this section consists mostly of verbatim excerpts from the Draft Report of the Pilot Study, Volume 1, of the Systemic Evaluation 2001/2002 presented at its International Colloquium on 24–25 April 2001 (DoE, 2001a).

- explaining why some schools are performing better than others and *vice versa*
- informing policy evaluation and development
- benchmarking – nationally and internationally
- determining a baseline to measure improvement and decline nationally
- ensuring public accountability and mobilising South Africans in a great national effort to raise standards

By implication, SE is concerned about providing political accountability on the delivery of education and training, covering the sub-sectors of both the mainstream and learners with disabilities and all the levels of the system. Such assessment is based on the national political aspirations as are enshrined in the Constitution and the respective national education laws.

### *(b) The method*

The SE Programme identified two sets of instruments that would need to be developed: learner achievement instruments and contextual instruments.

Learner achievement instruments were developed for the three Learning Areas dealt with in Grade 3, namely, language and communication skills (listening, reading and writing skills), numeric skills and life skills. The instruments were developed from curriculum specifications that were ratified by the Department of Education and submitted for international benchmarking.

Contextual instruments were developed to gather data on the contextual variables that affect learner achievement. The contextual instruments comprise separate questionnaires for the learners, parents, educators, principals, district officials and hostels. The questions address the principles of access, equity, redress and quality.

For the mainstream, the instruments and administration processes were piloted in the mainstream, followed by item selection and final editing and translation. Data were collected from a stratified convenience sample of 5% mainstream schools.

## 6. Including Learners with Special Educational Needs in the SE Programme

### *(a) The process*

*(1) Preamble*

Recognising the values in the Constitution as cross-cutting in the various education policy documents, underscores the integration which has been achieved at policy level in respect of education for learners with disabilities and other barriers to learning and participation, as demonstrated in the development of the EWP 6.

Incorporating learners with disabilities and other barriers to learning and participation in a SE of an inclusive education system is no routine or simple matter. All performance measures need to be carefully developed and administered to ensure equal access for all learners to every assessment item, and the results need to be interpreted with specialist knowledge to determine their reliability. All contextual indicators must be aligned with policy, to look at the form and quality of inclusive education so far achieved.

The 'LSEN'-component of the SE Programme, however, got off to a late start, having been left out of the initial phase of planning, including budgeting and conceptualisation. Also, the long delay in publishing the EWP 6 has made it impossible to fully align all instruments with policy in the current exercise.

In the present round of developing adapted assessment instruments and procedures, the focus has been only on learners with disabilities who are attending special schools. Once an inclusive education and training system has officially been set on course, we could expect the SE Programme to include investigating whether processes, systems and resources could be better organised to improve the performance of learners with disabilities in full-service and ordinary schools and for the system increasingly to meet the requirements of all learners with disabilities.

The categories of disability for which accommodations were developed, are blindness, partial sight, deafness, specific learning disability and physical disability.

*(2) Principles of accommodation*

By the very nature of inclusive education and participation, its form, extent and quality have been found to be strongly context-specific to both the particular school and classroom (Dyson & Milward, 2000). But certain principles which underpin inclusive practice, including those in respect of accommodations in the assessment of the performance of learners with disabilities, apply in all contexts.

- At the Grade 3-level, the development tasks of learners with disabilities would still seem to target the optimum development of their self-assistive (intact) abilities and the mastery of assistive learning skills (such as more acute development of the intact senses and language-cum-cognitive skills), rather than the curriculum content which is freely accessible to those learners who are not disabled.
- Since Grade 3 learners with a disability are expectedly less able to function fairly independently in a formal assessment situation than learners without a disability, the amount of assistance and support generally afforded them (such as adapting both the format of questions and the process of administering the assessment instruments) should be determined and allowed in the SE Programme.
- The assessment instruments would need to have some open questions. Multiple-choice questions might be restrictive in that the target response as well as the distracters sharply define the areas of knowledge and experience in terms of which learners would be expected to demonstrate their learning. In restricting the mode and content of the response, and if learners with disabilities proved unable to answer the mainstream assessment questions, what they had actually learned would remain unclear.

- At the Grade 3-level, the number of items (as a function of both time and effort) would be important in assessing learners with a disability. The assessment instruments as designed for ordinary schools might be too long – suggesting selection of perhaps only one item per question type and/or extending the assessment over more than one session per day per instrument.
- For learners with multiple disability, the full spectrum of barriers would need to be accommodated; it would not be equitable to accommodate only one disability.

These principles of accommodation clearly show how equitable, accommodating assessment practices were developed.

*(3) Instrument development plan*
The instrument development phase involved operationalising the accommodation principles in each instrument for the respective disabilities, developing a per-item (that is step-by-step) administration manual for each disability, pilot testing the instruments and analysing the results. The adaptation of the instruments comprised the following steps:[4]

- The dynamics of learning and facilitation of learning to learners with disabilities was observed and qualitatively analysed in authentic classroom situations and at the appropriate grade level, in order to gain some understanding of the modes, forms and levels of assessment at which the SE Programme instruments for learners with disabilities should effectively be pitched.
- In-depth, semi-structured interviews were conducted with teachers and therapists dealing with learners with disabilities in Grade 3. Discussion centred on the learners' cognitive development and levels of competence, and on the forms and extent of the adaptations to learning opportunities and materials which were required for this stage of development.
- Accommodations for each category of disability were workshopped with the research team and a first round of item adaptations for each category of disability was attempted.
- The accommodations were also workshopped with the 'LSEN' National Working Group.
- *It was agreed to address the expected curriculum problem later, during a process of joint item selection after the Pilot Studies, when the data on learners with disabilities would be utilised to direct the choices in terms of appropriate curriculum content for all.*
- All the instruments were developed using the English language.
- *The instruments were to be translated and back-translated by qualified translators into the other formal languages required by the sample.*

4 Steps italicised could not be carried out, for reasons of a budgetary and/or contractual nature. They are included to give the full picture of what it would entail fully to include learners with disabilities in the SE Programme.

- For each category of disability, a separate manual on the administration of the four instruments was developed, providing a detailed step-wise description of the procedure per item (that is issues of format) and instructions to be given *verbatim.*
- *It was judged necessary to introduce an element of norming while operationalising and piloting the assessment accommodations for learners with disabilities in Grade 3, by using a sample of special schools selected from those which are well-resourced and have a tradition of effective education of learners with disabilities, that is to obtain data not contaminated by disadvantaged learning opportunity (other than the learners' disabilities) which could mask the effect of the accommodations to be tested.*
- To criterion-reference assessment instruments accurately, frequently necessitates their norm-based development as a first step. This was especially true in developing accommodations for learners with disabilities in the Foundation Phase of the curriculum, where a disability might be casting up barriers to their learning of content/skills at the criterion pace or in the customary ('normal') sequence associated with each criterion, and where failure on an item might therefore occur on account of various reasons in addition to possible inadequacies in the accommodations which had been made. Trying to determine potential levels of performance in ill-resourced special schools in the pilot phase would obviously be counterproductive in that it would provide an inadequate base of comparison to evaluate the measures of accommodation as well as the issues of equity and redress. And that was again sure to lower the long-term sights for learners with disabilities, because of a limiting effect on the degree to which they could actually meet the criteria.
- *The process of item selection for learners with disabilities was problematical from a methodological perspective, since the results of the 'LSEN' Pilot Study were not incorporated in the item selection for the mainstream schools for the Main Study as intended.*

*(4) Adaptations for each category of disability*

To illustrate the practical implications of equitable, non-discriminatory, fair and valid accommodation of the assessment of learners with special educational needs, the following accommodations and appropriate technical adaptations for learners who are partially sighted are presented as an example:

- font type and size
- quality and heaviness of lines in illustrations and fonts
- clarity of illustrations and avoidance of clutter
- colour of pages
- positioning of the parts which constitute each item relative to each other
- length of words and sentences
- careful structuring of assessment procedures and instructions (developed to be given *verbatim*)

*(5) The pilot study*
The 'LSEN' Pilot Study tested the accommodation and administration of the instruments for each of the five categories of disability, looking at the following:

*Learner assessment instruments for learners with disabilities*

- accessibility per item at the Grade 3-level to learners with each category of disability, in respect of format (presentation, sensory abilities required, cognitive operations required, layout, question type, typographical accuracy), formulation (communicative and linguistic comprehensibility, readability, translations) and content (availability of experiential base and learning opportunities, including cultural considerations)
- appropriateness of the length of the instrument; number and spacing of rest intervals
- appropriateness and feasibility of methodology of instrument adaptation, sampling and data collection

*Administration of instruments to learners with disabilities*

- identification and training of the instrument administrators per disability
- identification and accommodation of additional factors hampering accessibility which were not provided for in the adapted instruments
- effectiveness of the manual per item and per disability

*Organisation and logistics*

- sampling procedure: availability and accuracy of learner information
- translation, printing and brailling products per instrument

*(b) Preliminary findings*

The Assessment Tasks were administered in 46 schools, and 587 learners with disabilities in Grade 3 and 4 participated. Completion of Assessment Tasks was terminated because of disability factors (such as epileptic seizure, slow speed of work and exhaustion) for an average of 17.8% learners on Listening Comprehension, Literacy, Numeric and Life Skills, suggesting that the issue of task length for Grade 3 learners with disability should be revisited to realise equitable assessment.

Interpretation of achievement data of learners with disabilities requires caution on account of the following considerations:

- The individual nature of the various adaptations per disability and per item, complicating interpretation of variance and consistency across disabilities; and
- The mixed and undefined constitution of the sample (that is from well- and ill-resourced schools), which introduces multiple, mostly unrecognisable contextual factors and makes it impossible to evaluate the accommodations against a normed frame of performance to explain good and poor achievement.

- The communication difficulties still experienced by learners with disabilities during the Foundation Phase especially at the expressive level, frequently limiting speed, lucidity and volume of responses.
- The split between many learners' home language and their language of learning especially during the Foundation Phase, further exacerbates the already serious barrier to communication and learning experienced by most learners with disabilities in this phase.
- The small sample size per school, holding the danger of unreliable or over-interpretation since a few weak or strong learners in any subgroup could have had a significant influence on the results.

Only 315 learners (53.7% of the total number) did the assessment tasks in their home language. Since special schools are not within easy reach of all learners with disabilities in South Africa, it is to be expected that many learners in special schools are receiving education through a language other than their mother tongue. All that can be said with reasonable assurance, is that the large second language factor in the sample might have led to somewhat depressed mean performance scores.

The findings for learners with disabilities in special schools were generally more positive than for learners in the Mainstream Pilot Study in respect of the mean performance in Listening comprehension, Literacy, Numeracy and Life Skills. Reasons to explain the positive findings include the following:

- Learners with disabilities in ordinary schools were not excluded from the population before sampling, which might have depressed the scores in the ordinary schools.
- The small number of learners per site made it possible to give individual attention and maintain good discipline, which could have helped to make the unfamiliar procedure of formal assessment run more smoothly.
- Being educators for learners with disabilities, the administrators might have brought more professional expertise to the task of administering the instruments than their counterparts in mainstream education, and might consciously or unconsciously have helped their learners to answer questions correctly.
- Nearly all administrators had received training at first hand.
- Better learning may indeed be taking place in the special schools in the country than in the ordinary schools.
- Adaptations for the various categories of disability might in some cases have over-accommodated for the disability.

The performance data as well as the discrimination data showed irregularity across disabilities, with those for the learners who are blind, deaf and partially sighted often being lower than for learners who are learning disabled or physically disabled. Possibilities to consider in contemplating the data per item include the following:

- The relatively small sample size per category of disability caused the data to be extremely vulnerable to irregularity in the sample composition, which is to subgroup-effect. The data should be taken chiefly to indicate trends.

- The adaptations to the instruments or to specific questions might have been more appropriate in terms of some categories of disability than others.
- Some knowledge and/or skills addressed by some questions might have been less familiar or attainable to learners in some categories of disability than others.
- The barriers to learning cast up by some categories of disability generally or in respect of a particular area of knowledge or skill may be reflected in the results.
- The effect of a multiple disability in a considerable proportion of the sample may be in evidence, leading to questions of whether and how the item(s) should be adapted to accommodate additionally for the noted deficit.

The reliability/unreliability of the instruments appears to cluster in meaningful patterns, clearly illustrating the importance of empirically developing reliable measures to assess learners with disabilities in SE. As an exemplar, the item analysis of the Listening Comprehension Assessment Task in respect of the results of learners who are blind is included. The results show the importance of non-discriminatory, fair and valid accommodations to make the assessment equitable. Item analyses of all the other Assessment Tasks for learners in all the categories of disabilities addressed in the research are available from the authors on request.

The proportion of intact/successful items on Listening Comprehension, as adapted for learners who are disabled from the Assessment Task for ordinary schools, ranges from 50% (learners who are learning disabled) to 65% (learners who are physically disabled). For each category of disability, the qualities of the items display a particular scatter across the 3 sets of question types which could be related to the particular barrier(s) of the category of disability and/or suggest shortcomings in the adaptation(s) for that category of disability.

The first set (Items 1–6) assesses literal word knowledge by means of line drawings in a multiple-choice format. For learners who are blind, descriptions (also in a multiple-choice format) were substituted for the pictures. The first set is completely acceptable for learners who are partially sighted and learners who are physically disabled and has two (different) poor items for learners who are deaf and learners who are learning disabled, whereas only one item appears to be reliable and to discriminate well for learners who are blind. The second set (Items 7–12) assesses the understanding of finite statements by means of line drawings in a multiple-choice format, again substituted by descriptions for learners who are blind. This set is acceptable for all categories of disability, except that Question 7 decreases Cronbach Alpha for learners who are blind and learners who are partially sighted and is therefore not reliable. The final set (Items 13–20) comprises a story with multiple-choice questions. In this set, no item has achieved full clearance across the full sample. Except for learners who are blind, for whom 5 out of the 8 questions have proved both to be reliable and have good discrimination ability, a very high ratio of the items decreases Cronbach Alpha and/or has poor discrimination ability.

Judging by the scatter between poor and intact items for learners who are blind, it would seem that these learners are effective listeners, well versed in the processing of context-embedded information as occurs in sentences (Set 2) and coherent text (Set 3). However, the decreased Cronbach Alpha in 5 out of 6 items in Set 1 suggests that the barrier cast up by their disability still complicates their formation of concepts at the Grade 3-level, so that they might have difficulty in achieving word knowledge and/or demonstrating this skill by identifying the appropriate description.

During the 'LSEN' Pilot Study, it had become apparent from the feedback of the administrators that a considerable number of learners with physical disabilities are also learning disabled and this fact was taken partly to explain why all their instruments yielded unreliable results. In the main study, when the Grade 3 learners with both physical and learning disabilities were administered the instruments for learners who are learning disabled, the items for learners who are physically disabled emerged as the most reliable of all categories of disability, certainly underscoring the imperative to accommodate multiple disability in assessment.

### *(c) Discussion*

The Process-Provisions prescribed by the Framework Document on Systemic Evaluation do not refer to learners with disabilities and need to be extended as follows, to take all possible measures to prevent marginalisation of these learners:

- *Instrument Development*: Separate adaptations (including detailed adaptations of the manuals) should be made per disability.
- *Analysis*: Items should be identified and adapted for learners with disabilities, to be comparable to those included in the battery of items developed and selected for the mainstream schools.

When considering whether and/or how learners with disabilities are to be included in the evaluation of a system, and when the results of SE are interpreted in respect of learners with disabilities, a number of fundamental and complex questions will have to be addressed:

- How is the system affecting learners with disabilities and other barriers to learning and participation?
- And how are the learners with disabilities and other barriers to learning and participation affecting the system?
- What measure of inclusion of learners with special educational needs and other barriers to learning and participation has the system succeeded in achieving?
- The topic regarding focus on learner assessment *versus* broad quality assurance imperatives in SE is even more at issue when contemplating the assessment of learners with special educational needs than of regular learners – criteria such as the social and emotional development of learners with special educational needs (a vital rationale for inclusive education) are not yet being addressed.

On another level, considerations of a more pragmatic, but rigorously methodological, nature are also at issue. It would be well to obtain essential baseline data on the current achievement of learners with special needs who are in special schools, by which to understand and steer the future development of inclusive education in South Africa. Various elements in the data suggest that placement in a special school might indeed on occasion be the least restrictive environment for such learners.

Other issues also come into play when considering the presence of learners with disabilities in the mainstream schools participating in SE:

- To obtain reliable and uncontaminated performance data from the mainstream schools which could really inform on how well the system is running, learners with disabilities in those schools should either be presented with the instruments accommodating their disabilities, or they should be excluded from the assessment. Failing this, the results for the mainstream can be expected to be depressed and/or skewed and the particular needs of learners with disabilities who are presently in the mainstream by default will not be noted for future planning and provision.
- In future rounds of SE, the particular barriers to learning and participation to be accommodated will regularly have to be decided anew.

## 7. Conclusion

Much can be said about policy development and policy implementation. Eventually, the learners, as important stakeholders in the education system, often bear the brunt of policy implementation. The aim of accommodations in the assessment of learners with special educational needs can be posed as a question: How do we deal with inequity to create equity without discrimination? (based on Füssel, 2001).

To reiterate what was stated in the introduction: As the proof of the pudding is in the eating, so the worth of policy is demonstrated in its implementation. One great challenge in policy implementation is to achieve congruency between the values ensconced in the policy and the effects of policy implementation. Systemic evaluation of the education system, as part of policy implementation, without accommodations for special educational need, will work against the values of human dignity, the achievement of equality, and the advancement of human rights and freedoms ensconced in policy.

## References

Booth T, Ainscow M, Black-Hawkins K, Vaughan M and Shaw L. 2000. *Index for Inclusion: Developing Learning and Participation in Schools*. Bristol: Centre for Studies on Inclusive Education (CSIE).

Bruininks R, Thurlow ML and Ysseldyke JE. 1992. Assessing the right outcomes: Prospects for improving education for youth with disabilities. *Education and Training in Mental Retardation, 27*: 93–100.

Burns E. 1998. *Test Accommodations for Students with Disabilities*. Springfield, IL: Charles C Thomas.

Crockett JB and Kauffman JM. 1999. *The Least Restrictive Environment. Its Origins and Interpretations in Special Education*. London: Lawrence Erlbaum Associates.

Department of Education (DoE). 1996. *National Education Policy Act No* 27. Pretoria, South Africa: Department of Education.

Department of Education (DoE). 1997. *Quality Education for All. Overcoming barriers to learning and development. Report of the National Commission on Special Needs in Education and Training (NCSNET) and National Committee on Education Support Services (NCESS)*. Parow, South Africa: CTP printers.

Department of Education (DoE). 1998. *Assessment Policy in the General Education and Training Phase Grade R-9 and ABET*. Pretoria, South Africa: Department of Education.

Department of Education (DoE). 2001a. *Draft Report of the Pilot Study, Volume 1, of the Systemic Evaluation 2001/2002*, International Colloquium on 24–25 April 2001. Pretoria, South Africa: Department of Education.

Department of Education (DoE). 2001b. *Education White Paper 6. Special Needs Education. Building an Inclusive Education and Training System*. Pretoria, South Africa: Department of Education.

Department of Education (DoE). 2001c. *Framework Document on Systemic Evaluation*. Augustus 2001. Unpublished manuscript, Department of Education.

Dyson A. 1999. Inclusion and inclusions: Theories and discourses in inclusive education. In: Daniels H and Garner P. 1999. *Inclusive Education*. London: Kogan Page.

Dyson A and Milward A. 2000. *Schools and Special Needs. Issues of Innovation and Inclusion*. London: Paul Chapman.

Füssel HP. 2001. *The Legal Target in Europe 'Special Educational Needs'*. 30 November 2001. Paper presented at the 9th European Association for Education Law and Policy (ELA) Conference, 30 November 2001–2 December 2001, Brussels, Belgium.

Hallahan DP, Kauffman JM and Lloyd JW. 1996. *Introduction to Learning Disabilities*. Boston: Allyn & Bacon.

Mardulier T. 2001. *The Overall Agenda on Special Educational Needs in Europe: Priorities and Strategies*. Paper presented at the 9th European Association for Education Law and Policy (ELA) Conference, 30 November 2001–2 December 2001, Brussels, Belgium.

Muthukrishna N. 2000. *Transforming the System: The Development of Sustainable Inclusive Education Policy and Practice in South Africa*. Keynote Paper presented at the International Special Education Congress (ISEC), 24–28 July 2000, University of Manchester.

Persson B. 1998. Who needs special education? *International Journal of Educational Research, 29*(2): 107–117.

Republic of South Africa (RSA). 1996a. *Constitution of the Republic of South Africa, Act No. 108*. Government Gazette, vol. 378, no.17678. Pretoria, South Africa: Government Printer.

Republic of South Africa (RSA). 1996b. *South African Schools Act, Act No. 84*. Government Gazette, vol. 377, no. 17579. Pretoria, South Africa: Government Printer.

UNESCO. 1994. *The Salamanca Statement and Framework for Action on Special Needs Education*. World Conference on special needs education: Access and quality, 7–10 June 1994, Salamanca, Spain.

JOHAN BECKMANN,[1] ELMENE BRAY,[2] SIMEON MAILE[3]

# Aspects of Equality and Special Needs Education[4] in South Africa: Reflections on Education White Paper 6 of the South African Department of Education: Special Needs Education – Building an Inclusive Education and Training System (July 2001)

## 1. Introduction

The Constitution of the Republic of South Africa, Act 108 of 1996 (hereinafter CRSA) (preceded by the interim Constitution of 1993) ushered in a new legal order which abolished the previous apartheid system and constituted a sovereign democratic state founded on the fundamental values of human dignity, equality and freedom.[5] The newly-founded democracy has had a profound impact on the lives of all people in South Africa.

South Africa is still in the throes of transition. Old apartheid structures and ideologies are being restructured and transformed. New democratic foundations are being built to uphold the founding principles of the Constitution and the fundamental rights and freedoms of every person. The transformation of education has, without doubt, been the most intensive and expansive in the country's history. In 1996/7 a new democratic school system, of which the growing pains of reform are still being experienced, was introduced. This system underscores the democratic principles of

1 Head: Department of Education Management, University of Pretoria, and Director: Interuniversity Centre for Education Law and Education Policy.

2 Professor of Law in the Department of Constitutional, International and Indigenous Law, University of South Africa.

3 Lecturer in the Department of Education Management and Policy Studies, University of Pretoria.

4 Parts of this article are based on Bray, Elmene and Maile, Simeon. 1999. Equal treatment and opportunities in special needs education. *Education and Law Journal* 9(2): 249–273.

5 Section 1 of CRSA.

*Jan De Groof and Gracienne Lauwers (eds.), Special Education*, 111–135.

participation, transparency and accountability, and guarantees the protection of basic human rights. Notwithstanding transitional obstacles, the school system is meant to evolve into a truly democratic system.

It is against this background that "special needs" education and the application of the equality principle in this sphere will be explored. The place of this sphere of education in the education system, and the status and range of learners accommodated within this sphere, have been vociferously debated from international and national platforms for many years. The advent of, *inter alia*, a human rights consciousness has profoundly changed the traditional attitudes and approaches towards learners who are experiencing special needs in education as well as the quality of education they receive. Nevertheless, there are still many uncertainties regarding the content and scope of "special needs" and "learners who are experiencing special needs" in education in South Africa. Traditional terminology caused much confusion and led, among others, to the exploitation of these learners; many became exposed to labelling, stigmatisation and prejudice.[6]

With the transition to a democratic legal order and the concomitant paradigm shift in South African education, new and different terminology had to be devised to replace traditional and discriminatory concepts. For example, in the sphere of special needs education, Mahlangu[7] identifies different categories of learners with special needs: visually handicapped, deaf and hard-of-hearing, orthopaedically and other health impaired, emotionally disturbed, speech impaired, disadvantaged, disabled, mentally retarded. Kokot[8] also emphasises giftedness as a category of special needs. The White Paper on an Integrated National Disability Strategy points out, *inter alia*, that not all learners with disabilities have special needs, as they do not experience a learning breakdown. Special needs in education therefore exist in both ordinary and specialised learning centres, and special needs also exist outside the classroom.[9] Recent descriptions recommended for learners with special needs, namely "learners who are experiencing barriers to learning and development", must be understood in the context of the proposed new integrated education system which would accommodate diversity (*inter alia*, through the outcomes-based approach) and ensure that all learners achieve their full potential and become dignified and useful persons in society.[10]

What this article sets out to do is to provide answers to the question whether new policies and provisions in South Africa contribute to equality of educational

[6] Republic of South Africa. 1997. White Paper on An Integrated National Disability Strategy. Office of the Deputy President: November 1997, p. 1.

[7] Mahlangu, DMD. 1989. Educating the special child. Pretoria: De Jager & HAUM, p. 3.

[8] Kokot S. 1996. In defence of elitism. Excedo, 1(3): 2.

[9] Republic of South Africa. 1997. White Paper on An Integrated National Disability Strategy. Office of the Deputy President: November 1997, p. 38.

[10] Department of Education. 1997(2). Quality education for all: Overcoming barriers to learning and development. Report of the National Commission on Special Needs in Education and Training (NCSNET) and National Committee on Education Support Services (NCESS). Pretoria: Department of Education, pp. iv–v.

opportunities and to equal access to such opportunities for learners with special education needs. In order to explore the question as to the relationship between equality of educational provision and the influence of special needs education policy in this regard, attention will be given to the following in the rest of this article:

(1) Education White Paper 6, 2001
(2) Special needs education in South Africa and international trends
(3) The current situation regarding special needs education in South Africa
(4) Equal treatment and opportunities for learners experiencing special needs
(5) Assessment, conclusion and future challenges.

## 2. EDUCATION WHITE PAPER 6 SPECIAL NEEDS EDUCATION – BUILDING AN *INCLUSIVE EDUCATION AND TRAINING SYSTEM*, 2001[11]

### *2.1. History of the White Paper*

In October 1996 the Ministry of Education appointed the National Commission on Special Needs in Education and Training (NCSNET) and the National Commission on Education Support Services (NCESS). The Minister of Education received a joint report on the findings of these two commissions in November 1997 and the final report was published in February 1998 for public comment and advice.[12] The investigations found that specialised education and support have been provided to a small percentage of learners with disabilities within special classes and schools. Such education and support were provided on a racial basis with the best "human, physical and material resources" reserved for whites.[13]

In August 1999 the Ministry of Education released a consultative paper.[14] The submissions and feedback emanating from this consultative paper informed the writing of White Paper 6. The White Paper was published in July 2001.

The history of White Paper 6 suggests a number of significant changes in the approach to, and conceptualisation of, the accommodation of special needs education.

### *2.2. Considerations which informed the recommendations in the White Paper*

- 280,00 disabled children younger than 18 years are not in schools or colleges.[15] That is enough to fill 848 special schools accommodating approximately

[11] All references to White Paper 6 in this section are to Department of Education, 2001. *Education White Paper 6 Special Needs Education – Building an Inclusive Education and Training System*. Pretoria: Department of Education, July 2001.

[12] Department of Education. 2001. *Education White Paper 6 Special Needs Education – Building an Inclusive Education and Training System*. Pretoria: Department of Education, p. 4.

[13] Ibid.

[14] Department of Education. 1999. Consultative Paper No. 1 on Special Education: Building an *Inclusive Education and Training System*. Pretoria: Department of Education, p. 6.

[15] White Paper 6, p. 4.

330 learners each. The estimated upper limit of disabled and impaired learners is about 400,000 while approximately 64,200 learners with disabilities and impairments are accommodated in special schools.[16] Special schools cannot be the only answer as they raise issues of funding and also of unequal treatment.

- The NCSNET and NCESS investigations found that in the past (in the so-called apartheid era) specialised education and support were provided to a small percentage of learners with disabilities within special classes and schools. Such education and support were provided on a racial basis with the best "human, physical and material resources" reserved for whites.[17] Race and disability were both used as segregating criteria (p. 9). Only 20% of learners with disabilities were accommodated in special schools – there were about 380 special schools.[18]
- Learners with special education needs are most vulnerable to barriers to learning and to exclusion.[19]
- The development of an inclusive system needs to take into account the incidence and spread of the HIV/AIDS pandemic and other infectious diseases.[20]
- The unequal provision of special needs education is reflected in Table 1.

*Table 1:* Distribution of special schools, learner enrolment and per learner expenditure on special needs education[21]

| *Province* | *No. of special schools* | *No. of learners in special schools* | *% of learners in special schools* | *% of total No. of special schools in province* | *Per learner expenditure (R)* |
|---|---|---|---|---|---|
| Eastern Cape | 41 | 6,483 | 0.28 | 10.79 | 13,746 |
| Free State | 19 | 3,127 | 0.40 | 5.00 | 22,627 |
| Gauteng | 96 | 25,451 | 1.62 | 25.26 | 11,049 |
| KwaZulu-Natal | 58 | 7,631 | 0.28 | 15.26 | 21,254 |
| Mpumalanga | 15 | 2,692 | 0.29 | 3.95 | 17,839 |
| Northern Cape | 8 | 1,392 | 0.68 | 2.11 | 15,749 |
| Northern Province | 19 | 4,250 | 0.23 | 5.00 | 16,609 |
| North West | 42 | 4,364 | 0.46 | 11.05 | 13,015 |
| Western Cape | 82 | 9,213 | 0.96 | 21.58 | 28,635 |
| Totals | 380 | 64,603 | 0.52 | 100.00 | 17,838 |

16 Ibid., p. 9.
17 Ibid., p. 4.
18 Ibid., p. 9.
19 Ibid., p. 7.
20 Ibid., p. 8.
21 Ibid., p. 13.

- One can deduce that learners in certain geographical areas are more likely to be disadvantaged (discriminated against). The disparities in provision are illustrated by figures such as the following:[22]
  - The disabilities in the Eastern Cape constitute 17.39% of the national disabled population, yet the province has only 10.79% of the number of special schools.
  - Gauteng has 17.14% of the disabled population but 25.56% of the schools.
  - The Western Cape has 17.14% of the disabled population but has 21.58% of the schools.
- The varying expenditure per learners suggests inefficiency in the use of resources and indicates the absence of a "uniform renouncing strategy and national provisioning norms for learners with disabilities".[23]

### *2.3. Proposals regarding an inclusive education and training system*

#### *2.3.1. Concerns*

The policy appears to be driven by concerns about "what kind of educational experience would be available to learners with moderate to severe disabilities in mainstream education".[24]

#### *2.3.2. Vision*

The main vision is:

- Providing educational experiences to learners with moderate to severe disabilities in "vastly improved special schools, as part of an inclusive system".[25]
- The overhauling of the process of identifying, assessing and enrolling learners in special schools and its replacement by structures that acknowledge the central role played by educators, learners and parents.[26] Early assessment, identification and intervention will be pursued.[27]
- Making available the expertise and resources invested in special schools to neighbourhood schools, especially "full-service schools and colleges".[28]
- Making special schools, "in an incremental manner", part of district support services where they can become resources for all schools.[29]

[22] Ibid., p. 14.
[23] Ibid., p. 15.
[24] Ibid., p. 3.
[25] Ibid.
[26] Ibid.
[27] Ibid., pp. 32–33.
[28] Ibid., p. 3.
[29] Ibid.

- Countering the many fears accompanying inclusion by "further professional and physical resources development, information dissemination and advocacy".[30]

*2.3.3. Definition*

Inclusive education and training is defined as:[31]

- Acknowledging that all children and youth can learn and need support.
- Acknowledging and respecting differences in learners due to e.g. age, gender, ethnicity, language, class, disability, HIV AIDS or other infectious diseases.
- Acknowledging that learning also occurs in other than formal educational settings.
- Changing attitudes, behaviour, teaching curricula and environments to meet the needs of all learners.

*2.3.4. School and system conversion*

The "phased conversion" of 500 out of 20 000 mainstream primary schools to "full-service schools" will be done to develop models for later system-wide applications.[32] This will begin with the 30 school districts that are part of the national district development programme.[33] Depending on needs and the availability of resources more than 500 full-service institutions may be developed.[34] Segregation will be based on categories of disability and full-service schools will have biases towards particular disabilities depending on need and support[35] – this builds on the realisation that mainstream schools will not be able to provide the "intensive levels of support" required by certain categories of learners.[36] This learner-centred approach to learning and teaching is central to the policy and is also consistent with "a systemic and developmental approach to understanding problems and planning".[37] The Ministry envisages the "establishment of an inclusive education and training system as a cornerstone of an integrated and caring society" for the 21st century.[38] Eventually further education and training and higher education institutions will also be made part of the system.[39]

30 Ibid.

31 Ibid., pp. 6–7, 16.

32 This means that, at best, more learners will have access to appropriate opportunities. These opportunities are not guaranteed to all.

33 Ibid., pp. 4–8.

34 Ibid., p. 22.

35 Ibid., p. 10.

36 Ibid., p. 21.

37 Ibid., p. 19.

38 Ibid., p. 10.

39 Ibid., pp. 28, 31, 42.

*2.3.5. Orientation within mainstream education*

The management, governing bodies and professional staff within mainstream education will be oriented and introduced to the inclusion model.[40]

*2.3.5.1. Distinction between mainstreaming and inclusion.* Certain distinctions, notions and policy shifts from earlier position papers are implicit in the White Paper. For example the notion that the mainstream system must accommodate each and every individual learning almost irrespective of disability seems to have made way for the notion that the system must be changed to become an inclusive system. The emphasis changes from endemic handicaps in individual learners that prevent them from fitting into the system to recognising that learners can also be handicapped by the system and that the system needs overhauling. In previous position papers there seemed to be a rather naïve notion that access to mainstream schools would as such ensure quality learning opportunities for disabled learners. White Paper 6 seems to acknowledge that access *per se* does not guarantee quality learning opportunities but rather what is offered in the system. Apart from these implicit shifts to inclusive education, the White Paper also provides explicit comparisons of differences (Table 2).[41]

*2.3.6. Human resources development*

Classroom educators are primary resources for achieving the goals of an inclusive system. Staff development at the school and district levels will be crucial.[42] Education support personnel at district level will be oriented and trained in their new roles.[43]

*Table 2:* Mainstreaming compared to inclusion

| *Mainstreaming or integration* | *Inclusion ("system change")* |
|---|---|
| Getting learners to fit into a system (integrating them into the system) | Recognising and respecting differences among all learners and building on similarities |
| Giving learners support so they can fit into normal classroom routine – such as individualised support programmes | Supporting all learners and the system as a whole to meet the full range of learning meets |
| Changes in the learner so that the learner can "fit in" | Overcoming barriers in the system that prevent it from meeting the full range of learning needs. Adapting support systems available in the classroom |

40 Ibid., p. 8.

41 Ibid., pp. 17–19.

42 Ibid., p. 18.

43 Ibid., p. 19.

*2.3.7. HIV AIDS infected learners*

It is noticeable that learners with HIV AIDS and other infectious diseases are regarded as learners with disabilities (special needs).[44] The same does seem to not apply to gifted children and early developers (see *Doreen Harris v Minister of* Education[45] where the court decided that an age restriction regarding school entry was unconstitutional – yet all applications outside the prescribed age limits must be handled as individual and exceptional cases in terms of amendments to the South African School Act (SASA) in 2002).

*2.3.8. Onus on government*

Government has the onus of ensuring that all human resources are developed to their fullest potential.[46]

*2.3.9. Inter-departmental co-operation*

The successful implementation of inclusive education policies will also depend on co-operation with other state departments such as Public Works, Health and Welfare.[47] Barrier-free physical environments are an aspect that may have to be dealt with at an inter-departmental level.[48] This suggests a type of diffused or disguised accountability for special needs education which is not necessarily good for a purposeful pursuit of the improvement of a national system for such education. Such accountability requires, among others, an innovative and sophisticated system of administration that is hard to foresee in the light of current constraints in South Africa, e.g. the under-staffing of executive education departments.[49]

*2.3.10. Review of existing legislation and policies*

Existing legislation and policies will have to be reviewed with a view to the establishment of an inclusive system of education and training.[50]

*2.3.11. Funding strategy*

A twenty-year developmental approach is assumed and funding for new and additional needs is to depend on new conditional grants from the national government, funding from the line budgets of provincial education departments and donor

44 Ibid., p. 23.

45 Doreen Harris v Department of Education (CCT 13/01) (5 October 2001).

46 Ibid., p. 25.

47 Ibid.

48 Ibid., pp. 28, 32.

49 In 1999 only two provinces had retained the same HODs since 1995. In the KwaZulu-Natal province 25% of the positions in the management echelon were vacant, in Limpopo there were 28% vacancies and in Mmpumalanga there were 54% vacancies. See Department of Education, 1999. First Report of the Minister of Education to the President, 30 November 1999. Pretoria: Department of Education, pp. 11–12.

50 Ibid., p. 27.

funds.[51] Where new posts have to be created, a top-slicing model will be followed and post provisioning will be within current post-establishment models (or revisions thereof).[52] Financial resources will be targeted towards those with the greatest need. This will include targeting on the basis of poverty, income and socio-economic status.[53]

*2.3.12. Time frames*

The White Paper envisages short-term (2001–2003), medium-term (2004–2008) and long-term (2009–2021) steps.[54]

- *Short term.* These steps include advocacy, outreach programmes, completing audits of special schools, conversion of 30 special schools, conversion of 30 primary schools to full-service schools, implementing district support teams, orientation of management, governing bodies and professional staff, implementing early identification systems and procedures.
- *Medium term.* Transforming higher and further education and training institutions, expanding the number of full-service schools and colleges and special schools.
- *Long term.* Expanding to reach target of 380 special schools/resource centres, 500 full-service schools and colleges and district support teams and 280,000 out-of-school children and youth.

While it makes sense to phase in provision, access to suitable educational opportunities are *de facto* almost indefinitely postponed for many learners.

*2.3.13. Co-operative government*

The national and provincial departments of education departments will embark on inclusive education and training in a co-operative fashion in line with the Constitution.[55]

## 3. Special needs education in South Africa and international trends

### *3.1. Pre-Constitution situation in South Africa*

Pre-1993 education in South Africa has been branded as a discriminatory and segregated system which legitimised privileged "white" education at the expense of education for other South Africans who were of a different race or ethnic group (e.g., the so-called "Bantu education" system provided inferior education to the vast

[51] Ibid., pp. 39–40.
[52] Ibid., p. 41.
[53] Ibid., p. 38.
[54] Ibid., p. 42.
[55] Ibid., pp. 46–47.

majority of South African learners). Within the main education system, very little attention was given to learners who experienced special needs in education. As a matter of fact, education and training offered to these learners revealed similar discriminatory and fragmented features, amplified and reinforced not only by racial criteria but also by discrimination on the basis of disability, capability, age, sex and gender, to name but a few.

To conclude, within the apartheid education system(s), a segregated and secluded "special education system" developed. Although it is generally accepted that learners who experience special needs in education comprise a heterogeneous group(s) and require differentiated education treatment and opportunities, within the context of apartheid, "differentiation" was relegated to discrimination as a result of its "segregated" and "secluded" nature and its low priority vis-à-vis "mainstream" education. Such discriminatory treatment deprived these learners of their right to equal treatment and opportunity in education.[56]

There is no doubt that the previous situation under apartheid education could no longer be tolerated in a new constitutional dispensation based on democratic principles and fundamental values. In fact, the new legal order requires a different mindset of all South Africans, particularly with regard to the protection of all learners in education, their right to education and to equal treatment and opportunities in education. International (and national) pressures on South Africa, and its isolation from international participation and co-operation, contributed significantly to the constitutional struggle and the achievement of a new democratic state.

### *3.2. International trends in special needs education*

The international development of a human rights culture in education, and its application in the sphere of special needs education, is well documented in many international legal instruments. For example, the United Nations (UN) Universal Declaration of Human Rights of 1948 emphasises that every person has the right to education; the UN Declaration on the Rights of Mentally Retarded Persons of 1971 declares that states should provide the mentally retarded with education opportunities; the UN Declaration on the Rights of Disabled Persons of 1971 calls upon states to provide disabled persons with equal educational opportunities. Finally, the UN Convention on the Rights of the Child of 1989 states in article 23 that … "a mentally or physically disabled child should enjoy a full and decent life under conditions which:

- ensure dignity
- promote self-reliance, and
- facilitate the child's active participation in the community."

In the African context, the Organisation of African Unity (OAU) justifies the protection of human rights in its African Charter on Human and People's Rights.

[56] Department of Education. 1997(2), p. 21 et seq.

Article 2 provides: "Every individual shall be entitled to the enjoyment of the rights and freedoms recognised and guaranteed in the present Charter without distinction of any kind such as race, ethnic group, colour, sex, language, religion, political or any opinion, national and social origin, fortune, birth or other status".

The place of special needs education in the education system and the legal status of learners who are experiencing special needs in education, have also been (and still are) a bone of contention, both internationally and in South Africa, as mentioned above. In 1990 at the Jomtiem World Conference which dealt with the theme *Education for All: Meeting basic learning needs*, the Conference stated its commitment to a child-centred concept of education in which individual differences are accepted as a source of diversity, a challenge and not a problem; and to a developmental, intersectoral and holistic approach to education and care of primary school children. The *Salamanca Statement* of 1994 also states that

> regular schools with an inclusive orientation are the most effective means of combating discriminatory attitudes, creating welcoming communities, building an inclusive society and achieving education for all. Moreover, they provide an effective education to the majority of children and improve the efficiency and ultimately the cost-effectiveness of the entire education system.

It further identifies learners who experience special needs in education as follows:

- those who are currently enrolled in primary school but for various reasons do not progress adequately
- those who are currently not enrolled in primary schools but who could be enrolled if the schools were responsive, and
- the relatively smaller group of children with more severe physical, mental or multiple impairments who have more complex special needs that are not met.

In terms of sections 39 and 233 of CRSA international legal instruments have a direct impact on South African law and, consequently, on the way in which education will develop in the future. The latest international views on special needs education and the status of learners who are experiencing special needs (i.e. the promotion of an integrated and diversified education system), have been incorporated into recent policy and strategy documents of the Department of Education.

## 4. The Current Situation Regarding Special Needs Education in South Africa

### *4.1. Legal framework*

In 1996 the new South African Schools Act (SASA) was promulgated. This Act brought the school system in line with the new constitutional framework and established the new democratic school system.

CRSA provides that school education is a matter over which the national legislature and provincial legislatures have "concurrent" legislative powers.[57] Notwithstanding that, provincial school education laws will generally prevail over national laws unless the matter is of national interest (e.g., uniform national norms and standards for all schools and national school policy).[58]

In terms of SASA, a public school may be an ordinary public school or a public school for learners experiencing special education needs (section 12(3)). In terms of section 12(4), the Member of the Executive Council (MEC) of a province, must, where reasonably practicable, provide education for learners who experience special education needs at ordinary public schools and provide relevant education support services for such learners. The MEC must take all reasonable measures to ensure that the physical facilities at public schools are accessible to disabled persons (section 12(5)). Parents' choice of school must be taken into account, especially in the case of learners experiencing special education needs even if the principal and the HOD do the placement of such learners (sections 3(1) and 5(6)).

Individual provincial school laws also refer to aspects of special needs education in a particular province.[59]

It is apparent that there is, at present, no comprehensive legal framework for a properly integrated and diversified education (school) system. Nevertheless, as was mentioned before, both national and provincial legislative initiatives seem to favour "inclusion". Inclusion should not be understood as incorporating all learners into a type of "mainstream" education, but to accommodate them in an integrated and intersectoral education system which would fulfil their diverse and differentiated educational needs and enable them to achieve their full potential as learners, and as adults in society.

Education authorities and various NGOs are getting increasingly involved in research in the sphere of special needs education (e.g., the South African Federal Council on Disability (SAFCD), National Co-ordinating Committee on Disability, National Commission on Special Needs in Education and Training (NCSNET) and the National Committee for Education Support Services (NCESS)). The National Qualifications Framework (NQF), established in terms of the South African Qualifications Authority Act of 1995, intends to manage the equal treatment of all learners by utilising what is called an "outcomes-based" approach. This approach focuses on the end results of education and endeavours to assist each learner to learn effectively according to his/her own ability by using the appropriate content, learning support and assessment procedures.[60] It seems that outcomes-based education will

[57] Schedule 4 of CRSA.

[58] Also see the discussion of the Bill of Rights below.

[59] Provincial legislation will not be discussed in this article.

[60] Killen R. 1996. Outcomes-based education: Rethinking teaching. Paper presented at the University of South Africa: 15 October, pp. 1, 5; Burden A. 1997. Special needs

provide a process of learning in which the learner who experiences special needs in education, would be able to reach his/her full potential in an integrated and diversified education environment. Recent discussion documents and policy strategies support an integrated and diversified system in which outcomes-based assessments are used, but also stress that the school system (actually the entire education system) will have to be reconsidered if the new "systems-change" approach (compared to the previous "change-the-person" approach – see below) is to succeed.[61]

Despite the latest developments and the growing awareness of human rights in education in South Africa, special needs education remains an under-researched and neglected field and social attitudes that traditionally stereotyped and labelled these learners, still prevail today.[62] As a result, learners who are experiencing special needs in education are still being excluded (in a secluded system) or included in a "mainstream" system which offers very little or no scope for differentiation with regard to curriculum, tuition, support services, etc. For example, the hard-of-hearing learner may cope well in an ordinary "mainstream" school, depending on his/her ability/capability, the flexibility/adaptability of the curriculum, the size of the class, the teacher's expertise, and so on. On the other hand, deaf learners need additional support, thus a more specialised form of education and training which they will almost certainly not get in the present system of "mainstream" schooling. Whether the lack of differentiated educational opportunities in these illustrations, is in fact discriminatory, depends on the facts and circumstances of each case.

### *4.2. The Constitution, equality and learners who experience special needs*

The South African Constitution is the supreme law of South Africa and incorporates a justiciable Bill of Rights (Chapter 2) which guarantees most of the individual fundamental rights found in modern constitutions of the world (e.g., Canada, USA and Germany).[63] Any court (and specified tribunals or independent *fora*) may judge upon

---

education in terms of the outcomes-based approach of the National Qualifications Framework. Paper presented at the Southern African Society for Education Conference: 4–6 September, p. 7.

61 See e.g. Republic of South Africa. 1997. White Paper on an Integrated National Disability Strategy; Department of Education. 1997. (1) Pretoria: Department of Education; Department of Education. 1997. (2) Quality education for all: Overcoming barriers to learning and development. Report of the National Commission on Special Needs in Education and Training (NCSNET) and National Committee on Education Support Services (NCESS). Pretoria: Department of Education.

62 White Paper on an Integrated National Disability Strategy, 1997: 4.5.

63 Waal, J, Currie, I & Erasmus, G. 1998. The Bill of Rights Handbook, Cape Town: Juta, pp. 1–9; Rautenbach, IM & Malherbe, EFJ. 1996: What does the Constitution say? Pretoria: JL van Schaik, p. 11 et seq, p. 279 et seq.

a case where human rights are being infringed or threatened, but the Constitutional Court remains the most authoritative and final court for the adjudication of human rights issues.[64]

Section 1 of CRSA (Founding Provisions) stipulates that South Africa is a sovereign, democratic state founded on fundamental values which include:

1(a) Human dignity, the achievement of equality and the advancement of human rights and freedoms.
(b) Non-racialism and non-sexism…

The equality clause in section 9 of the Bill of Rights states that

(1) Everyone is equal before the law and has the right to equal protection and benefit of the law.
   (1) Equality includes the full and equal enjoyment of all rights and freedoms. To promote the achievement of equality, legislative and other measures designed to protect or advance persons, or categories of persons, disadvantaged by unfair discrimination may be taken.
   (2) The state may not unfairly discriminate directly or indirectly against anyone on one or more grounds, including race, gender, sex, pregnancy, marital status, ethnic or social origin, colour, sexual orientation, age, disability, religion, conscience, belief, culture language and birth.
   (3) No person may unfairly discriminate directly or indirectly against anyone on one or more grounds in terms of subsection (3). National legislation must be enacted to prevent or prohibit unfair discrimination.
   (4) Discrimination on one or more of the grounds listed in subsection (3) is unfair unless it is established that the discrimination is fair.

In short, the equality clause in section 9 (section 8 in the Interim (1993) Constitution) has five subsections: (1) deals with the principle of equality before the law and the right to equal protection and benefit of the law; (2) deals with affirmative action; (3) contains the prohibition of unfair discrimination on "listed" (and unlisted) grounds (including disability); (4) extends the prohibition of unfair discrimination to the horizontal level; and (5) presumes public or private discrimination on the listed grounds to be unfair. The South African constitutional commitment to equality is evident throughout the Constitution (i.e. the Founding Principles, sections 7, 36 and 39) and is regarded as one of the central and fundamental (inherent) values of the new constitutional order. The Constitutional Court has held that: There can be no doubt that the guarantee of equality lies at the very heart of the Constitution. It permeates and defines the very ethos upon which the Constitution is premised.[65]

[64] CRSA, section 167.

[65] Fraser v Children's Court, Pretoria North 1997 (2) SA 261 (CC), par 20).

The Bill of Rights also protects children (defined as persons under the age of 18 years) and recognises their need for additional and special protection (i.e. not to be subjected to neglect, abuse or degradation) (section 28 of CRSA). A "child's best interests are of paramount importance in every matter concerning the child" (section 28(2)).

Every person's right to education is guaranteed in section 29 of the Bill of Rights: *inter alia*, "Everyone has the right (a) to a basic education, including adult basic education; and (b) to further education, which the state, through reasonable measures, must make progressively available and accessible". Section 4 of the National Education Policy Act of 1996, gives an assurance that no person is denied the opportunity to receive an education to the maximum of his or her ability as a result of physical disability. Section 3(2) of the SASA provides that the national Minister of Education must, by way of an official notice, determine the ages of compulsory attendance at schools for learners who experience special needs in education and, in terms of section 5(1), a public school must admit learners and serve their educational requirements without unfairly discriminating in any way. Finally, all education legislation must be in line with the Constitution in guaranteeing the promotion of fundamental rights, equal treatment and opportunities, and protection against unfair discrimination of all persons in education.

The right to equal treatment and opportunities in education (as most other rights) does not apply absolutely, and has to be weighed up (or balanced) against other competing (or conflicting) rights in a given situation. For example, the hard-of-hearing learner in an ordinary public school has (like every other learner [and the teacher]) a right to equal treatment and opportunities in education. The learner may complain that she is being discriminated against because she has to work so much harder to cope in overcrowded classes and without additional attention from the teachers. Certain factors will have to be considered to determine whether a "limitation" can be placed on her right to equal treatment/opportunities in education (e.g. because there are no other facilities and resources available). If she demands individual, specialised tuition in all her subjects, it could result in the unfair treatment (e.g. neglect) of the other learners (i.e. the class would get behind in their work). To resolve issues like these, one has to determine what would be reasonable and justifiable under the circumstances, and section 36 of the Bill of Rights (the limitation clause) provides a proportionality test to determine when, how, and to what extent, a limitation would be permissible. Section 36 reads

(1) The rights in the Bill of Rights may be limited only in terms of law of general application to the extent that the limitation is reasonable and justifiable in an open and democratic society based on human dignity, equality and freedom, taking into account all relevant factors, including
   (1) the nature of the right;
   (2) the importance of the purpose of the limitation;
   (3) the nature and extent of the limitation;

(4) the relation between the limitation and its purpose; and
(5) less restrictive means to achieve the purpose....

From the preceding discussion it is apparent that learners who are experiencing special needs in education (or, barriers to learning and development) comprise a heterogeneous group (or groups) and need differentiated treatment, depending on their particular (individual) educational needs (see below). The proposed integrated and diversified system advocated in the latest policy documents, will to a large extent accommodate all learners in the "systems-change" approach and enable them to enjoy equal treatment and opportunities in education (e.g. each learner in this integrated and diversified environment in which an outcomes-based approach to education is being followed, will be in a position to achieve his/her full potential and become a dignified and useful person in society). However, to say that unequal treatment will not occur, is wishful thinking.

## 5. Equal treatment and opportunities for learners experiencing special needs

The South African Constitutional Court has in a few recent cases (see below) given judgment on the equality clause, but has not yet had the opportunity to apply it in an education context. Equality should be regarded as a dynamic concept, in the sense that it has to meet the aspirations of a developing South African society. To accommodate such evolutionary development, the Constitution (including the equality clause) must be interpreted in a contextual (purposive) manner (section 39).[66]

In this discussion a few guidelines are given on the content, interpretation and possible application of the equality clause to learners who are experiencing special needs in education. It must be stressed that generalisation and oversimplification must be avoided: each case or incident has to be evaluated in terms of its own facts and circumstances – so-called "model" solutions almost invariably fail.

### *5.1. Substantive equality*

Section 39 of the Bill of Rights promotes a contextual (purposive) approach to constitutional interpretation and, therefore, supports a substantive (contextual) conception of equality rather than a formal (narrow) approach.[67]

Equality in the "formal" sense, simply means that all persons are equal bearers of rights irrespective of the actual social and economic disparities between groups and individuals: it therefore promotes sameness of treatment (e.g. where the law treats all learners in the same manner regardless of ability, capability, circumstances, etc.).

[66] De Waal et al. 1998: p. 99 et seq.

[67] De Waal et al. 1998, p. 155.

Clearly such treatment (e.g. where all follow the same curriculum) may in fact discriminate against learners who are experiencing special needs in education, thus resulting in unfair treatment of and unequal opportunities for them.[68]

Equality in a "substantive" form, on the other hand, requires an examination of the actual social and economic conditions of groups or individuals to determine whether the Constitution's commitment to equality is being upheld. Consequently, one has to consider the unique circumstances of learners who are experiencing special needs and the law has to ensure equality of outcome (e.g. the physically/mentally disabled learner should follow a differentiated school programme to enable him to reach his full potential in society). It seems that the result or effect of a particular conduct is highlighted rather than its mere form.[69]

The paramountcy of equality in its substantive form has been accepted in the Constitutional Court and illustrated by O'Regan J as follows:[70]

> The policy of apartheid, in law and in fact, systematically discriminated against black people in all aspects of social life. ... Senior jobs and access to schools and universities were denied to them; ... Instead separate and inferior facilities were provided. The deep scars of this appalling programme are still visible in our society. It is in the light of that history and the enduring legacy that it bequeathed that the equality clause needs to be interpreted.

Therefore, to realise the right to equality in education of learners who are experiencing special needs in education, it may be necessary to treat them differently to other learners, as mentioned above.[71] It also means that differentiation in education (e.g. differentiated treatment and opportunities) does not necessarily imply inequality in education. However, it is quite possible that individual learners (or certain groups) could experience discrimination under such circumstances (see below).

### 5.2. *Differentiation*

Laws almost invariably differentiate and it is virtually impossible to regulate the affairs of people and the state without differentiation and without classifications which treat people differently and which impact on people differently.

Generally speaking, the equality clause allows for two instances in which a law or conduct might differentiate between people: differentiation which does not involve any discrimination (or "mere" differentiation: as propounded in CRSA

68 De Waal et al. 1998, pp. 154–155.

69 Albertyn, C & Kentridge, J. 1994. Introducing the right to equality in the interim Constitution. South African Journal of Human Rights, pp. 152–155; Loenen, T. 1997. The equality clause in the South African Constitution: Some remarks from a comparative perspective. South African Journal on Human Rights, p. 403.

70 Brink v Kitshoff NO 1996 6 BLCR 759 (CC); 1997 3 SA 1012 (CC), para 21.

71 Loenen, op. cit., pp. 404–405.

section 9(1)); and differentiation which does involve constitutionally impermissible discrimination (in section 9(2)–(5)).[72] In short, in the substantive context, "unfair" discrimination does not simply distinguish between different kinds of differentiation, but between permissible and impermissible discrimination. This means that discrimination would be "fair" (permissible) if it is justifiable in relation to the purposes underlying the value of equality itself, as discussed below.[73]

Why then do we distinguish between discrimination which is "permissible" and "impermissible"? Is discrimination not in itself a pejorative concept and therefore unjustified and unfair? Albertyn & Kentridge[74] explain this qualification as follows: "a simple prohibition of discrimination ... knows no distinction between discrimination against members of subordinate groups and discrimination against the privileged". This conception of discrimination acknowledges that harm caused by measures which disadvantage vulnerable and subordinate groups is, indeed, a greater evil which merits more suspicion than measures which disadvantage powerful and otherwise privileged groups.[75] If one looks at the sphere of special needs education in this context – its apartheid remnants, traditionally "secluded" nature and present state of transitional turmoil – one cannot but conclude that it represents a vulnerable "disadvantaged education minority".

The Constitutional Court has identified criteria to distinguish legitimate differentiation from constitutionally impermissible differentiation. In *Harksen v Lane*, the Court asked whether the alleged discriminatory provision in question, differentiates between people or categories of people.[76] If it does, one should ask whether the differentiation has a rational connection to a legitimate government purpose. If it does not, a violation of section 9(1) has occurred. Even if a rational connection exists, the differentiation might nevertheless amount to discrimination. For example, the previous government defended a separate system of "special (and specialised) education" because it was cost-effective and promoted "equal" opportunities for "disabled" learners to reach their maximum potential. Although a separate system might have seemed rational in view of the government's purpose (i.e. cost-effectiveness, differentiation, achievement of full potential), large-scale discrimination occurred as a result of its "secludedness" (and state of neglect) and prevented many learners from enjoying equal treatment and opportunities in education and in society.

To determine whether such discrimination should be tolerated (be permissible), one must apply section 36 to examine if the limitation of the right to equality (e.g. the alleged discrimination) will be reasonable and justifiable (see above).

[72] Prinsloo v Van der Linde 1997 6 BCLR 759 (CC), paras 23, 28.

[73] Van Reenen, T. 1997. Equality, discrimination and affirmative action: an analysis of section 9 of the Constitution of the Republic of South Africa. South African Public Law, pp. 156–159.

[74] Op. cit., pp. 16–17.

[75] Loenen, op. cit., p. 408.

[76] Harksen v Lane NO 1997 11 BCLR; 1998 1 SA 300(CC), para 53.

In applying the proportionality test, arbitrary differentiation should be avoided and prescribed factors used to try and balance the situation (i.e. the nature of the right at stake, the importance of the purpose of limiting it, the nature and extent of the limitation, the means-end relationship and the question of whether less restrictive means are available to achieve the purpose). If, for example, the state proves that the inherited "special education" system cannot be incorporated overnight into a diversified and integrated education system (not yet in place), that a serious lack of resources is contributing to this problem, but that it will alleviate the situation by providing further state-subsidised career-orientated programmes and increase job opportunities for these learners, the alleged discrimination could under the circumstances be permissible.

South Africa's history is chequered with examples of differentiation used more often than not for purposes of exclusion rather than inclusion. Classifications of all sorts (including legal, educational, etc.) have excluded non-whites, women and the disabled, to name a few, on the basis of their differences. A guiding factor should be that the worse the disadvantage suffered by the group, and the more sensitive to harm the group affected, the stricter the test of permissibility should be. Finally, in weighing up the "degrees" of discrimination, special protection should be offered against classifications of a suspect or sensitive nature.[77]

### *5.3. Unfair discrimination*

When the concept "unfair discrimination" is analysed, it may be defined as "treating persons differently in a way which impairs their fundamental dignity as human beings who are inherently equal in dignity".[78] For the purpose of this discussion, discrimination in education on the basis of disability, sex and race, may be the most glaring examples of unfair discrimination.

In terms of the equality clause in section 9, differentiation, which involves unfair discrimination, may be based upon

- the enumerated grounds in section 9(3), in which case there is a presumption of unfairness (in terms of section 9(5));
- other grounds (not enumerated in section 9(3)) in which case there is no presumption of unfairness.[79]

The second stage of the inquiry applied in *Harksen v Lane*[80] is much broader than the first one (above). It investigates whether discrimination amounts to "unfair discrimination" and comprises two stages: Does the differentiation amount to "discrimination" and, if it does, does it amount to "unfair discrimination"?

77 Loenen op. cit., p. 406.

78 Prinsloo v Van der Linde 1997 6 BCLR 759 (CC), para 31.

79 Prinsloo v Van der Linde 1997 6 BCLR 759 (CC), paras 23, 28.

80 Harksen v Lane NO 1997 11 BCLR; 1998 1 SA 300(CC).

*5.3.1. Does the differentiation amount to "discrimination"?*
Differentiation that is based on a specified ground (in section 9(3)) seems to be discriminatory. For example, refusing the hard-of-hearing learner admission to an ordinary school, seems to be discriminatory – discrimination on the basis of her disability.

If the differentiation is not based on a listed ground, then whether or not there is discrimination will depend on whether, objectively speaking, it is based on attributes and characteristics which have the potential to impact on the human dignity of the person as a human being or affect such a person adversely in a comparably serious manner.[81] "Attributes and characteristics" should not be narrowly defined and guidance in this regard is obtained from the attributes and characteristics of the listed grounds in section 9(3). The listed grounds relate to immutable biological attributes or characteristics (e.g. race, sex or pregnancy), some to the associational life of humans (e.g. sexual orientation, culture), or to intellectual, expressive and religious dimensions (e.g. disability, language or religion), and in some cases a combination of one or more of these features (e.g., disability).[82] For example, a boy who suffers from epilepsy is prohibited from participating in sports activities. It seems that such an act encroaches upon his human dignity as a person (as well as his right to equal treatment and opportunities in education). In practice, bad "attitudes" from other learners and teachers towards these learners have often encroached upon their dignity and integrity.

*5.3.2. If the differentiation amounts to "discrimination", does it amount to "unfair" discrimination?*
If discrimination is on a specified ground (section 9(3)), then unfairness will be presumed. For example, the refusal to admit the hard-of-hearing learner to the ordinary school (above) is presumed unfair, unless the contrary is proved.

If discrimination is on an unlisted ground, unfairness will have to be established by the complainant. The unfairness test focuses primarily on the impact of the discrimination on the complainant and other persons in a similar situation. For example, the hard of hearing boy (above) is an athletic boy who excels in sports. He is devastated by the teacher's decision and becomes withdrawn and aggressive. Such discrimination affects his human dignity and self esteem and would be unfair, especially in the light of the fact that epilepsy is medically treated and the teacher, as a professional person, should have acted with more insight.

Discrimination can be blatantly and obviously (directly) unfair, or can have indirect unfair results. For example, the institution of higher school fees at a school for the deaf may seem neutral but could have unfair results if it discriminates against a large group of deaf learners (e.g. black learners). O'Regan J warned that "the more vulnerable the group affected by the discrimination, the more likely the discrimination will

[81] Harksen v Lane NO 1997 11 BCLR; 1998 1 SA 300(CC), para 46.
[82] Harksen v Lane NO 1997 11 BCLR; 1998 1 SA 300(CC), para 49.

be held to be unfair. Similarly, the more invasive the nature of the discrimination upon the interests of the individuals affected, the more likely it will be held to be unfair".[83] In the *Hugo* case the Constitutional Court also rejected the idea that equality demanded equal treatment in all circumstances and held that an unfair discrimination enquiry requires an assessment of whether the overall impact of the discriminatory action "furthers the constitutional goal of equality" or not.[84]

If, at the end of the second stage of the enquiry proposed in the *Harksen* case, the differentiation is found to be "fair", there will be no violation of sections 9(3) and (4). For example, the refusal to admit the hard-of-hearing learner to the ordinary school (above) is presumed unfair. However, if the school authority proves that the school has overcrowded classes, a shortage of teachers and no support services, and that another school which is more suitable to the learner's needs is available in the district, the "discrimination" (refusal to admit) would be "fair" (or, would constitute legitimate differentiation). In the same vein, one would presume that deaf learners (above) who receive no support services in their school, are treated unfairly unless the school authority proves that the shortage of support services and specially trained teachers is of a temporary nature, and that no other schools in the area could accommodate these learners in the interim.

If discrimination is found to be unfair, the next question is whether such unfair conduct may be justified in terms of the general limitation clause in section 36. For example, if the hard-of-hearing learners (above) are instructed to follow an inferior programme in the ordinary (or special) school which has an unfair impact and effect on their lives and future careers, such treatment would constitute unfair discrimination. If the state argues that all the ordinary state schools in the area (district) lack facilities and support services, and that no money is available to upgrade the ordinary schools or provide integrated and diversified education, one has to consider such limitation(s) and the purpose and effect of it on their right not to be discriminated against in education on the basis of their disability. Other alternatives that are available here, and which steps could be taken that would have the least disruptive impact should also be considered. It is apparent that within the context of the situation, the "unfair" discrimination may be reasonable and justifiable, particularly in the face of other more intrusive or disruptive options (i.e. long-distance travelling to schools in larger centres).

### *5.4. Affirmative action*

Affirmative action (or, positive action/discrimination) is used as a broad concept which encompasses all measures directed at improving the position of sensitive

[83] President of the Republic of South Africa and Another v Hugo 1997 6 BCLR 708 (CC), para 113.

[84] President of the Republic of South Africa and Another v Hugo 1997 6 BCLR 708 (CC), para 41.

groups (e.g. blacks, women and the disabled) previously disadvantaged by unfair discrimination.

If the substantive approach to equality is followed, the provision regarding affirmative action in section 9(2) is integrated into the broader goal of equality: "Equality includes the full and equal enjoyment of all rights and freedoms. To promote the achievement of equality, ...." Therefore, the frame of reference for equality (or, the question "equality of what?") should be equality to enjoy full and equal enjoyment of all rights and freedoms.[85] Used in this context, an affirmative action programme does not encroach upon the right against unfair discrimination, but must be regarded as a manifestation of the right to equality in its substantive sense.

The words "To promote the achievement of equality" suggests there should be a rational relationship between ends and means: it is therefore necessary to show that both the purpose of an affirmative action programme and the means selected for its implementation, are reasonably capable of meeting that purpose. If the purpose and means used do not "promote ... equality" (section 9(2)), the next question is whether such affirmative action amounts to "unfair" discrimination. Seen in this context, one may regard the entire pre-Constitution "special (or specialised) education" field (including the present situation) as a field representing a "disadvantaged education minority" in which individuals and groups of learners suffered degrees of deprivation depending on the system they were in (e.g. white or "Bantu" education) and whether they were white, black, Indian or coloured persons. If proportionately more resources are now allocated to improve the position of this minority, such "positive" discriminatory action (e.g. against "mainstream" education and its learners) will not be unfair discrimination, provided the measures and means used in this affirmative programme promote equality.

Groups of non-white learners who are experiencing special needs in education (especially black learners) are particularly vulnerable as a result of previous discriminatory and secluded (inferior) practices as well as racial discrimination against them as a group or individuals (or, sexual discrimination against female learners). Therefore, although it is correct to say that white learners who experienced special needs also suffered in this discriminatory system, they were not quite as vulnerable as other groups (particularly blacks). An affirmative action programme which focuses on preferential educational treatment for these non-white learners, for example, should promote the full enjoyment of their right to equality in education.

In *Motala v University of Natal*,[86] the Supreme Court (now High Court) dealt with preferential treatment in higher education. In this case the court allowed preferential treatment ("affirmative" university admission policy) of one disadvantaged group (Blacks) over another disadvantaged group (Indians) by applying the relevance of degrees of disadvantage suffered by each group. The judgment was given

[85] De Waal et al., op. cit., pp. 158–159.

[86] Motala and Another v University of Natal 1995 3 BCLR 374(D), at p. 375.

in favour of the black student but without consideration of the proportionality test (section 36) which could have drawn the line between acceptable and unacceptable forms of preferential treatment.[87]

If the means and measures used in the affirmative action programme are not reasonably capable of achieving equality, as discussed above, the programme may be unfair and amount to reverse discrimination, which is not the purpose of section 9(2). For example, if the programme benefits only white learners who are experiencing special needs or, in the case of preferential treatment (above), only a portion of black learners who had been fortunate to attend special private schools, the programme could be unfair towards other learners who are experiencing special needs in education, as well as towards all learners across the entire education spectrum (Van Wyk, 1997: 17ff; Loenen, 1997: 413). An affirmative action programme should therefore be inclusive and carefully constructed: it should not exclude learners who experience special needs but who were not "advantaged" (e.g. indigent white learners who could not afford special schools).

If the affirmative action programme amounts to unfair discrimination, the onus is on the education authorities to prove that such discrimination is reasonable and justifiable in terms of the limitation clause (section 36). For example, if the programme has the effect of benefiting only white learners who are experiencing special needs in education or only special schools with highly trained teachers, it would seem unfair towards the overall sphere of special needs education for which it was originally intended. However, if the education authorities prove, *inter alia*, that the measures to be implemented will initially benefit the entire spectrum of special needs education, but that the disadvantaged sectors and its learners will progressively enjoy increased benefits (as similar successful projects in neighbouring countries have proven), the programme may well be in line with the objective of promoting substantive equality in education.

In conclusion, the overarching (or ultimate) purpose of substantive equality in education necessitates an examination and correction of all forms of inequality, not by means of presumption, but through an investigation of the real situation (context) of individual learners, irrespective of their group affiliation (Van Wyk, 1997: 19; Grogan, 1997: 70–72).

## 6. ASSESSMENT, CONCLUSION AND FUTURE CHALLENGES

The field of special needs education is complex and diversified. It comprises a heterogeneous group(s) with diverse educational needs and it is, therefore, quite easy to fall into the trap of generalisation and oversimplification when explaining the application of the equality principle. That was not the aim of this discussion: it was merely to give some illustrations of how a system(s), group(s) and individuals

[87] Loenen, op. cit., p. 8; Van Reenen op. cit., p. 157.

interact in the achievement or deprivation of equal educational opportunities and treatment in the field of special needs education. The ultimate aim should be to promote the realisation of the full enjoyment of equality in education to enable learners to reach their full potential and become dignified and independent adults in society.

Education in South Africa is experiencing a period of transition, and the sphere of special needs education is no exception. Special needs education has been particularly vulnerable to transformation owing to the general neglect it has experienced to date. However, the new constitutional dispensation (and recent school legislation) has laid a solid foundation for the development of a democratic education system in which the human rights of all learners will enjoy equal respect and protection. Against this background, and in line with the latest policy and strategy proposals, special needs education should in future form part of an integrated and diversified education system, but fundamental changes still need to be done to transform the existing school system.

The proposed integrated and diversified school system will certainly provide a good basis for the realisation of the equality principle, but it is important that civil society's attitudes towards special needs education and its dated stereotyping and labelling of these learners, change.

When, and to what extent, special needs education will become fully integrated, depends on many factors of which resources (or the lack of), may be decisive (the delays being experienced in the implementation of the outcomes-based curriculum as a result of *inter alia* the lack of financial resources and a shortage of properly trained teachers, is but one example). The paucity of resources will play a significant role in the realisation of these learners' right to equal opportunities and treatment in education: it could be a direct cause of a "limitation" of the full enjoyment of their equality rights in education. The provision of support services in an integrated system (e.g. what kind of support services and the availability of facilities), in-service training to teachers and principals (e.g. to cope with diverse educational needs) and the implementation of such a system, must receive priority attention.

It is important that the implementation of integration and diversity in education be tackled within the legal context – all role-players must be aware of their legal responsibilities in working in a diversified and differentiated education environment. Special needs education is a historically disadvantaged and neglected field of education that needs urgent attention in the form of affirmative action programmes.

In the latest report on quality education and overcoming barriers to learning and development, the NCSNET and NCESS outline a future framework and strategy for learners who are experiencing barriers to learning and development (NCSNET & NCESS 1997 (2): 53ff). This comprehensive and well-researched report illustrates the paradigm shift that has occurred in education and underscores the basic values of the Constitution and application in education. With the emphasis on concepts such as "inclusiveness", "equality" and "differentiation" in the context of a future integrated and diversified education system (the "systems-change" approach), this report provides a sound constitutional and democratic basis for the development of education in South Africa.

Some of the proposals/recommendations of the report include:

- Equal access to a single, inclusive education system. Such a system would be responsive to diversity and learners would not be barred from participating in this system regardless of their physical, intellectual, social, emotional, language or other differences
- Access to the curriculum. There should be open participation to a flexible and adaptable curriculum (which is made possible by outcomes-based education)
- Community responsiveness. To ensure successful integration of all learners into society, communities should create an environment conducive to such integration
- Cost effectiveness. The need exists to create a system of education provision and support for all learners that is appropriate, effective, affordable, implementable and sustainable.
- Strategies for transforming the education system. Strategies and programmes traditionally aimed at meeting "special needs" in education must move away from the isolated focus of "changing the person", to a "systems-change" approach. This means that we should not see the system as fixed and unchanging, where individual learners need to fit in. Rather, we should see it as being able to be transformed so that it can accommodate individual differences among learners.
- Barriers to learning and development, and enabling mechanisms, would be placed within the context of general education transformation initiatives, influencing all aspects and bands of education. It means that all divisions or branches within the national and provincial departments would "infuse" the proposals outlined in the report into their transformation programmes.

Although policy and legal provisions seem to be pointing the education system in the direction of equal educational opportunities also for learners with special education needs, the achievement of such equality still seems distant if not unachievable.

# Part 2

# Questionnaire on Special Educational Needs and the Law in Europe

## Introduction

The primary objectives of special needs education are:

- The development of potential abilities through quality education which takes the special educational needs (SEN) of children and young people into account.
- The inclusion of children and young people with special educational needs in society.

Special needs education is therefore based on a strong respect for individual differences and not merely linked to a structure of (segregated) special education.

## 1. International law

Convention on the Rights of the Child
Declaration on the Rights of Mentally Retarded Persons
Declaration on the Rights of Disabled Persons
International Covenant on Economic, Social and Cultural Rights
United Nations, Resolution 48/96, The Standard Rules on the equalization of opportunities for persons with disabilities, New York, USA 1994.
UNESCO: The Salamanca statement and framework for action on special needs education, World conference on special needs education: access and quality. Salamanca, Spain, 7–10 June 1994.
European Commission, Helios II programme: European guide of good practice; Towards equal opportunities for disabled people, Brussels, Belgium, 1996.

How have these rules been introduced into national legislation? What influence do non-binding international rules have?

## 2. How does your national legislation implement the right to education for children with special educational needs?

### A. Essentials

***Right to education/right to access – Which groups are covered by legislation? Who is excluded? (Differences: age, private/public schools)***

Are there specific provisions which give the right to education of children with special needs extra weight? Sum up these provisions and give explicit examples.

*Jan De Groof and Gracienne Lauwers (eds.), Special Education*, 139–141.

Are there specific provisions to reinforce the right to education for children with special educational needs?

How are they incorporated into standard education and who is excluded from standard education? Who receives education in separate educational institutions/structures and which pupils receive no education at all?

Which categories of pupils are integrated in standard education and which categories are excluded?

Can a school refuse to accept children with special needs? Is there a difference between private and state education?

Is a school allowed to refuse children with special educational needs?

Are the rules concerning non-discrimination (e.g. discrimination on the basis of sex, ethnic background, etc.) applicable to the refusal of children with special educational needs?

Is the principle of freedom of choice also respected for children with special educational needs? (Freedom of choice means that the parents select freely between private and state schools on the basis of their philosophical outlook or other priorities, and that those responsible for running schools are in a position to organise them on the basis of a given philosophical outlook or other priority).

Is the principle freedom of choice also respected regarding children with special educational needs?

Are there examples in case law?

### *B. Education and care*

Care provided

*How are the legal principles put into practice in terms of the care provided? How is it financed?*

What rights do schools have if they accept pupils with special educational needs?

What are the legal duties of public authorities?

## 3. PROCEDURE

- The role of special centres: detection, diagnosis, consultation, referral, advice
- The role of home counselling services

What are the rights of parents of children with special educational needs?

What are the rights of the children?

- Legal remedies:
  - Rights of appeal: Are the procedures effective?
    Who is allowed to take responsibility for whom? (Authorities, schools, special centres, parents)

Role of a Special Educational Needs Tribunal
- Case law: discussion of certain interesting rulings

## 4. Lifelong learning for children and adults with special educational needs

Is there a need for co-ordination? Is there need for a more structured approach? What is the current situation? (Give a summary of the existing structures.)

**Recommendations to the Council of Ministers**

With a view to providing equal opportunities, it should be a policy priority to ensure that schools are as inclusive as possible, and more resources should be made available for implementing such a policy.

POL GHESQUIÈRE

# Belgium

## 1. Guarantee continuity in inclusion

Inclusive education is on the top of the political agenda in Europe. However, we must be aware that the success of inclusive education depends on the realisation of an inclusive society. Therefore it is necessary that there is some consistency in the different societal domains. It makes no sense of being together at school if we cannot work together or enjoy leisure time or social activities together. Thus, it is necessary to have figures about ***social inclusion*** of persons with special needs and about their ***transition to work***. Work must be done to realise inclusion also in this domains. The adaptation of EC rule 2000/78/EG of November 27, 2000 is very important in these.

## 2. Professional training of teachers

The success of inclusive education will depend in the efforts done in the domain of professional training of teachers, pre-service as well as in-service. Teachers should get some extra time to take refresher courses. Policy makers must further the opportunity of exchange of ideas and experiences, also in an international context. Therefore it is important to strengthen Comenius-projects and the work done by the European Agency on the development of special needs education.

## 3. International debate on educational standards

We must start an international debate on educational standards, stressing the paradox of high quality standards versus respect of diversity, and the paradox of academic output measures versus attention for special educational needs. Especially in countries were so-called '*league tables*' are used, this discussion is very important. We must create international standards on measuring '*quality of education*' and work has to be done to guarantee quality of education. Respect for diversity and special needs

*Jan De Groof and Gracienne Lauwers (eds.), Special Education*, 143–144.

must be an important part of it. It is an important question whether legislation is able to enhance quality education. There is a tension between legislation, administrative rules and personal rights on the one side and the way schools and society work out these rules and rights in practice on the other side.

## 4. International debate on child rights

The success of inclusive education depends also on the respect for child rights, especially the participation rights. We must stress the debate about this participation rights (also in educational matters) especially for children with special educational needs (e.g. children with mental retardation). In a lot of countries these children are not even part of the education system. International rules must be set up on this matter.

PAUL MEREDITH[1]

# England and Wales

## 1. International Law

None of these instruments has been incorporated directly into UK law, though most have been ratified. The extent to which they may influence legislators and courts in the UK in the absence of enforcement mechanisms is likely to be limited. Nonetheless UK courts will, when interpreting UK legislation which is ambiguous or unclear, apply an interpretative presumption to the effect that Parliament intended to legislate in conformity with the UK's international treaty obligations. This was of particular importance in respect of the European Convention on Human Rights before its (partial) incorporation under the Human Rights Act 1998.

Of the international instruments listed in the questionnaire, the most important so far as education law in the UK is concerned is almost certainly the Convention on the Rights of the Child. It does not however, have any direct method of enforcement, signatory governments merely being directed under Article 4 to undertake all appropriate legislative, administrative and other measures to implement the rights contained in the Convention. The reporting mechanism, under which governments are required to report at five yearly intervals to the UN Committee on the Rights of the Child on progress towards fulfillment of their obligations is, however, of considerable importance. The UK government's first such report, in 1994[2] came under some criticism as being superficial and evasive.[3]

[1] University of Southampton, UK.

[2] *The UN Convention on the Rights of the Child: The UK's First Report to the UN Committee on the Rights of the Child*, HMSO (1994).

[3] See Jane Fortin, *Children's Rights and the Developing Law*, Butterworths (1998), p. 45; Children's Rights Development Unit, the *United Kingdom Agenda for Children* (1994). See also the UK government's second report to the UN Committee, *UN Convention on the Rights of the Child: Second Report by United Kingdom*, HMSO (1999).

*Jan De Groof and Gracienne Lauwers (eds.), Special Education*, 145–149.

## 2. Implementation of National Legislation on the Right to Education for Children with Special Educational Needs

### *(a) Essentials*

*(1) General – definition of special educational needs*

The law on special educational needs in England and Wales is based essentially on Part IV of the Education Act 1996 (itself consolidating earlier provisions contained in the Education Act 1993) as amplified by the Code of Practice on Special Educational Needs issued by the Secretary of State under section 313 of the EA 1996. Very recently Parliament has enacted the Special Educational Needs and Disability Act 2001 which when in force will make significant amendments to the law. The provisions of Part IV of the 1996 Act impose considerable extra obligations upon LEAs and school governors in respect of children with special educational needs over and above those owed to children generally, in respect of identification of children with SEN, their assessment, making statutory Statements of special educational needs in appropriate cases, and making provision for those needs.

These special obligations are owed to children who fall within the statutory definition of those with "special educational needs". The legislation provides[4] that a child has "special educational needs" if s/he has a "learning difficulty" which calls for special educational provision. A child has a "learning difficulty" if

- s/he has a significantly greater difficulty in learning than the majority of children of his/her age; or
- s/he has a disability which either prevents or hinders him/her from making use of educational facilities of a kind generally provided for children of his/her age in schools within the area of the LEA.

*(2) Identification and assessment/statementing*

Where an LEA forms the opinion that a child for whom it is responsible has special educational needs and that it is necessary for the LEA to determine the nature, scope and substance of the special educational provision the child may require, the LEA must serve a notice on the child's parent informing him/her that they propose to make an ASSESSMENT of the child's special educational needs, and informing the parent that he/she has the right to make representations and submit written evidence to the authority.[5] Detailed provisions are set out in Schedule 26 to the 1996 Act in respect of the making of assessments.

If, in the light of the assessment and of any parental representations it is necessary for the LEA to determine the special educational provision which any learning

4 Education Act (EA) 1996, s 312.

5 EA 1996, s 323.

difficulty the child may have calls for, the LEA is required to make and maintain a STATEMENT of the child's EDUCATIONAL NEEDS.[6] The judgment as to whether a child's needs are sufficiently serious to justify making a Statement is a matter of great difficulty and frequently of dispute. Many children with special needs do NOT have such Statements. The Statement is required to give details of the LEA's assessment of the child's special educational needs and to set out the special educational provision to be made for the purpose of meeting those needs. The Statement specifies the type of school or other institution the LEA considers would be appropriate for the child.

Where a Statement is maintained for a child, unless the child's parent has made suitable arrangements, the LEA is *required* to arrange that the special educational provision specified in the Statement is made for the child, and the LEA *may* arrange that any non-educational provision specified in the statement is made for the child in such manner as it considers appropriate. *If a particular maintained school is named in the statement*, the governing body of the school is obliged to admit the child to the school.[7] This does not, however, prevent the headteacher/governing body from *excluding* such a child who is already a registered pupil at the school[8] on the basis of the child's conduct. The power to exclude pupils is, however, closely circumscribed by legislation.[9]

*(3) Choice of school*

Under Schedule 27 to the EA 1996, it is provided that, before making a Statement, the LEA must serve a copy of the proposed Statement on the parent.[10] The parent must be given the opportunity to express a preference as to the maintained school (which may be a maintained special school) at which s/he wishes education to be provided for the child, and to give reasons for the preference.[11] Where a parent has expressed a choice of school in accordance with these arrangements, the LEA must name that school in the Statement unless

- the school is unsuitable to the child's age, ability or aptitude or to his/her special educational needs, or
- the attendance of the child at the school would be incompatible with the provision of efficient education for the children with whom the child would be educated, or the efficient use of resources.[12]

6 s 324.
7 s 324(5)(b).
8 s 324(6)).
9 See School Standards and Framework Act 1998, ss 64–68.
10 para 2.
11 para 3(1).
12 para 3(3).

*(4) Integration*

The "principle of integration" of children with learning difficulties within mainstream schooling has hitherto been contained within section 316 of the EA 1996. Section 316 states that the relevant authorities – essentially LEAs and governing bodies) shall secure that a child with special educational needs should be educated in a school which is *not a special school* unless this is incompatible with the wishes of the child's parents, and so long as educating the child in a mainstream school is compatible with

- the child receiving the special educational provision which his/her learning difficulty calls for; and
- the provision of efficient education for the children with whom s/he will be educated; and
- the efficient use of resources.

These provisions in the Education Act 1996 are, however, now to be replaced by a new section 316, inserted by section 1 of the Special Educational Needs and Disability Act 2001. This will significantly strengthen the obligation to provide "mainstream" education for children with special educational needs. This provides that, in the case of children with special educational needs but for whom a Statement has not been made, the child MUST be educated in a mainstream school. In the case of statemented children, the child must be educated in a mainstream school unless this is incompatible with the wishes of his/her parent, or with the provision of efficient education for other children.

*(5) Non-discrimination*

Provisions of the law prohibiting discrimination on the grounds of sex or race would apply to children with special educational needs as they would in relation to children generally. The Special Educational Needs and Disability Discrimination Act 2001 will bring schools within the ambit of the anti-discrimination measures contained in the Disability Discrimination Act 1995.

### *(b) Education and care*

The LEA is under a statutory obligation[13] to ensure that the educational provision specified in a statemented child's Statement of special educational needs is met. A Statement in essence provides a guarantee as to educational provision. The resources come out of the LEA's overall budget – there is not a separate budget for children with special educational needs. More money spent in this area will mean less money to spend elsewhere on schools provision. This is a fundamental tension that pervades the whole system.

[13] EA 1996, s 324(5)(i).

*Procedure*

The Code of Practice on Special Educational Needs, promulgated by the Secretary of State under section 313, EA 1996 (and to which LEAs and governing bodies (among others) must have regard) deals with the responsibilities of school special educational needs co-ordinators and co-operation between the different agencies involved in the identification, assessment and statementing process, including, very importantly, the LEA educational psychology service. Parents themselves have a right to be consulted at key stages of assessment and statementing.

Parents have a right of appeal against decisions taken by the LEA to the Special Educational Needs Tribunal (SENT) in specified circumstances. The SENT is constituted under sections 333–336 EA 1996. The SENT operates on a national basis with a centralised administration under the overall control of a national President. Individual tribunals within the system sit locally, each tribunal comprising a legally qualified chair sitting with two members who, although not legally qualified, have extensive experience in the field of education, special needs and local government. Parents have a right to appeal to SENT in a range of circumstances, of which perhaps the most important are the right of appeal against a decision by an LEA not to make a Statement of special educational needs following assessment;[14] the right to appeal against the contents of a Statement;[15] and the right to appeal against a decision by an LEA not to make an assessment of a child.[16]

From a decision of a SENT the parent (but not the child) may appeal on a point of law to the High Court).[17]

[14] s 325.

[15] s 326.

[16] s 329.

[17] Tribunals and Inquiries Act 1992, s 11(1).

ANDRE LEGRAND

# France*

## 1. Droit international

L'application des dispositions internationales en droit français est soumise à deux conditions: leur ratification ou leur approbation, suivie de leur publication au Journal Officiel, qui conditionne leur entrée en vigueur dans l'ordre interne; la constatation de leur caractère directement applicable. Il appartient au juge de trancher si telle ou telle disposition est susceptible de recevoir directement application et si, à ce titre, elle est invocable ou non devant lui par les justiciables. C'est à la lumière de ces principes que doit être envisagée la réponse à la question posée, s'agissant des différents textes évoqués.

1.1 *La convention sur les droits de l'enfant* a été ratifiée par la France et publiée par le décret n° 90-917 du 8 oct. 1990. Elle a donc été introduite dans le droit français à cette date.

La jurisprudence a cependant été amenée à plusieurs reprises sur les effets exacts de cette convention dans notre ordre juridique. La position adoptée par la Cour de cassation n'a pas été la même que celle du Conseil d'Etat. La première a en effet globalement rejeté la possibilité d'invoquer directement ce texte devant l'ordre judiciaire (Cass. 1$^{ère}$ civ., 10 mars 1993, *Lejeune*, RGDI publ. 1993, p. 1051, note Alland). Se fondant sur l'art. 4 de la convention, qui prévoit que les Etats parties s'engagent à prendre les mesures législatives, administratives et autres qui sont nécessaires pour mettre en œuvre les droits reconnus dans la convention, elle regarde celle-ci comme privée d'effet direct dans son ensemble.

Au contraire, le juge administratif se livre, pour répondre à la question, à une analyse détaillée disposition par disposition. Ainsi admet-il par exemple l'invocabilité directe de l'art. 3-1 de la convention (CE 22 sept. 1997, *Melle Cinar*, RFD adm. 1998, p. 562, concl. Abraham; JCP 1998.II.10051, note A. Gouttenoire-Cornut; Petites affiches, 1998 n°11, p. 18, note Reydellet; RGDIP 1998, 208, note Alland).

* Président de l'université de Paris X Nanterre.

*Jan De Groof and Gracienne Lauwers (eds.), Special Education*, 151–160.

En revanche, depuis l'arrêt du 29 juil. 1994, *Préfet de la Seine Maritime* (Rec., tables p. 1084), il considère que nombre d'autres dispositions, si elles créent des obligations pour les Etats, n'ouvrent pas de droits aux particuliers. Ainsi, il refuse la possibilité d'invoquer directement l'art. 16 sur l'absence d'immixtions illégales dans la vie privée (CE 10 mars 1995, *Demirpence*, Rec., tables p. 810); les art. 12-1, 12-2, 14-1, et 30 (CE, 3 juil. 1996, *Paturel*, Rec., p. 256); ou encore celle de l'art. 24-1 sur le droit de l'enfant à jouir du meilleur état de santé et de bénéficier de services médicaux et de rééducation, l'art. 26-1, qui lui reconnaît le droit à bénéficier de la sécurité sociale et l'art. 27-1 qui consacre le droit à un niveau de vie suffisant pour permettre son développement physique, mental, spirituel, moral et social (CE, sect., 23 avr. 1997, *GISTI*, RFD adm 1998, p. 562, concl. Abraham; AJDA 1997, p. 482, chron. Chauvaux et Girardot; RGDIP 1998, p.208, note Alland); ou encore celles des art. 6 et 28, ce dernier concernant en particulier le droit à l'éducation (CE 29 déc. 1997, *Epx Soba*, Rec., tables p. 626); ou enfin, celles de l'art. 10 (CE, 1er avr. 1998, *Mme Aublé*, Rec., tables p. 952).

La Haute juridiction a généralement considéré ces dispositions comme insuffisamment précises pour être directement appliquées en droit interne. On peut donc penser, en particulier à la lumière de l'appréciation portée sur l'art. 26, que les dispositions de l'art. 23 appelleraient la même conclusion.

1.2. La situation est assez parallèle en ce qui concerne *le Pacte des Nations Unies sur les droits économiques, sociaux et culturels*, publié par le JO le 1er fév. 1981. Beaucoup de ses dispositions ne comportent que des engagements très généraux s'efforçant de "mettre en œuvre certains avantages au profit de leurs ressortissants, ou encore des droits au profit des individus qui n'ont manifestement qu'un sens programmatoire, tels que 'le droit qu'a toute personne d'obtenir de gagner sa vie par un travail librement choisi ou accepté' (art. 6 du pacte)" (G. Burdeau, note sous CE, 29 janv. 1993, *Mme Josefa Bouilliez*, AJDA 1993, p. 365). Le juge administratif refuse donc aux particuliers la possibilité d'invoquer les art. 2, 9 ou 10 du Pacte sur l'absence de discrimination fondée sur la fortune, ou le droit à la sécurité sociale ou le droit de la famille à une assistance (CE, ass., 5 mars 1999, *Rouquette*, Rec., p. 37). Saisi d'une demande concernant la possibilité d'appliquer les dispositions de l'art. 26 du Pacte sur les droits civils et politique (principe de non-discrimination) aux droits reconnus par le Pacte sur les droits économiques, il a considéré que cet art. ne pouvait s'appliquer qu'aux droits consacrés par le Pacte dont il était issu (CE, ass., avis, 15 avr. 1996, *Mme Doukouré*, RFD adm. 1996, p. 808, concl. Martin).

1.3. A la différence des conventions, les déclarations ne constituent pas des dispositions ayant un caractère direct s'imposant à l'autorité nationale (v. par ex. pour la déclaration universelle des Droits de l'Homme, CE, 15 avr. 1951, *Elections de Nolay*, Rec., p. 310; ass., 23 nov. 1984, *Roujansky*, AJDA 1985, p. 216, concl. Labetoulle). Elles ne sont donc pas susceptibles d'être directement invoquées devant les tribunaux. Il en va ainsi de *la Déclaration des droits du déficient mental de 1971*, comme de *la Déclaration des droits des personnes handicapées de 1975*.

1.4. *La déclaration de Salamanque et le cadre d'action pour l'éducation et les droits spéciaux* sont des dispositions de même nature, auxquelles on peut appliquer les mêmes principes.

## 2. Mise en œuvre du droit à l'éducation par la législation nationale

### *2.1. Principes: Droit à l'éducation*

*2.1.1. Textes législatifs applicables*
La loi fondamentale est la loi n° 75–534 du 30 juin 1975 d'orientation en faveur des personnes handicapées. Selon son art. 1er, "la prévention et le dépistage des handicaps, les soins, l'éducation la formation et l'orientation professionnelle … constituent une obligation nationale … Les familles, l'Etat, les collectivités locales, les établissements publics, les organismes de sécurité sociale, les associations, les groupements, organismes et entreprises publics et privés associent leurs interventions pour mettre en œuvre cette obligation … L'Etat coordonne et anime ces interventions." A quoi l'art. 4 ajoute que "les enfants et adolescents handicapés sont soumis à l'obligation éducative".

Le principe du droit à l'éducation a été repris dans la loi n° 89-486 du 10 juillet 1989 d'orientation sur l'éducation. Affirmant dans son art. 1er que "l'éducation est la première priorité nationale", elle précise en particulier par la suite que "l'intégration scolaire des jeunes handicapés est encouragée".

Cette loi est complétée par un rapport annexé qui, comme l'indique l'art. 35 de la loi énonce "les objectifs de la politique nationale pour l'éducation pour la période 1989 à 1994". Le Conseil d'Etat a jugé que ce rapport n'est pas revêtu de la valeur normative qui s'attache aus dispositions de la loi (CE, ass., 5 mars 1999, *Confédération nationale des groupes autonomes*, AJDA 1999, p. 462, chr. Raynaud et P. Fombeur). Sous cette réserve, dans un paragraphe spécifique, il rappelle et développe la priorité affirmée par la loi de 1975 sur l'accueil des enfants et des adolescents handicapés et "l'importance capitale" de leur intégration scolaire dans le processus d'intégration sociale et professionnelle des personnes handicapées.

L'éducation spéciale s'adresse aux enfants et adolescents qui ne peuvent suivre une scolarité normale: handicapés physiques, sensoriels ou mentaux, qui constituent le public visé par la loi de 1975, malades ou enfants en grande difficulté et le principe largement affirmé est celui de l'intégration scolaire. Née au début du vingtième siècle, avec la création des classes et des écoles de perfectionnement, destinées aux "enfants arriérés et déficients", l'éducation spécialisée se développera, après la seconde guerre mondiale, avec la multiplication de multiples formations de formateurs spécialisés par types de handicaps en direction de "l'enfance inadaptée". Après 1965, on renversera les perspectives en mettant l'accent sur la notion "d'adaptation et d'éducation spécialisée" (AES) aux lieu et place de "l'inadaptation" antérieure.

Et c'est en 1980 qu'apparaît la vision actuelle de l'éducation spécialisée, avec la substitution, dans la droite ligne de la loi de 1975 précitée, de l'AIS (adaptation et intégration scolaire) à l'AES. C'est l'accent mis sur l'idée d'intégration qui fait clairement apparaître la notion essentielle. Comme toutes les évolutions historiques, celle-ci ne réalisera pas les principes à l'état pur. Chacune des phases décrites laissera subsister, en développant le principe nouveau, certains sédiments des périodes antérieures et la situation actuelle est donc la résultante d'un développement complexe.

*2.1.2. L'intégration scolaire: un principe non exclusif*

En fixant le statut légal de l'intégration scolaire, le législateur a exprimé une préférence pour l'idée de scolarisation dans un établissement ordinaire. Mais il n'en fait pas la solution exclusive et il ouvre concomitamment des possibilités alternatives. Les dispositions des lois précitées comportent certaines dispositions caractéristiques qui en témoignent. Ainsi l'art. 4 de la loi de 1975 prévoit que "les enfants et adolescents handicapés ... satisfont à l'obligation éducative en recevant soit une éducation ordinaire, soit, à défaut, une éducation spéciale". A quoi l'art. 5 ajoute que "l'Etat prend en charge les dépenses d'enseignement et de première formation professionnelle des enfants et adolescents handicapés

1) soit, de préférence, en accueillant dans les classes ordinaires ... tous les enfants susceptibles d'y être admis malgré leur handicap.
2) soit en mettant du personnel qualifié relevant du ministère de l'Education nationale à la disposition d'établissements ou services créés ou entretenus par d'autres départements ministériels, par des personnes morales de droit public, ou par des groupements ou organismes à but non lucratif conventionnés à cet effet".

Dans le même esprit, les textes réglementaires qui fixent, dans ce qu'on appelle, par référence au décret n° 56-284 du 9 mars 1956 auquel elles étaient rattachées, les annexes XXIV, les conditions d'autorisation des établissements et services mentionnés ci-dessus prévoient la prise en charge des enfants ou adolescents handicapés à temps partiel ou à temps plein, dans un établissement scolaire ordinaire, "chaque fois que c'est possible" (ex. art. 6 de l'annexe XXIV bis dans la rédaction du décret n° 89-798 du 27 oct. 1989).

*2.1.3. Les populations concernées*

Il résulte de ces textes que tout enfant handicapé, physique, sensoriel ou mental doit avoir la possibilité de fréquenter un établissement scolaire ordinaire. Ce sont en revanche d'autres dispositions législatives ou réglementaires qui s'appliquent aux élèves connaissant des problèmes sociaux ou aux populations relevant de la protection judiciaire de la jeunesse. S'agissant donc des handicapés au sens strict, les circulaires n° 82–2 et 82–048 du 28 janv. 1982, impliquant à la fois les ministres de l'Education nationale et de la solidarité nationale recommandent de "décloisonner le dispositif institutionnel existant dans une perspective d'intégration ... en lui assignant prioritairement, mais non exclusivement, un objectif de réinsertion en milieu scolaire ordinaire chaque fois que possible avec, si nécessaire, les soutiens spécialisés pédagogiques et thérapeutiques appropriés". Bien entendu, l'obligation d'instruction étant générale, et le principe d'égalité ayant une valeur constitutionnelle, il ne saurait être question de discrimination en raison du sexe ou de la race.

Une question particulière se pose cependant à propos des déficients intellectuels. Les structures qui leur sont offertes dans les établissements scolaires, qu'elles soient ordinaires ou spécialisées, ne sont ouvertes qu'aux déficients intellectuels légers ou moyens. Le handicap intellectuel lourd ne relève pas de la compétence des établissements de l'Education nationale, mais d'instituts placés sous la tutelle du ministère des Affaires sociales (Instituts Médico-éducatifs pendant la période d'obligation scolaire, Instituts Médico-professionnels ensuite).

La frontière entre les deux types d'institutions s'est donc déplacée à l'occasion de la remise en cause, dans les années 80, de la définition antérieure de déficience intellectuelle légère par l'Organisation Mondiale de la Santé. Cette modification de la définition du handicap a donc sensiblement accru la population justiciable des institutions de l'Education nationale.

*2.1.4. L'organisation de l'accueil*

Le principe posé (v. par ex la circulaire n° 65–348 du 21 sept. 1965) est l'idée de la scolarisation "dans des conditions aussi proches que possible de la normale en évitant de ..séparer (les enfants) de leur milieu naturel, familial et scolaire". Trois solutions sont donc ouvertes:

- l'intégration individuelle dans une classe ordinaire: c'est le principe, en particulier dans l'enseignement primaire, rappelé par ex. par la circulaire interministérielle n° 76–156 et 31 du 22 avril 1976, confirmé par la circulaire n° 82-2 ét 048 du 28 janv. 1982, qui y voit « une priorité ». Au prix, le cas échéant d'enseignements de soutien, d'adaptation et d'un appui particulier des groupes d'aide psycho-pédagogique,[1] l'enfant relève des classes normales d'un établissement scolaire ordinaire.
- la création de classes spéciales d'externat annexées aux établissements scolaires ordinaires des différents niveaux, dans les cas où la nature des handicaps l'exige et la concentration des effectifs le permet. Généralement adoptée dans l'enseignement primaire, où elle prend la forme des classes d'intégration scolaire (CLIS), elle existe aussi largement dans l'enseignement secondaire, où se sont par exemple développées des sections d'éducation spécialisées (SES), devenues sections d'enseignement général et professionnel adapté (SEGPA), au sein des collèges.
- la création d'établissements spécialisés avec internat quand la complexité ou la nature du handicap rend indispensable le placement dans un établissement spécialisé ou quand la dispersion de la population fait obstacle à la mise en place d'un

[1] Transformés, depuis la circulaire n° 90-082 du 9 avril 1990, en réseaux d'aides spécialisées aux élèves en difficulté (RASED).

dispositif cohérent.. Certains relèvent de l'Education nationale (comme les écoles régionales d'enseignement adapté – EREA – au niveau collège ou les écoles nationales de perfectionnement – ENP- au niveau lycée) et sont régis par les règles émanant de ce ministère. D'autres sont des établissements médico-éducatifs relevant du ministère des Affaires Sociales. Ce sont eux qui sont visés par les annexes XXIV, dont les dernières rédactions, par le décret de 1989, déjà cité, placent la volonté éducative avant même l'activité de soins. Se rattache à cette dernière solution la possibilité de créer un service d'éducation spéciale et de soins à domicile (SESSAD)[2] généralement rattaché à l'établissement ou, exceptionnellement, autonome. Dans le cas des structures relevant de ce ministère, les textes favorisent largement la coopération avec les services de l'Education nationale, soit en ouvrant des possibilités d'intégration partielle, soit en favorisant la mise à disposition de personnels enseignants par convention avec les établissements.

*2.1.5. Modalités d'affectation des enfants handicapés*

L'art. 6 modifié de la loi de 1975 instaure une commission de l'éducation spéciale dans chaque département, compétente à l'égard des enfants handicapés de 0 à 20 ans. Selon son paragraphe I (devenu art. L. 351-2 du code de l'éducation), cette commission "désigne les établissements ou les services.... dispensant l'éducation spéciale correspondant aux besoins de l'enfant ou de l'adolescent et susceptible de l'accueillir. La décision de la commission s'impose aux établissements scolaires ordinaires et aux établissements d'éducation spéciale dans la limite de la spécialité au titre de laquelle ils ont été autorisés ou agréés". Il résulte donc de ce texte que l'établissement concerné n'a pas la possibilité de s'opposer à la décision de la commission.

Le principe de la liberté de choix des parents est reconnu. D'une part, sauf le cas exceptionnel où un seul établissement ou service est à même de correspondre aux besoins de l'enfant, la commission doit laisser le choix entre plusieurs d'entre eux. A cela s'ajoute l'obligation pour elle de faire figurer au nombre des établissements ou service qu'elle désigne, dès lors qu'il correspond aux besoins de l'enfant et qu'il est en mesure de l'accueillir, et quelle que soit sa localisation, celui pour lequel les parents ou représentants légaux de l'enfant expriment leur préférence.

Le décret n° 75-1166 du 15 déc. 1975 précise et complète les dispositions législatives. Son art. 7 crée des commissions de circonscription compétentes pour les enfants relevant de l'enseignement préscolaire et élémentaire (les CCPE) et son art. 9 des commissions équivalentes pour l'enseignement secondaire (les CESD). Ces commissions agissent par délégation de la commission départementale.

Il revient à ces diverses commissions de décider, dans l'exercice de leurs compétences respectives, de l'orientation des enfants et, soit de constater qu'un enfant ne relève pas de la compétence d'un établissement de l'éducation nationale et de

2 Là encore, l'ordre des termes est tout à fait caractéristique.

l'orienter vers un institut médico-éducatif, soit d'opter, sous les limites indiquées plus haut quant au choix des parents, entre les diverses solutions ouvertes au sein de celle-ci.

*2.1.6. Contentieux*

La loi, comme cela a été dit, repose sur un principe de préférence et n'établit pas une obligation absolue. Ce fait entraîne des conséquences juridiques non négligeables. La première est que, du côté de l'éducation nationale, la plupart des dispositions précises sont émises sous la forme de circulaires, les dispositions législatives et réglementaires ne posant que des principes à caractère général. La seconde est que le volume du contentieux sur l'orientation des élèves est finalement très faible.

Il n'en existe pas moins et il concerne deux types de questions. La loi de 1975 et ses textes d'application confient aux tribunaux judiciaires le contentieux des recours contre les décisions relatives à l'éducation spéciale (juridictions du contentieux technique de la sécurité sociale: tribunal du contentieux de l'incapacité, puis, en appel, Cour nationale de l'incapacité ...). Appelées à connaître du contentieux de la légalité de ces décisions, elles soint aussi compétentes pour juger les recours en indemnisation qui se fonderaient sur l'illégalité des décisions d'orientation ( Cons. d'Et. 23 janv. 1984, *Min. de la solidarité c/ Mme Rodriguez*, Rec. p. 18; Trib. Confl. 19 oct. 1999, *Bernardet c/ min. Educ. Nat.*, G.P. 11-12 avr. 2001, p. 12, concl. Sainte-Rose).

Le rôle de la CDES est cependant multiple. A côté de sa compétence d'orientation, elle a aussi une fonction d'attributions d'aides financières qu'à la différence de la précédente elle ne peut pas déléguer. C'est elle qui, à ce titre, accorde l'allocation d'éducation spéciale (AES) destinée à compenser une partie des frais d'éducation supplémentaires occasionnés par le handicap et susceptibles de varier selon sa nature ou sa gravité. Le contentieux de cette attribution est de la compétence des juridictions spécialisés dans le domaine de la Sécurité sociale. Le recours en cassation porté contre les décisions des juridictions d'appel est de la compétence de la Chambre sociale de la Cour de Cassation.

## *2.2. Education et soins*

2.2.1. L'accueil repose sur deux logiques différentes, selon qu'on se situe dans des établissements relevant de la tutelle des affaires sociales ou de l'autorité de l'Education nationale. Les premiers sont des établissements de soins et leur *financement* est assuré par la sécurité sociale selon le système du prix de journée (art. 7 – I de la loi de 1975,[3] même si le traitement des enseignants mis à disposition est assuré

[3] "Les frais d'hébergement et de traitement dans les établissements d'éducation spéciale et professionnelle ainsi que les frais de traitement concourant à cette éducation dispensée en dehors de ces établissements, à l'exception des dépenses incombant à l'Etat en application de l'art. 5, sont intégralement pris en charge par les régimes d'assurance maladie, dans la limite des tarifs servant de base au calcul des prestations".

sur le budget de ce ministère. Le financement des seconds repose entièrement sur le budget de l'Etat.

2.2.2. La scolarisation s'accompagne généralement de *services d'accompagnement*. Ceux-ci peuvent être par exemple des services de soutien à l'éducation familiale et à l'intégration scolaire, qui sont généralement rattachés à l'établissement d'accueil. Mis au service de la scolarisation en milieu ordinaire, en particulier au niveau de l'école maternelle, leur objectif est de permettre un maintien de l'enfant dans sa famille. Ils peuvent aussi être des services d'éducation spéciale et de soins à domicile qui ont pour objectif de faciliter la coordination de tous les moyens médicaux, paramédicaux, psycho-sociaux, éducatifs et pédagogiques adaptés.

L'Etat a l'obligation d'assurer gratuitement un certain nombre de prestations d'éducation spéciale et, en particulier des mesures de soutien pédagogique. Saisi d'un recours présenté par un établissement privé sous contrat d'association, le Tribunal administratif de Toulouse lui a reconnu le droit de réclamer à l'Etat la prise en charge des rémunérations des enseignants qui les ont assuré (8 nov. 1988, *Lafitte*, Rec., tables p. 825).

## 3. Procédure

### *3.1. Le rôle et les droits des acteurs*

C'est un point qui a déjà été largement abordé dans les développements précédents. Pour le reste, les questions principales touchant à l'organisation des enseignements adaptés ont tourné, dans ces dix dernières années, autour de deux points. Ils concernent surtout les structures d'accueil pour déficients intellectuels.

3.1.1. *Eviter toute dérive au niveau du recrutement des structures d'enseignement adapté*. Dans le cadre de l'évolution récente de la doctrine concernant les conceptions de l'intégration scolaire, évoquée ci-dessus (n° 2.1.1.1.), les textes réglementaires ont été modifiés et en particulier ceux des annexes XXIV. Les nouvelles annexes résultent donc des décrets n° 88-428 du 22 avril 1988 concernant les élèves atteints de déficiences auditives ou visuelles, et 89–798 du 27 Oct. 1989 concernant les élèves atteints de déficiences intellectuelles ou motrices. Dans ce cadre, une circulaire interministérielle du 30 Oct. 1989 rappelle que les établissements spécialisés relevant de cettc annexe ne sont pas des structures de traitement de la difficulté scolaire et que leur vocation n'est pas d'accueillir des enfants qui connaissent des difficultés scolaires du seul fait des difficultés sociales auxquelles ils sont confrontés, le traitement de celles-ci relevant de la vocation normale des établissements scolaires ordinaires.

De la même manière, deux circulaires Education nationale comportent des passages significatifs. Celle du 6 fév. 1989 (n° 89-036), qui fixe les orientations concernant les enseignements généraux et professionnels adaptés constate "que la SES est encore trop souvent sollicitée pour accueillir des élèves que rien ne prédestine à recevoir un enseignement spécialisé. La sur-représentation des élèves étrangers, maîtrisant mal la langue française, en est un exemple". Celle du 20 mars 1990 (n° 90-065) rappelle aux commissions de circonscription du second degré (CCSD) la nécessité de veiller à ce que les SES et les EREA ne deviennent pas "des voies de relégation scolaire" et leur recommande de ne pas y envoyer "des élèves dont l'échec n'est dû qu'à des problèmes de comportement ou de maîtrise de la langue".

C'est le même esprit qui conduit à la substitution aux classes de perfectionnement et autres classes spécialisées des classes d'intégration scolaire. "Les CLIS accueillent de façon différenciée; dans certaines écoles élémentaires ou exceptionnellement maternelles, des élèves handicapés physiques ou handicapés sensoriels ou handicapés mentaux ou handicapés mentaux qui peuvent tirer profit, en milieu scolaire ordinaire, d'une scolarité adaptée à leur âge et à leurs capacités, à la nature et à l'importance de leur handicap" (circ. n° 91-304 du 18 nov. 1991).

Les classes de perfectionnement étaient vécues comme des lieux de relégation où l'on hésitait à placer les élèves. La CLIS est une classe pour élèves handicapés, ayant pour objectif de permettre à ses élèves de suivre totalement ou partiellement un cursus ordinaire. La circulaire sus-nommée crée quatre catégories de CLIS, en fonction du handicap concerné.

3.1.2. Affirmer la priorité de *l'adaptation pédagogique*, collective et différenciée, sur la mise en place de structures fermées visant à particulariser à l'extrême les élèves en difficulté. C'est le sens de la substitution par la circulaire n° 90-082 du 9 avr. 1990 des réseaux d'aides spécialisées aux élèves en difficulté (RASED) aux groupes d'action psycho-pédagogique (GAPP). L'idée générale est de situer l'action au plus près de la classe et d'impliquer au maximum le maître "ordinaire" en coopération avec les intervenants spécialisés pour la prévention des difficultés scolaires.

La circulaire distingue deux modalités d'aides: les actions à dominante "pédagogique" et celles à dominante "rééducative". Les premières peuvent prendre la forme de "classes d'adaptation" à effectif réduit regroupant de façon permanente des élèves en difficulté dans le but de les réinsérer, le plus rapidement possible, dans une classe ordinaire; ou de "regroupements d'adaptation", rassemblant de façon temporaire, pour des actions pédagogiques décidées en commun, des élèves en difficulté qui continuent à fréquenter une classe ordinaire. Les secondes font, pour l'essentiel, intervenir des intervenants spécialisés.

### *3.2. Les recours légaux*

Un décret avait instauré un dossier scolaire destiné à recevoir toutes indications utiles sur le comportement des élèves, les handicaps et les inégalités dont ils peuvent souffrir. Le Conseil d'Etat a jugé que l'institution de ce dossier ne violait pas le secret médical, dans la mesure où il ne comportait que des éléments médicaux non confidentiels et qu'il n'était consultable que par l'élève, ses représentants légaux ou des agents ou organismes internes à l'établissement (CE, 6 fév. 1980, *Guihaumé*, Rec., tables p. 748). Elle ne porte pas non plus atteinte aux principes fondamentaux de l'enseignement, mais vise au contraire à leur donner leur plein effet en mettant à la disposition de ceux qui apportent leur concours à l'œuvre éducative un instrument propre à favoriser la prévention des difficultés scolaires, à dépister les handicaps et à compenser les inégalités (CE, 6 fév. 1980, *Confédération synd. des familles*, ibid.).

## 4. Handicapés et formation tout au long de la vie

Il y a peu de dispositions spécifiques sur ce point au sein des textes français. Les handicapés[4] ont tous les droits à la formation professionnelle auxquels ont droit les travailleurs valides. Et leur état doit pouvoir être pris en compte à partir de l'application du principe d'individualisation de la formation qui caractérise un certain nombre de textes sur la formation continue.

Les points essentiels relèvent de la loi n° 87-517 du 10 juillet 1987 en faveur de l'emploi des travailleurs handicapés. Rerédigeant une partie du code du travail, elle impose, par l'art. L. 323-1 de celui-ci, à tout employeur occupant au moins vingt salariés, de compter, parmi ses salariés employés à temps plein ou partiel, au moins 6% de personnes relevant d'une des huit catégories énumérées à l'art. 323-3. Parmi celles-ci, figurent en premier lieu les travailleurs reconnus handicapés par décision de la commission technique d'orientation et de reclassement professionnel, créée par l'art. 323-11. Si une entreprise n'atteint pas ce chiffre, elle peut s'acquitter de son obligation d'emploi en versant une contribution annuelle, proportionnelle à l'importance du "déficit" à un fonds de développement pour l'insertion professionnelle géré par une association agréée, l'association nationale de gestion du fonds pour l'insertion professionnelle (AGEFIPH). Celle-ci, créée par l'art. L. 323-8-3 peut notamment consacrer les sommes ainsi recueillies à le compensation du coût supplémentaire des actions de formation et au financement d'actions d'innovation et de recherche au bénéfice des travailleurs handicapés.

De la même manière, la COTOREP est consultée (art. R. 325-5 du code du travail) sur toutes les demandes ou propositions de rééducation ou de réadaptation d'un travailleur handicapé. Elle donne un avis sur la nature, les modalités et la durée de la formation. A ce titre, elle peut demander l'extension de la durée réglementaire d'une formation et, lorsque celle-ci est organisée au profit d'un demandeur d'emploi handicapé.

4 Est travailleur handicapé toute personne dont les possibilités d'obtenir ou de conserver un emploi sont effectivement réduites par suite d'une insuffisance ou d'une diminution de ses capacités physiques ou mentales (art. L. 323-10 du code du travail).

ANTONIO EMBID IRVJO AND FERNANDO GURREA CASSAMAYOR[1]

# Spain

## 1. International Law

Convention on the Rights of the Child
Declaration on the Rights of Mentally Retarded Persons
Declaration on the Rights of Disabled Persons
International Covenant on Economic, Social and Cultural Rights
United Nations, Resolution 48/96, The Standard Rules on the equalisation of opportunities for persons with disabilities, New York, USA 1994.
UNESCO: The Salamanca statement and framework for action on special needs education, World conference on special needs education: access and quality. Salamanca, Spain, 7–10 June 1994.
European Commission, Helios II programme: European guide of good practice; Towards equal opportunities for disabled people, Brussels, Belgium, 1996

How have these rules been introduced into national legislation? What influence do non-binding international rules have?

Spain's constitutional system (the 1978 Spanish Constitution) provides for a broad protection of fundamental rights. In particular, the right to education is recognised in article 27.1 and, as will be seen in the rest of this questionnaire, within this right to education there are contents that apply to people with physical or sensorial disabilities.

In addition, art. 49 of the Constitution requires the Public Authorities to carry out a policy of care, treatment, rehabilitation and integration in favour of the physically, sensorially, and mentally handicapped, who must be provided with the specialised attention that they need, and the rights that all citizens enjoy under Chapter I of the Constitution must be safeguarded. This provision does not recognise any type of fundamental right of citizens; it merely rules on how the public authorities should act in this field.

[1] Antonio Embid, Professor of Administrative Law. University of Zaragoza (Spain) & Fernando Gurrea, General Secretary of the Aragon Government Cabinet Office.

*Jan De Groof and Gracienne Lauwers (eds.), Special Education*, 161–165.

The Constitution also establishes in art. 10.2 that "the regulations with regard to fundamental rights and freedoms recognised under the Constitution shall be interpreted in accordance with the Universal Declaration of Human Rights, and international treaties and agreements on these matters ratified by Spain".

There is no ruling from the Constitutional Tribunal with regard to non-binding international regulations.

## 2. How does your national legislation implement the right to education for children with special educational needs?

### *A. Essentials*

***Right to education/right to access – Which groups are covered by legislation? Who is excluded? (Differences: age, private/public schools)***

Are there specific provisions which give the right to education of children with special needs extra weight? Sum up these provisions and give explicit examples.

Are there specific provisions to reinforce the right to education for children with special educational needs?

The right to education established in the Constitution (art. 27.1) has a particular content established by the *Ley Orgánica Reguladora del Derecho a la Educación* – The Right to Education Act (1985, modified in 1995). One of the rights of students is the right "to receive an education that will ensure full development of their personality" [art. 6.1.a)]. This expression "full development of their personality" also appears in art. 27.2 of the Constitution as an object of education, and we believe that this completely covers the basic constitutional aspects that concern the purposes of this report.

How are they incorporated into standard education and who is excluded from standard education? Who receives education in separate educationai institutions/structures and which pupils receive no education at all?

Which categories of pupils are integrated in standard education and which categories are excluded?

Can a school refuse to accept children with special needs? Is there a difference between private and state education?

Is a school allowed to refuse children with special educational needs?

Are the rules concerning non-discrimination (e.g. discrimination on the basis of sex, ethnic background, etc.) applicable to the refusal of children with special educational needs?

Is the principle of freedom of choice also respected for children with special educational needs? (Freedom of choice means that the parents select freely between private and state schools on the basis of their philosophical outlook or other priorities, and that those responsible for running schools are in a position to organise them on the basis of a given philosophical outlook or other priority).

Is the principle freedom of choice also respected regarding children with special educational needs?

Are there examples in case law?

There is legislation (Royal Decree 732/1995, of 5 May, establishing the rights and obligations of students and internal rules of educational establishments) which addresses these issues in detail, bearing in mind that *it applies only to publicly-funded centres* (in other words, State schools and Direct Grant schools). Thus, it does not apply to schools without public funding. Art. 12.2.a) of this Decree establishes a principle of equality of opportunity consisting of:

> non-discrimination for reasons of birth; race; sex; economic status; social level; political, moral or religious convictions, as well as for physical, sensorial and mental disabilities or for any other personal or social situation or circumstance.

To this effect, the Decree rules on a series of policies to be carried out.

From the above, it may be deduced that a fully private educational establishment may reject a student with special educational needs, since student selection is at their discretion. However, for this reason alone, a State or Direct Grant school may not do so. But it must be borne in mind that from time to time the press reports on problems of integration concerning children with certain illnesses (Aids, for example, although there is no case law in this respect). In the Direct Grant schools (private schools funded with public money) it is doubtful whether the principle of non-discrimination is applied as scrupulously as in the State schools.

### *B. Education and care*

Care provided

*How are the legal principles put into practice in terms of the care provided? How is it financed?*

What rights do schools have if they accept pupils with special educational needs?

What are the legal duties of public authorities?

There exists in Spain the concept of "compensatory (remedial) education" to designate the set of measures that may be adopted by the public authorities to attend to children with special educational needs within the educational system. These special educational needs refer to economic necessities as well as physical or mental disabilities. They include schoolchildren in particular circumstances (e.g. travelling people – gypsies – or those in hospital). The legislation dealing with these measures is Royal Decree 299/1996 of 28 February, concerning actions aimed at compensating for inequalities in education. It should be borne in mind that this is a piece of State legislation, and that the Autonomous Communities – who have powers to act in the field of education – may have their own specific policies with regard to this.

Compensatory education programmes involve economic support for schools that have integration programmes. They receive financial grants, remedial staff, technical resources, etc.

In addition, there is a piece of legislation which to some extent is a specific manifestation of the above, and which attempts to address a global consideration of special educational needs. This is Royal Decree 696/1995 of 28 April, concerning the regulation of the education of children with special educational needs. The content of this legislation will be dealt with in the next section.

## 3. Procedure

– The role of special centres: detection, diagnosis, consultation, referral, advice
– The role of home counseling services

What are the rights of parents of children with special educational needs?

What are the rights of the children?

– Legal remedies:
  - Rights of appeal: Are the procedures effective?
    Who is allowed to take responsibility for whom?
    (Authorities, schools, special centres, parents)
    Role of a Special Educational Needs Tribunal
  - Case law: discussion of certain interesting rulings

Royal Decree 696/1995, mentioned above, includes gifted children who have special educational needs as well as those who have mental, motor or sensorial handicaps. *It applies to publicly-funded schools only*, and therefore, not to private schools.

It aims to detect these cases immediately and adopt the corresponding measures. This task is given to educational and psycho-pedagogical orientation teams who are responsible to the educational authorities (which today are the Autonomous Communities). Thus, this task is not the responsibility of the Schools, although these teams work in collaboration with the Schools.

The general principle of the regulation is that attention to children with special needs is given in ordinary schools under an integration system. For this, schools may be provided with remedial teachers and syllabus changes may be effected for certain students.

There will only be schooling in special centres when any adaptations that may be necessary are extreme or impossible to carry out in an ordinary school. In these special centres, students will be given the basic compulsory education plus training to help them make the transition to adulthood.

In the case of gifted children, their period of schooling may be flexible.

## 4. LIFELONG LEARNING FOR CHILDREN AND ADULTS WITH SPECIAL EDUCATIONAL NEEDS

**Is there a need for co-ordination? Is there need for a more structured approach? What is the current situation? (Give a summary of the existing structures.)**

These long-term or lifelong educational needs are dealt with in Spain, not by the educational system, but by the Social Services. They fall within the bounds of social work, not education. There are several types of centre, both public and private, but once again, not within the educational system, and therefore, no official educational qualification of any type may be obtained there.

**Recommendations to the Council of Ministers**

With a view to providing equal opportunities, it should be a policy priority to ensure that schools are as inclusive as possible, and more resources should be made available for implementing such a policy.

HANS-PETER FÜSSEL

# Germany

## 1. Relations between the International Law and the National Law

The International Conventions became as far as the German Federal Legislation had accepted them part of the German Federal Law (see Art. 59 Par. 2 of the Federal Constitution, the Basic Law).

Following Art. 31 of the Basic Law the Federal Law is overruling the Law of the Länder. Also with the right to legislation in educational matters the Länder are bound by these international conventions which became by adopting part of the German Federal Law.

Many of the International Conventions include more declarations and intentions than concrete and binding legal obligations. Therefore these International Conventions become important in direction of the interpretation of the Law of Education in the Länder; in most cases the International Conventions will not be quoted directly in the School Acts of the Länder.

The HELIOS II-programme was a programme of co-ordination and co-operation; the German Länder had been included via the Kultusministerkonferenz and states played an active role in this network together with members from the other states.

## 2. Right to Access

The Right to Education is a right of all pupils; this means that all pupils – with special educational needs or without – have this right, but they also have to attend the compulsory school-education.

Children with special educational needs have in all School-Acts of the Länder and also the daily reality in all Länder their own and individual rights – following a special procedure of testing their specific abilities and skills (see No. 4). These rights are fixed in special provisions in the different School-Acts of the Länder and unlike the general understanding of the right to education in Germany

*Jan De Groof and Gracienne Lauwers (eds.), Special Education*, 167–170.

these rights of Children with special educational needs are real, concrete and individually orientated.

The instruments of special educational needs are quite different following the different needs of the children.

In an integrative system (class or school) the single child will get the necessary kinds of help and assistance either in the normal school lessons – for example by a second, in special education especially trained teacher – or also separated for a time.

A separated and also specialised school for different kinds of handicap will have special opportunities and possibilities to help the single child and also the group of children/class.

Pedagogical integration in this way in Germany is distinguished in an equal learning goal-system and a different learning-goal-system for the children with special educational needs (always compared with the learning conditions of children without special educational needs). But not in all of the German Länder a system of different learning-goals for children with special educational needs is accepted by the legal regulations.

All kinds of integration of children with special educational needs in regular schools will under legal provisions only be accepted if the regular schools can fulfil the necessary conditions of special conditions by their teaching, the technical and also their financial possibilities; if this will not be possible the School Inspectorate may refuse the acceptance of a child with special educational needs in a single school – this rule had been accepted by the German Federal Constitutional Court and is not in contradiction to Art. 3 Para 3 of the Basic Law: "no person shall be disfavoured because of disability" (decision from 28 October 1997, BVerfGE 96, 288).

In general all children with special educational needs will be given a chance of being integrated – also the number of children with special educational needs in a class will be limited depending on the kinds and conditions of the special education needs. Differences relating to their needs normally will not be made, at least from a legal perspective; in reality heavily multiple-handicapped children sometimes can not be integrated because schools can not fulfil the necessary conditions like mentioned before.

The decision if a child with special educational needs has to attend a regular or a special school had to be taken by the School Inspectorate, not by the single school. Therefore not the parents choose the school for their child but the School Administration has to decide. But it is against the already quoted rule of Art. 3 Para. 3 of the Basic Law if the School Inspectorate decides against the wish and will of the parents who want an education of their child with special educational needs in a regular school and this can be fulfilled by the conditions in this concrete school – under these conditions the German Federal Constitutional Court has voted for a preference for "integrated education" for children with special educational needs.

The only choice parents may have is that they decide that their child with special educational needs will attend a private school – but because of the fact that in Germany private school in general are in a clear minority the real chances of parents to make their choice in this way is quite small because a specialised private school must be found in an acceptable distance of the families home (also because of the specialised state schools for children with special educational needs these children sometimes have to be transported for a longer distance day by day – e.g. if there is only a special school for blind children in an area of 50–60 km children from all around – especially from the rural areas – have to be transported to this special school and that may take more than just one hour each way; the only solution then may be a boarding school-system – but also this system includes then at least an even greater social segregation from their families for these children).

## 3. Education and Care

Social welfare and social insurances also give rights to children with special educational needs. The problem by now is a system of non-co-ordination between the rights of children with special educational needs out of their situation as pupils and the rights as persons with a handicap and therefore also special needs which may be fulfilled by social welfare institutions.

How the legal relation between these different rights had to be described, if there is any preference and how far these rights may be combined is still not yet solved – the jurisdiction of the different law-courts in Germany on that field is quite different, sometimes also contradictory. An understanding that there where the school-authorities are responsible for the child/pupil the social welfare institutions must not give any assistance or help is quite widespread – last but not least also for financial reasons …

## 4. Procedures

In a special procedure the individual educational needs of a child will be tested. Doctors, teachers and also psychologists are involved in the procedure of testing, also the parents. This procedure may take part in some special educational centres; in most cases the special schools will do this procedure.

At the end the School Inspectorate has to decide which kind of special educational needs a single child needs and should get; and also the place where these needs will be fulfilled will be defined by the School Inspectorate: whether it will be the regular school or a special school (in Germany most of the children with special educational needs will have to attend a special school – only about 5% are allowed to go to a regular school, to become "integrated"; and the possibilities of integration become worse the older the child is : in secondary schools the rate is still lower than these 5% in general …).

Parents have by the jurisdiction of the German Federal Constitutional Court a right to know the concrete reasons why their child with special educational needs cannot attend schooling at a regular school. This decision may be proofed by the law courts. The courts then will have to see if the reasons mentioned by the School Inspectorate that the regular school will not be able to fulfil the conditions of special educational needs in this concrete case can be accepted or not. This system is effective – because not only some general information and some general reasons given by the School Inspectorate may justify the refusal of a parental wish of integration.

Insofar as special educational centres had been founded in some of the Länder these centers are responsible for testing, for the teacher-training on the field of special education, they do advisory services for parents and regular teachers and they are also the institution for the co-ordination of the necessary special education given to children with special educational needs in the regular schools; sometimes also children with special educational needs will be educated for a time in these centres and not in their regular schools. Therefore these centres are an important institution for the integration of children with special educational needs in regular schools – in the interest of these children, but also in the interest of the regular schools.

## 5. Lifelong learning

The older a person becomes the more the institutions of social welfare and social insurances will have to take care. A new Law – "Sozialgesetzbuch, 9.Buch" – has been adopted and came into force in the middle of the year 2001; co-ordination in the interest of persons with disabilities is one of the main aims of this new law. It is too early to say anything about the success because the implementation of this law has just started.

Integration in social life is a general aim of all legal instruments – and this aim only can be reached if all institutions co-operate.

## 6. Recommendations

Co-operation and co-ordination seem the most important aspects to provide equal opportunities – and this aim must be fulfilled by the co-operation of institutions and by the co-ordination of the legal instruments.

RAINER FANKHAUSER[1]

# Austria

## 1. INTERNATIONAL LAW

How have these rules been introduced into national legislation? What influence do non-binding international rules have?

The Convention of the Rights of the Child and the International Covenant on Economic, Social and Cultural Rights have been transformed into national law by acts of Parliament. Additional legal steps were not taken as Austria already meets the obligations laid down in these documents.

Moreover, the Federal Constitutional Law (*Bundes-Verfassungsgesetz*) contains a provision stipulating that the general recognised rules of the International Law are regarded as part of the Federal Law.

It should be noticed in this connection that the European Convention of Human Rights and Freedoms including its protocols are part of the Austrian constitutional law.

Non-binding international rules may serve as guideline for interpretation.

## 2. HOW DOES YOUR NATIONAL LEGISLATION IMPLEMENT THE RIGHT TO EDUCATION FOR CHILDREN WITH SPECIAL EDUCATIONAL NEEDS?

Are there specific provisions which give the right to education of children with special needs extra weight? Sum up these provisions and give examples.

The Austrian school legislation contains various provisions concerning children with special educational needs. They are laid down in different laws, the most important being the Compulsory School Act (*Schulpflichtgesetz*), the School Organisation Act (*Schulorganisationsgesetz*) or the School Instruction Act (*Schulunterrichtsgesetz*). None of them, however, is endowed with an extra legal weight. In order to obtain extra weight a law must either be on constitutional level or the law maker must give it special prevalence.

[1] Ministry of Education, Science and Arts, Vienna.

*Jan De Groof and Gracienne Lauwers (eds.), Special Education*, 171–177.

In Austria there is also a rule of interpretation saying that in case of *conflicting* regulations the one which is more specific prevails the more general.

**Are there specific provisions to reinforce the right to education for children with special educational needs?**

There are specific provisions of this kind. They comprise

- The procedure by which it is determined whether a child needs special educational assistance.
- The position of his/her parents in this procedure. This includes the right of the parents to make an appeal *vis-à-vis* the superior educational authority or the Administrative Court.
- The types and categories of Special Needs Schools (*Sonderschulen*).
- The possibility to integrate children with special educational needs outside the system of Special Needs Schools.
- The possibility to have an additional classroom teacher if such an integration takes place.
- The possibility to reduce the maximum number of pupils in classes where children with special educational needs are integrated.

**How are they incorporated into the standard education and who is excluded from standard education? Who receives education in separate educational institutions/structures and which pupils receive no education at all?**

From a legal perspective Special Needs Schools and the integration of children with special educational needs into the so-called standard system are equivalent. According to the framework provided by the School Organization Act both Special Needs Schools as well as the integration are belonging to the standard system. Regarding the rights provided there is no difference between these two possibilities.

The integration of children with special educational needs can take place at a Primary School (*Volksschule*), a Lower Secondary School (*Hauptschule*) or at the lower cycle of a Secondary Academic School (*Unterstufe der allgemein bildenden höheren Schule*). Therefore all schools covering the ages from 6 to 14 are open to integration. For the moment we do not have integration at vocational schools. Vocational schools cover the age range from 15 to 17/18/19. There are, however, Colleges for Engineering (*Höhere technische Lehranstalten*) and Colleges for the Occupation in the Business Sector (*Handelsakademien*) that are especially adapted to the needs of physically disadvantaged students. Colleges take pupils from 14/15 to 19. They last five years an end with a "*Reifeprüfung*" – Examination that gives unrestricted access to universities and *Fachhochschulen*.

Parents may choose between a Special Needs School and the integration of their children into the standard school system. In principle this choice is bound to the condition that there is a school providing integration within easy reach of a child's home. The educational authorities must advise parents on these schools. But the Compulsory School Act goes even a step further. In order to allow in as many cases as possible for the choice just described it obliges the responsible educational authorities to take all reasonable measures within their sphere of competence when the parents of a child ask for integration in an area where such a possibility does not yet exist. This does not give the child or his/her parents a subjective right to integration but it compels the educational authorities to do everything that can reasonably be justified.

Whether a child needs or does not need special educational care has to be decided by the responsible District Educational Authority (*Bezirksschulrat*) through a formal procedure laid down in the Compulsory School Act. The procedure is started on the request of the parents or the principle of the school the child attends or is going to attend. The reason for providing special educational care is mental and/or physical disadvantages. They must be serious enough to prevent a child from following instruction at a Primary or Lower Secondary School. Ordinary learning difficulties will never justify a decision that a child is in need of special educational care. The Austrian school legislation tries to keep the number of children who receive no education at all as low as possible. Therefore, the School Organization Act also provides for Special Needs Schools for extremely disadvantaged children.

**Which categories of pupils are integrated in standard education and which categories are excluded?**

As stated above a categorisation of this kind does not exist. As soon as it is determined that a child requires special educational care his/her parents may choose between a Special Needs School or integration. In principle it depends on the parent which way a child goes. If no school providing integration is available the district school authorities have to take all reasonable measures to equip at least one school for accepting disadvantaged children.

In Austria there are the following types of Special Needs Schools:

- Special Needs Schools for physically disadvantaged children
- Special Needs Schools for children with speech problems
- Special Needs Schools for children who are hard of hearing
- Special Needs Schools for deaf children
- Special Needs Schools for partially sighted children
- Special Needs Schools for blind children
- Special Needs Schools for problem children

Moreover, Special Needs Schools may also have classes for multi-disadvantaged children.

**Can a school refuse to accept children with special needs? Is there a difference between private and state education?**

State schools cannot refuse children with special needs. As soon as a formal decision is taken in this respect the child has acquired a subjective right to attend a Special

Needs School suited for his/her disadvantages or to be integrated into the standard system under the conditions already explained. The child's obligation to start or to continue his/her compulsory school education corresponds to the right to receive a suitable education within the public school system.

In contrast to public schools, private Schools can refuse children. Pupils are admitted to a private school by a private law contract. It therefore lies within the autonomy of private law that a school accepts.

**Is a school allowed to refuse children with special educational needs?**

Compare answer to the above question.

**Are the rules concerning non-discrimination (e.g. discrimination on the basis of sex, ethnic background, etc.) applicable to the refusal of children with special educational needs?**

The Federal Constitutional Law contains a general provision, which interdicts all kind of wilful treatment on the basis of gender, race, religion etc. The protection of the disadvantaged is specifically mentioned. The respective clause says that the Republic (Federation, *Länder* and municipalities) will ensure an equal treatment of disadvantaged and non-disadvantaged people in all spheres of life.

As basic rights are if not stated otherwise mainly orientated towards the state and do usually not extend to acts based upon private law, rules concerning non-discrimination do not refer to private schools. Therefore, private schools may refuse to take children with special educational needs.

**Is the principle of freedom of choice also respected for children with special educational needs?**

In the private school system parents can chose within the whole range of schools but none of them is compelled to accept a request for admission. Concerning the special priorities of parents private schools do not have right to demand additional revenues from the state in order to meet them.

With regard to state revenues there are two categories of private schools. Private schools maintained by a recognised church or religious body have a right to receive the teachers they need free of charge. The teachers will give instruction at the private school but remain to be employed by the state (the Federation or a *Land* depending on the type of school). The right of these schools to receive the necessary teaching staff is guaranteed by the Private School Act (*Privatschulgesetz*). Concerning other expenses (non-teaching staff, building costs, school equipment etc.) the state may conclude a private law treaty with the body maintaining a private school but cannot be obliged to do so.

Private Schools which do not belong to a recognised church or religious body relay entirely on the will and the capacity of the state to support them. In contrast to the first category of private schools they have no right to receive their teaching staff free of charge. This unequal treatment of private schools has already been put forward to the Constitutional Court. Up to now the Court has refused to consider the matter. According to the Constitutional Court Act (*Verfassungsgerichtshofsgesetz*) the Court may refuse to enter into a complaint if she thinks that the clarification of a question of constitutional law is not to be expected.

In the public school sector the parents of a child with special educational needs may as a rule choose any suitable education. If they decide for a Special Needs School it must be one adequate for the child's disadvantage. If the parents want their child to be integrated and integration is offered by the local Primary School than this school should be taken as Primary Schools have a catchment area. However, if a public Primary School outside the catchment area is willing to accept the child he/she may attend it. While a Primary School within the catchment area must take the child, a school outside can. The size of catchment areas is determined by the legislation of the *Länder*. A catchment area may dispose of one or more Primary Schools. The Vienna School Act for example determines that the entire city of Vienna constitutes one single catchment area.

**Is the principle of freedom of choice also respected regarding children with special educational needs?**

Compare the answer given to the question above.

**Are there examples in case law?**

No.

**What rights do schools have if they accept children with special educational needs?**

According to the Austrian concept of law a right is a legal position on the basis of a law or a contract which can be sued in court. Public schools are not endowed with a legal personality of their own. They are institutions depending on the state (Federation and/or the *Länder*) and are therefore not entitled with subjective rights. They are submitted to their responsible superior authorities. As public schools have no legal personality they cannot conclude contracts with the educational authorities. They are part of the educational administration which is considered a unit. If schools need assistance because they have children with special educational needs they cannot force the authorities to give them what they are asking for. Even if the educational authorities should not fulfill their legal commitments *vis-à-vis* a school (teaching staff; school equipment) the school may not go to court. It may only inform the administrative level superior to the one it has run into conflict with. It is than up to this level to ensure the laws being implemented correctly. In doing so the higher unit can also introduce disciplinary measures against members of the lower level.

If a superior level should constantly cover legally doubtful positions of the level below with respect of the provision of teachers or equipment it is imaginable that in the end a complaint of parents would be accepted by the Administrative or, depending on the circumstances, even by the Constitutional Court. The Courts may be willing to investigate although in a case like this the law infringed would be an objective one which is directed towards the school administration and not a subjective one protecting individual positions of parents or pupils.

With private schools the situation may be different. As mentioned before schools maintained by a recognised church or religious body have a right to receive the teaching staff they need free of charge. The maintaining organisation of a private school, which integrates pupils with special educational needs, is therefore in a relatively strong position. In staff matters it may invoke a subjective right provided by the Private School Act. The same applies if a private law contract is concluded between the body running a private school and the state. In this case it is irrelevant whether the maintainer of a private school is a recognised church or any other organisation.

**What are the legal duties of public authorities?**

The duties of the public authorities in connection with children with special educational needs refer to the school building, the school equipment and the staff (teaching as well as non-teaching).

In connection with Primary and Lower Secondary Schools the legislation of the *Länder* may determine that classes in which children with special educational needs are integrated may be given a second classroom teacher. This means that two teachers are in the classroom at the same time. The second teacher who should have a specific training may either be a permanent one or simply be present for several hours or days a week.

Referring to the lower cycle of Academic Secondary Schools the provisions concerning the use of additional and specifically trained classroom teachers are issued by the federal legislation.

Schools holding children with special educational needs have a reduced maximum number of pupils per class. For Primary and Lower Secondary Schools this number is again fixed by the legislation of the *Länder*. It also determines how many pupils with special educational needs a class may have. One of the criteria imposed on this respect by federal law is the degree of disadvantages.

With regard to the lower cycle of Academic Secondary Schools these numbers are stipulated by federal legislation. The current legislation says that classes in which integration takes place should at least hold five pupils with special educational needs. Each of them reduces the maximum number of pupils per class by two.

In standard Primary, Lower Secondary and Academic Secondary Schools the maximum number of pupils admissible to a class is 30.

## 3. Procedure

The decision whether or not a child needs special educational assistance is taken by the District Educational Board (*Bezirksschulrat*) at the request of the parents or the principal of the school the child is already attending or is going to attend. Following this request the District Educational Board opens a formal procedure which has to be oral on the parents' demand. The Board must inform the parents about this possibility. In the course of the procedure the District Educational Board has to consult expert opinion on the child's needs. If the Board deems it necessary and the parents agree a school physician will also be consulted. During the procedure the parents are entitled to submit to the Board the expert opinion of people having provided or still providing pedagogical, psychological or medical care to their child. Although the Board is not obliged to follow the views expressed it must consider them when making its decision. To consider an expert opinion in a formal decision means that one has to discuss the arguments put forward, explaining why one follows or does not follow them.

On the request of the parents the Board may suspend the procedure agreeing that the child attends a Public or Lower Secondary School for a period of up to five months before the matter is finally decided. The District Educational Board has to hand out its decision in writing. Parents may appeal against it at the Provincial Educational Board (*Landesschulrat*) the decision of which can be brought before the Administrative Court in Vienna. An appeal to the Constitutional Court is possible if the constitutional rights of the child have been infringed.

## 4. Lifelong learning

Lifelong learning belongs to adult education which in Austria is entirely conferred to the private sector.

STIG KLINGSTEDT

# Norway

## 1. International Law

The special education legislation in Norway is in accordance with the goals and rights set forth in the declarations and conventions mentioned in the letter.

Soft law has no binding influence on national legislation. But it will be of great importance to the Norwegian government to ensure that our legislation is in accordance with the goals and ambitions set forth in these declarations.

## 2. National legislation concerning children with special educational needs

First some facts about the Norwegian educational system:

The Norwegian system of education is divided into four main categories:

- Primary and lower secondary education – This is compulsory education for pupils aged 6–16.
- Upper secondary education – Students aged 16–19.
- Higher education
- Adult education

Norway is divided into

- 19 counties
- 435 municipalities

The municipalities are responsible for the running of pre-school, primary and lower secondary education.

The counties are responsible for providing upper secondary education.

In autumn of 1999 a new education act[1] came into force. This act covers primary, lower secondary and upper secondary school for all ages.

[1] Act relating to Primary and Secondary Education (Education Act) last amended 30 June 2000. www.dep.no/kuf/engelsk/regelverk/lover/014101–200002/index-dok000-b-n-a.html

*Jan De Groof and Gracienne Lauwers (eds.), Special Education*, 179–185.

It is laid down in this act, in section 2-1, that every child has a right to primary education. There is no difference between children who need special education and children who do not. The act also states, in section 3-1 that young people have a right to secondary education. This is a legal right to up to five years of education and training when the need for this is documented.

A very important goal in this act is that teaching shall be adapted to the abilities and aptitudes of the individual pupil. To reach this objective it is laid down in the act, in section 5-1, that pupils who can't benefit satisfactorily from the normal education are entitled to special education.

If special education is given it is to be given in accordance with the principles of integration, participation and decentralisation.

- **Which groups are covered by legislation?**

It is clearly stated in the act, section 2-1, that *all* children and young people in Norway are given a right to education, regardless of their special needs. This is not just an ambitious goal – this is reality.

In Norway children start school at the age of six. They usually finish upper secondary education at the age of 19. But also young people and adults older than this are given a right to education.

- **Specific provisions for pupils with special educational needs:**

The education act states in section 5-1 that pupils who can't benefit satisfactorily from the ordinary education have a right to receive special education. Special education is only given if the child or its parents give their consent.

Special education is given based on an expert assessment by the educational-psychological counselling service. Their report shall give reasons why the pupil is in need of special education. It shall also describe the content of the special education, the extent and how it ought to be organised.

The report from the educational-psychological counselling service gives advice to the municipality or county on how the measures taken for the student can ensure that pupils will get an equivalent educational situation to that of the other pupils. If the municipality or county do not follow the advice given, the reason for this must be documented.

Based on the report, the school works out an individual educational plan (IEP) for this pupil. This plan must take into consideration the advice of the educational-psychological counselling service, but also adapt the special needs education to the curriculum taught to the rest of the class.

Section 5-4 in the educational act states that both the child and its parents shall be involved when the organisation and content of the special education is decided.

The education act makes no distinction between different forms of special education.

It is clearly stated in section 8-2 that all pupils have a right to be a member of a class. As a result of this the majority of pupils with special educational needs are given their adapted education in the mainstream school to which the pupil belongs, usually within his or her own class.

Pupils with special educational needs may be taught in smaller groups or - individually. Special education can be given in the form of an extra teacher or individually adapted educational plans that can be very different from what we normally associate with education.

A combination of these methods is practised for many pupils.

The local educational-psychological counselling service assists teachers in developing suitable programmes for the different pupils

The support system for mainstream schools consists of the educational-psychological services in the municipalities and the 20 national resource centres. These resource centres constitute the national support system.

If the municipality or county lack the required competence they can ask the resource centres for guidance.

To accommodate the needs of the deaf, sign language training has been introduced. It is stated in the act, in sections 2-6 and 3-9, that pupils who have sign language as their first language have the right to receive tuition in both the use of sign language and through the medium of sign language.

To ensure that the blind receives adequate education the use of books on tape and the use of Braille are increasing.

Books on tape are also used to accommodate the needs of pupils with dyslexia.

The use of digital media has been increased in order to improve the learning possibilities for disabled pupils and students.

- **Integration in the standard education**

It is a fundamental principle in the educational act that pupils who need special education shall receive this, as far as possible, in their local schools and preferably in their own class. There are very few special schools left in Norway, except schools for the deaf. We have got six schools which take special care of the needs of the deaf.

We also have some schools, which give pupils with severe behavioural disorders a more practical oriented education.

In co-operation with parents and guardians the school shall provide the pupil with educational facilities adapted to his or her needs. These needs may lead to teaching in smaller groups or individual counselling.

In the year 2000 less than one percent of the pupils in Norway attended special schools. This tells us that the majority of the pupils who receive special education have their needs covered within ordinary schools. The use of special classes and - special schools are more common in the big cities and in densely populated municipalities.

- **Public and private schools**

In Norway the majority of pupils attend public schools. Private schools are not very common.

A public school cannot refuse to accept children with special educational needs. The same rules apply to private schools that receive state funding according to the private school act. It is stated in this act, in section 7, that schools who receive funding must accept everyone who has a right to attend public schools. Since public schools cannot refuse to accept a pupil with special educational needs, neither can a private school that receives state funding.

- **Non-discrimination rules**

The education act clearly states that everyone is entitled to an education. If a school refuses to accept a child with special educational needs this will be a breach of the principle that all children have equal right to education regardless of their special educational needs.

- **Freedom of choice**

The principle of freedom of choice is applicable to a certain extent. As mentioned Norway does not have many private schools. However, the parents are free to choose between state and private schools. As mentioned earlier, a private school, which receives state funding, must accept all children, regardless of their special needs.

Parents cannot choose freely between public schools. The main rule is that a pupil shall attend the school closest to its home. This also prevents that pupils with special educational needs are all sent to the same schools.

However, section 8-1 in the education act states that on application, the pupil may be accepted for another school than is designed for the area where he or she resides.

- **Case law**

We do not have a lot of case law in this area. This is probably a result of a very good educational policy in Norway. Everybody is given a right to education according to his or her needs and abilities. The fact that we have hardly any case law tells us that our educational policy is working.

*Education and care*

- **What rights do schools have?**

All public and many of the private schools are subsidised by the central government.

There is no separate national funding system for special education. The municipalities have the same responsibility for all the pupils in their area.

The municipal authorities divide the grants taking into account the number of pupils and classes and the number of pupils with special educational needs in the previous school year. The allocated resources shall cover adapted education in the form of divided classes, a two-teacher system, individual lessons and group teaching.

If a municipality wants to have a special school this has to be financed through the mainstream municipal school budget.

As mentioned a school cannot refuse to accept a child with special educational needs. If a school has got pupils with such needs they will have to finance it through the ordinary school budget.

- **Legal duties of public authorities**

The legal duties of the public authorities are listed in chapter 13 of the education act. They shall provide an adequate education to all children and young people. To achieve this they are given a lot of obligations.

- The municipalities must provide standard and special education for all students at primary and lower secondary level. This is stated in section 13-1 of the education act.
- The county must provide standard and special education at upper secondary level. This is stated in section 13-3 of the education act.
- Each municipality and county is responsible for providing an educational-psychological counselling service. This is stated in section 5-6 of the education act
- They are responsible for arranging transportation for certain groups of pupils. This is stated in chapter 7, and section 13-4 of the education act.
- According to section 14-1 of the education act the state shall supervise the education given to pupils with special educational needs. If conditions are discovered that are in violation of the education act, the state may order the correction of such conditions.
- It is stated in section 5-9 of the education act that the state shall ensure that textbooks and other educational resources are prepared for special education.

## 3. Procedure

- **The role of special centres**

The roles of the special centres have changed dramatically in the last ten years. Until 1992 Norway had 40 national schools for special education. As a part of the re-organisation of special education 20 have been closed and the remaining 20 special schools have been turned into state resource centres. As mentioned these resource centres constitute the national support system.

We have got resource centres for pupils with certain disabilities including visual and hearing impairment, dyslexia, behavioural and emotional disorders, severe learning difficulties and mental disabilities. In collaboration with the ministry of Health and Social affairs, four regional resource centres have been established for persons born both deaf and blind. An autism programme and a national resource centre for MBD/ADHD, Tourette's syndrome and narcolepsy have also been started.

The national resource centres shall help to make sure that the institutions responsible for education, the municipalities and the county, receive advice and support in order to assure the quality of the education provided.

The resource centres shall also develop special educational expertise for groups of students with serious and special needs. They shall achieve this goal through investigations, diagnosis, advice and development work.

If the schools do not have the necessary knowledge to help pupils with such needs, they can ask the resource centres for help.

In Norway it is a goal to identify children with special educational needs as early as possible. The special centres do not do this. This is done by local health centres in co-operation with the educational-psychological service centres. Many children with such needs are identified before they start school.

- **The role of home counselling services**

Home counselling services do not play an important role in this area. Outside the school support is given by the educational-psychological counselling service and the national resource centres. The support is mainly addressed to the parents.

- **The rights of parents/children with special educational needs**

It is stated in section 5-4 of the education act that the parents or the pupil can demand that the school perform the necessary investigations in order to find out if the pupil is in need of special education.

As mentioned earlier it is the educational-psychological counselling service that gives an expert assessment of the pupil's needs. Before this assessment is made, and before special education commences, the parents or the pupil must give their approval.

The parents and the pupil are also entitled to see the content of the specialist report, and they are given a right to express their views before any decision is made.

The content of the special education shall be decided in co-operation with the pupil and its parents, and their views shall be given a lot of weight.

According to section 5-5 of the education act, the school must make a written report every six months on what kind of special education the pupil has been given and an evaluation of the pupils' progress. This report shall be sent to the pupil and its parents.

- **Legal remedies**

Section 15-2 of the education act states that the ministry of Education, Research and Church affairs is the appeal body in these cases. This power has been delegated to the national educational offices. There is one such office in each county.

If the parents or the pupil aren't satisfied with the result of the first appeal they can appeal the educational offices decision, and take them to court.

As mentioned earlier we have hardly any case law in this area. This indicates that the procedures of appeal are effective.

- **Special educational needs tribunal**

In Norway we do not have a special educational needs tribunal. As mentioned the pupil or its parents can complain to the state education offices. After this they can take their case to the ordinary courts.

- **Case law**

As mentioned we have hardly any case law in this area. We have only two interesting rulings by the Supreme Court.

The first judgement is published in Rt. 1993 p. 811.

This ruling concerned a 28 years old mentally retarded and physically challenged woman and her right to further training. In the appeal to the Supreme Court she invoked her right after the adult education act to undergo further training on the primary school level.

The Supreme Court found that she had been given an adequate primary education, and that she had no legal claim to undergo further training on the primary school level.

## 4. Lifelong learning

Equal opportunities of education for adults and lifelong learning are the two major tenets of the Norwegian adult education policy. The education policy aims to raise the general level of education within the adult population regardless of their special needs or where in the country they live.

The act on adult education (voksenopplæringsloven) and the education act (Opplæringsloven) regulate adult education. These acts place the responsibility for the adult education with the public authorities responsible for the various levels of education and adult education associations such as Folkeuniversitetet.

The municipalities are responsible for the adult education at primary and lower secondary level, and the counties at upper secondary level. In addition the adult education associations and distance education institutions also provide courses at these levels, as well as courses in higher education.

THEODORE FORTSAKIS[1]

# Greece[2]

After a short analysis of the definition of the persons with special needs (**1**) and the description of specific impairments (**2**) we will outline the basic modern policy Issues (**3**) and the relevant legal provisions (**4**). Furthermore, we shall attempt a description of the relating projects (**5**), the relevant non-governmental organisations (**6**) and finally the participation of Greece in research and educational programmes (**7**).

## 1. Definition of persons with special needs

Persons with special educational need are by no means a readily – defined group with common characteristics. Until today there is no generally accepted description of the terms "handicapped" and handicap. This leads to further difficulties regarding the pedagogical approach, where several theoretical views conflict with one another. Furthermore, there are many kinds of disabilities, which influence the educational programmes adopted. Nowadays, the use of a general definition of special education is avoided. The prevailing argument is that the education system should treat the student with special needs like any other student, i.e. like a complex personality and not like a disability student. Furthermore, the personality of the student is not considered anymore as deviating from normal. It is respected without an effort to "normalise" it.

According to article 1 of Law 2817/2000 a person is considered to have special educational needs according to the difficulties he/she faces in learning. Article 1 gives a definition of persons with special educational needs which states in paragraph 1 that "Persons with special education needs under the meaning of the present Law are considered to be persons that have a significant difficulty in learning and adapting due to physical, mental, psychological and social problems. Paragraph 2 specifies the categories that include persons with mental incapacity or immatureness,

[1] Professor of Public Law in the Faculty of Law of Athens, Attorney at Law

[2] The author thanks Ms. Eleni Gouliou, LL.M. Cambridge, for her legal research of the relevant materials.

*Jan De Groof and Gracienne Lauwers (eds.), Special Education*, 187–201.

persons with significant impairment of view or hearing, with neurological or orthopaedic problems, with problems of speech, persons with difficulties in learning, like dyslexia, difficulties in numeracy and literacy and finally persons with complex emotional, social and learning difficulties as well as autistics and persons with other development impairments. Paragraph 3 broadens the scope of this Law as to also include children of pre-school and school age (both in their childhood and puberty) that do not fall under one of the aforementioned categories but need a (temporary or lifelong) special care and approach in education. No other persons should be considered to fall under this category. In particular, persons who have difficulties in education because their mother language is not Greek do not fall under the categories of people with special needs. The "Centres for diagnosis, evaluation and support" (K.D.A.Y.) determine whether a person satisfies the aforementioned conditions and can be characterised as a person with special education needs.

## 2. Description of specific impairments

### *(i) Deafness*

Deaf is the person who even with a hearing aid cannot perceive a conversation through the channels of hearing. A deaf person mainly uses his/her sight in order to understand the speakers (lip reading, sign language, written language). A person with a hearing impairment is a person that even with hearing aid has difficulty in perceiving a conversation by hearing channels only.

### *(ii) Autismus*

Autismus is a lifelong development disorder due to a biological malfunction of the brain or the central nerve system, the exact nature of which still remains unclear. Its effect is unusual or abnormal behaviour that varies from apathy to aggression and severe problems in communication and social skills.

### *(iii) Mobility problems*

Mobility problems can be caused by damage to the central nerve system (brain paralysis), by orthopaedic damage and by epilepsy. The nerve – muscular disorders can take the form of tetraplegia, paraplegia, hemiplegia etc and can be accompanied by other difficulties, for example, in speech, vision, hearing, memory, etc.

### *(iv) Vision impairment – Blindness*

Blind persons are the persons who cannot read written material with the use of their vision. Persons with impaired vision are those who can partly see written material when magnified and can thus access knowledge by the channel of sight.

### *(v) Mentally retarded persons*

The term "retarded" means that the specific skill (different in each case) is significantly below average. Difficulties can arise relating to social and vocational skills as well as to basic necessary skills.

### *(vi) Learning difficulties*

The term "learning difficulties" is a general term referring to a heterogeneous group of disorders, which can cause significant difficulties to the learning and use of speech, reading, writing, logic or numeracy. These skills are caused by a malfunction of the central nerve system. Although sometimes learning difficulties can exist concurrently with other impairments, they are not the consequence of these impairments.

## 3. Basic modern policy issues

### *(i) Early identification and early intervention*

Early identification and early intervention is the best way to tackle educational disadvantage. When educational failure becomes entrenched, pupils can move from demoralisation to disruptive behaviour and truancy. But early diagnosis and appropriate intervention improve the prospects of children with special educational needs and reduce the need for expensive intervention later on. For some children, giving more effective attention to early signs of difficulties can prevent the development of special educational needs. The majority of children with the most severe disabilities will be identified well before they start school. But health and social services should also look for other factors, which may lead to an educational disadvantage. An integrated approach by child health professionals, social services and education staff is needed right from the start.

### *(ii) Inclusion*

The term integration is used to signify the systematical placement of one element inside another, and the completion of the first as an internal part of the whole. The term mainstreaming signifies the effort to incorporate an element to the whole, whereby the element acquires the characteristics of the whole and loses its own special characteristics. The difference is that in integration the basic characteristics are maintained, whereas in mainstreaming they are wiped out by the characteristics of the whole.

The general trend in the last years is to use a new term in pedagogical terminology, the term "inclusive education", which signifies the education that takes into consideration the individual needs and abilities of all persons. The term "inclusive" indicates a permanent struggle in order to establish better and more effective education systems. Inclusion is an expansion of the term "integration", which becomes under this new theory only the means and not the object for the social change. However, in Greek educational reality integration was never an end in itself. It was the process that aimed towards the creation of a better school both for children with and without special needs, where the divergences between students would be accepted by the school community. Therefore, it is probable that the term "inclusive" will not add anything new to the theoretical basis of "integration". However, it carries within a new approach that suggests the will to change some social parameters and to reestablish the meaning of some terms.[3]

### *(iii) General objectives*

The objective of a special needs education is to contribute to the social integration of the disabled through school integration, with a view to enabling handicapped children to enjoy a more satisfying working life when they reach adulthood and to increase as far as possible the integration of the disabled into ordinary schools and to use specialised establishments only if necessary. According to the Resolution of the Council and the Ministers for Education meeting with the Council of 31 May 1990 concerning integration of children and young people with disabilities into ordinary systems of education, the Member States have agreed to encourage integration of pupils and students with disabilities, in all appropriate cases, into the ordinary education system. The work of special schools and centres should be seen as complementary to the work of the ordinary education systems. Furthermore, the Resolution promotes co-operation between all the bodies with an interest in and involvement with children and young people with disabilities. Moreover, it promotes the use of new technology as a means of education in order to aid communication and the development of language skills.

## 4. LEGAL PROVISIONS

### *(i) Historical background*

The first legal provision relating to special education is the Law 453/1937. This Law defined the meaning of the term "mentally retarded child" and regulates the founding of the first special school in Athens. Law 905/1951 follows later. This law deals particularly with the education of blind people and remains effectively in force for about fifteen years. From 1951 till 1981 a series of legal provisions are passed relating to special education.

[3] Athina Zoniou-Sideri, Integration of persons with special needs and analytical programmes, http://dolphin.dea.gr/DownLoad.

A very important legal turn is the constitutional recognition of the "rights of the disadvantaged child" in article 16 paragraph 4 of the Constitution of 1974. The State awareness regarding special education rises and in 1975 the first "Committee for the Study and Planning of Special Education" is being formed under the auspices of the Ministry of National Education and Religions with the participation of psychologists, psychiatrists, teachers and members of the Ministry. In a relatively short period of time, several structural changes take place, as the introduction of the role of the Special Inspector, today called School Advisor, the expansion of the special further training of the teachers from one year to two, etc.

Law 1143/1981 "On special education, special vocational training, employment and social care of the persons who deviate from normal and other educational provisions" aims to provide special education and special vocational training to persons with special needs as a separate section of the education system with separate legal form and programmes. Law 1143/1981 was supplemented by the Presidential Decree 603/1982 relating to the "Organisation and operation of special education units".

In a short period of time Law 1566/1985 on the "Structure and operation of primary and secondary education" was passed. For the first time special education is integrated in the general legal regime of primary and secondary education. Although the principle of integration was established in the Law 1566/1985 regarding "general education", it failed to solve many of the problems relating to pupils with special needs. The policy that was followed was the policy of a more subtle exclusion with an increase of the special classes (now inclusion classes). The ground was not prepared for a major educational change and moreover the social situation at the time was not suitable for such a change. The change in legislation was not followed by a carefully planned social and educational policy based on mutual acceptance and therefore it was not effective.

### *(ii) Legal provisions effective today*

#### *(a) The Constitution*

From the early times of the creation of the modern Greek state the issue of education was considered to be of major importance, especially among the drafters of the constitutional documents. Hence, all Greek constitutions since 1827 contain special provisions regarding education.[4] The present constitution in article 16 paragraph 4 section 1 states "All Hellenes have the right to a free education at all levels in state schools". The general freedom of education is the freedom of a person to decide if, where and how (as a matter of object and method) he/she is going to receive his/her education. This general freedom has several aspects, one of which is the freedom to

4 Articles 20 and 85 of the Constitution of 1827(in Trizina), article 11 of the Constitution of 1844, article 16 of the Constitution of 1864, article 16 of the Constitution of 1911, article 23 of the Constitution of 1927 and article 16 of the Constitution of 1952.

access education. No person can be prohibited from enjoying the right to education at any level. The first additional Protocol of the European Convention on Human Rights (ECHR) states in article 2 paragraph 1 that "No person shall be denied the right to education." Article 16 paragraph 4 section 2 states "The State supports … students that need help and special assistance according to their capabilities". These provisions also refer to persons with special educational needs, irrespective of their social standing and background. The constitutional legislator wanted therefore to protect all persons that need special assistance and protection according to their abilities.[5]

*(b) Laws, Presidential Decrees and Ministerial Decrees*

*b-1.* Presidential decree 420/5-3-1978 provides for the replacement of written examinations with oral examinations for persons with visual impairment or other persons if the health committee certifies that they are not able to undertake a written examination.

*b-2.* Law 1141/1981 still remains partly in force mainly relating to issues regarding the license necessary in order to found a private teaching unit for special education. According to article 20, both legal persons under public and private law or natural persons that offer special education or vocational training to persons deviating from normal without a license of foundation and operation are under the obligation to receive such a license. Otherwise, they are excluded from the right to provide special education and training. Furthermore, article 22 states that private educational units of any type and level should comply with Law 1141/1981.

*b-3.* Presidential decree 603/1982 (article 14) specifies the method of final evaluation of a pupil in his/her yearly report for primary school if he/she deviates from normal, as verified by the medical report of the service for child pedagogic.

*b-4.* Law 1351/1983 provides that persons that are blind, deaf, mute and anaemic are admitted to Universities as a surplus without any examination. These students can enrol at any department of their wish provided that the relevant department has not issued a decision otherwise justified by the reason that their participation will be hindered due to the nature of the specific course. Article 4 paragraph 1 of 1771/1988 and later article 2640/1998 adds further categories of handicapped persons to the list of people that can enrol in Universities without exams.

*b-5.* Presidential decree 465/1981 as amended by Presidential Decree 182/1994 regulates the method of evaluation for pupils in secondary education. An oral examination is provided where it is set by the relevant provisions.

[5] Panagiotis E. Poulis, *The Law of Education*, Ant. N. Sakkoulas Publishings, Athens – Komotini 1999, p. 102.

*b-6.* Article 34 of Law 1566/1985 states that the Minister of National Education and Religions is solely responsible for all issues relating to the education of persons with special needs.[6] Moreover, article 62 paragraph 7 states that this law is applied accordingly also to private school units both of primary and secondary level.

*b-7.* Article 33 of Law 2009/1992 states that the teaching personnel involved in special education is entitled to the same surplus benefits and compensation as for the teaching personnel of secondary education under the same terms and provisions.[7]

*b-8.* The Greek Parliament with Law 2430/1996 ratified the rules of the United Nations and the world programme of action. The elaboration of the national application plan was entrusted to a committee presided by the Minister of Social Security. Among others, an interministerial committee composed of the Ministers of diverse Ministries and presided by the Minister of Social Services, is charged with establishing the baseline of direction for the application of a global policy for handicapped persons. On the field of education, the approach was to reevaluate and reorganise the education system for pupils with special needs. Law 2430/1996 sets the 3rd of December as date dedicated to persons with special needs. Article 1 paragraph 2 provides that the National Confederation of Persons with Special Needs each year submits to the Chairman of the Greek Parliament a report regarding the exercise of human and social rights by persons with special needs. The events organised on this day are under the auspices of the Greek Parliament.[8] Article 3 adopts the world action programme as well as the equal opportunities rules for people with special needs, as these were approved by the General Assembly of the United Nations in 1993. Furthermore, article 3 paragraph 2 co-ordinates a committee entrusted with the supervision of the events as well as with the creation of a national application plan of the world action programme and the official rules for equal opportunities approved by the United Nations for persons with special needs. This committee is composed of the Minister of Health and Care or the competent Vice – Minister and a representative of each party with a seat in the Greek Parliament. This committee should also issue a yearly report regarding the application of United Nation rules for equal opportunities to persons with special needs.

*b-9.* Ministerial Decree YA G2b/1999 provides in article 5 that summer camps are allowed to host children with special needs if they hold a medical statement certifying that the condition of their health allows their participation in a summer camp.

[6] This is also supported by case law: Case Number 59/1999 of the Administrative Court of Appeal.

[7] This is also supported by case law (Case Nr. 59/1999 of the Administrative Court of Appeal).

[8] Article 2 paragraph 1 of Law 2430/1996.

*b-10.* Law 2817/2000 regulates the education of persons with special education needs. The Ministry of National Education and Religions is the exclusive competent authority for the education of persons with special educational needs. Furthermore, in the case of founding, operation and supervision of Centres and workshops of special vocational training for persons with special needs that fall under the authority of the Ministry of Health and Care, the Minister of National Education and Religions and the Minister of Health and Care are jointly competent if these institutions are also used by persons with special needs of school age.[9] The education of persons with special education needs is provided by state schools free of cost.[10]

The objectives of special education for persons with special educational needs is described in article 6 as the development of their personality, the improvement of their abilities and skills in order for them to be integrated or reintegrated in the mainstream education system, their vocational training, their participation in the production process and finally their mutual acceptance by society as a whole and equal social advance. In order for them to achieve the above goals the Greek State provides for services to the persons with special educational needs of a maximum age of 22 years in all school levels of primary and secondary education. Moreover, it is under the obligation to take measures in order to facilitate the learning process of such students and to apply in practice the principle of equal treatment of persons with special educational needs. Some of these measures include among others the application of special programmes and teaching methods, the acquisition of helpful equipment, the early diagnosis of the special educational needs, evaluation, pedagogical and psychological support, physiotherapy, ergotherapy, speech therapy, social and counseling services, etc.[11]

Article 1 paragraph 11 states that the education of people with special needs both general and technical–vocational is provided by the schools of primary and secondary education that are organised, equipped and supported accordingly as to make available the necessary teaching and psychopedagogical support of those persons. Pupils with special education needs can:

(a) attend the regular school class with concurrent support from a teacher of special education who is appointed either to the “Centres for diagnosis, evaluation and support” or to the school units of special education after a decision of the relevant “Centre for diagnosis, evaluation and support”.
(b) attend specially organised and equipped integration classes run by suitable personnel that operate within the ordinary schools of the general or technical education system.

9 Article 1 paragraph 10 of the Law 2817/2000.
10 Supra, paragraph 9.
11 Supra, paragraph 7.

However, article 1 paragraph 12 provides that in case that attendance of persons with special education needs in the ordinary schools provided by the education system or in the integration classes is difficult because of the nature or the extent of their impairment, these persons are educated:

(a) In separate schools of special education
(b) In schools or classes that either operate separately or as a part of other schools in hospitals, rehabilitation centres, institutions of education of minors or institutions of persons that suffer from long – term illnesses, if their residents or patients are children with special educational needs.
(c) At home in special circumstances, in which case the system of distance education is used. These persons are educated by the personnel of the "Centres for diagnosis, evaluation and support" or of the school unit for special education, which is specialised in the relevant impairment.

Article 1 paragraph 13 establishes the separate schools of special education, which are:

(a) kindergarten and primary school for infants and children with special needs from their 4th till their 14th year,
(b) junior high school (gymnasium) of special education from their 14th till the 18th year,
(c) high school (lyceum) of special education from their 18th till their 22nd year,
(d) technical – vocational training units (T.E.E.) of special education of the 1st Level, which includes a programme for the completion of the compulsory education (nine years duration) and the 1st Circle of Studies as set in article 2 of Law 2640/1988 regarding specialised technical and vocational skills. Graduates of primary school can enrol to these units. The programme has duration of at least five years from the 14th till the 19th year of the students.
(e) technical vocational training units (T.E.E.) of special education of the 2nd level, which include both the 1st and the 2nd Circle of Studies as set in article 2 of Law 2640/1988. Junior high school (gymnasium) graduates can enrol in the first grade of the first Circle. The programme has duration of two years for each Circle of Studies. Graduates of the T.E.E. of the 1st Level (mentioned above) can also enrol in the second Circle of Studies from their 19th till their 22nd year.
(f) workshop of special vocational training and instruction from their 14th till their 22nd year.

The School Units of Special Education (S.M.E.A.) and its personnel operate under the supervision of the relevant Department of Education according to their level (i.e. primary and secondary), in particular, the Workshops of Special Vocational Training and Instruction (E.E.E.E.K.) are supervised Department of Secondary Education.[12]

[12] Supra, paragraph 14.

Article 16 states that all schools, mentioned above under a, b, c, d and e are equivalent to the relevant schools of primary and secondary education. Apart from the daily instruction programmes, which are accordingly modified, these schools also offer a programme of creativity. Primary schools of special education include in their programmes activities of prevocational training, whilst secondary schools of special education include in their programmes courses on technical – vocational training and instruction. The object of these programmes is set by decisions of the Minister of National Education and Religions after recommendations of the Department of Special Education of the Pedagogical Institute.

The foundation, abolition, degradation and coalition of the aforementioned school units and the integration classes, the addition of new sectors and classes of specialisation in the T.E.E.s of special education, issues regarding its personnel and the increase or decrease of the positions are regulated by decisions of the Minister of National Education and Religions issued after recommendations from the relevant "Centres for diagnosis, evaluation and support" and other relevant organs.[13] The Minister of National Education and Religions issues decisions (either on his/her own or with joint authority) regarding several issues, among which are the following:

(a) the admittance, participation, and graduation of the students with special education needs in all categories of school units of special education and integration classes,
(b) the name, title and specified type of the schools of special education and the minimum amount of students that attend these units in each class and level,
(c) the method of home education,
(d) the specific duties and obligations of the special teaching personnel of the "School Units for Special Needs" and the "Centres for diagnosis, evaluation and support",
(e) the discovery, diagnosis, registration, transfer and placement of persons with special needs in the above mentioned schools.
(f) the weekly timetable of instruction and any other assignment of the personnel of special education employed in these schools,
(g) the start and end of the school year,
(h) the number of positions of the special teaching personnel and the special support and administrative personnel in each sector and specialisation for every Workshop of Special Vocational Training and Instruction,
(i) the process of establishing and operating parent groups, who will co-operate with the departments of the Ministry of National Education and Religions regarding the task of educating persons with special education needs,
(j) the operation of counselling and support services to the parents of children with special education needs, etc.[14]

13 Supra, paragraph 18.

14 Supra, para 20.

The issues relating to the examination and grading both of students that attend the School Units of Special Education and of students with special education needs that attend regular school classes[15] are regulated by Presidential Decrees issued following a proposal from the Minister of Education, after a recommendation from the Special Education Department of the Pedagogical Institute.[16]

Paragraph 23 recognises for graduates of the T.E.E.s of special education of both levels vocational rights following the procedure of article 6 paragraph 3 of Law 2009/1992.[17] The graduates of the Workshops of Special Vocational Training and Instruction receive a degree title, which carries the same weight as the certificate provided in article 6 of Law 2009/1992, and awards the same vocational rights.

Article 2 regulates the operation of the "Centres for diagnosis, evaluation and support" for persons with special education needs. These are organised in a form of decentralised civil authorities, which operate under the immediate supervision of the Minister of National Education and Religions.[18] The purpose of the "Centres for diagnosis, evaluation and support" is to provide services of diagnosis, evaluation and support for all students and especially those who have special education needs. Furthermore, their objective is to support, inform and raise the level of awareness of teachers, parents and society in general.[19] The "Centres for diagnosis, evaluation and support", have the following responsibilities:

(a) to conduct research in order to determine the type and extent of impairments that trouble the persons with special needs among the whole student community (and pre-school children community) with the assistance of the regional Health and Care Services.
(b) to recommend in co-operation with school advisors of special education, competent advisors (either at pre-school or at primary or at secondary school level), headmasters and special education personnel employed in the school units of special education in each case, the registration, placement and attendance in the school unit suitable for each student and to observe and evaluate the education progress of the students,
(c) to recommend the creation of individual or group programmes of psycho- pedagogic and teaching support, programmes of creativity and to apply any scientific,

15 Supra, para 21.

16 Supra, para 22.

17 The vocational rights (specified in the present law) of the holders of titles of vocational training and instruction according to specialisation and sector are issued by Presidential Decrees following a proposal from the Minister of National Education and Religions after a recommendation of the board of directors of the Organisation for Vocational Training and Instruction.

18 Supra, article 2 para 1.

19 Supra, para 2.

social or other method for students with special education needs. These programmes and methods can take place either in the schools, in the Centres or even at home,

(d) to provide counselling and information to the teaching personnel and to everyone participating in the education process and to organise information fairs for the parents and guardians of students with special needs,

(e) to determine the technical support equipment necessary to a person with special needs either for use at home or in school and to make suggestions for the improvement of the accessibility of school buildings,

(f) to recommend the substitution of written tests both at primary and secondary level with an oral examination or alternate methods of valuation for students, attending the school units of special education,

(g) to organise and apply programmes of early intervention in education, etc.[20]

The teaching personnel placed in the "Centres for diagnosis, evaluation and support" must hold a university degree in special education either at undergraduate or graduate level or a recognised equivalent title awarded by a foreign university or alternatively a degree of a two year conversion course in special education along with a three year work experience in a school unit of special education.[21]

Paragraph 13 establishes the Council for Special Teaching Personnel that belongs to the Central Service of the Ministry of National Education and Religions. This Council is competent to regulate issues of selecting, placing and appointing the special personnel as well as disciplinary and other issues regarding the personnel placed in the "Centres for diagnosis, evaluation and support" and the School Units of Special Education.[22] The composition of this Council is set in article 2 paragraph 14 following.

Article 2 paragraph 17 provides for the creation of a Special Education Department in the Pedagogical Institute. Its task is to conduct scientific research and studies relating to all issues of special education and to make proposals regarding the planning and application of policies in special education, to organise training programmes involving the personnel in special education, to establish the schedules and the analytical programmes of study and to process all teaching and support material for the education of persons with special needs, to evaluate the existing programmes of special needs in co-operation with the Department of Evaluation of the Pedagogical Institute, to promote the use of technology in special education, to provide scientific support to the school advisors of special education and to the programmes of school integration and finally to co-operate with scientific organisation both in Greece and abroad in order to promote awareness on special education.[23]

[20] Supra, para 3.

[21] Supra, para 5.

[22] Supra, para 13.

[23] Supra, para 18.

## 5. Relating Projects

### *(i) Acquisition, Installation and Operation of a Data Bank of Special Education of the Ministry of National Education and Religions and its connection to School Units of Special Education in the whole of Greece*

The project provides for the installation of a data bank in the Department of Special Needs of the Ministry of National Education and Religions, the collection of all relevant information, the acquisition of personal computers for School Units of Special Education and connection of these Units with the data bank. It is used by members of the Department of Special Education of the Ministry of National Education and Religions, by teachers in the school units of special education, by teachers in mainstream schools that deal with individual learning impairments, to pupils with special educational needs and finally to their parents. This project will give to the 167 Schools of Special Education the opportunity to receive information from the Data Bank in order for their teaching personnel to be kept up to date regarding scientific developments and teaching practices. It provides an opening to the field of information on a world-wide level through the Internet. Furthermore, it provides the opportunity to both teachers and pupils of special schools to communicate with other schools, exchange their views and experience and, hence, to exit from the isolation often experienced in special schools and to turn towards inclusion programmes in education. It enables the school community to access and communicate with the local authorities regarding activities outside school environment and finally it contributes to the modernisation of education programmes.

### *(ii) Seminars and Conferences*

The Ministry of National Education and Religions organises several conferences regarding specific issues on the education of persons with special needs (e.g. Conference on the awareness of the directors of education and of school advisors in mainstream and special education, Conference on the awareness and instruction of professionals in education and health services for the support of children when dealing with illness and death.) Seminars of further qualifications are also established either for certain categories of professionals (e.g. kindergarten teachers, teachers in special education, recently qualified (i.e. new) teachers, special personnel employed in the School Units of Special Education etc.). These seminars aim to raise awareness among the teaching community and to inform all personnel both in mainstream and special schools on issues relating to special education as to eradicate superstitions and to promote inclusion of children with special needs in the educational society. Other seminars focus on a specific handicap (deafness or blindness) or a specific emotional and social impairment. Seminars are also often organised for the parents of children with special educational needs.

### *(iii) Prevocational workshops*

Several prevocational workshops are established and maintained within special schools. These workshops aim at equipping the person with special needs with all skills and knowledge necessary in order for him/her to be self-sufficient and lead a life with decency.

### *(iv) Counselling Programme for Students with Special Needs regarding their studies*

The students' advisory centre organises a counselling programme regarding university students with special needs. The counsels will be students from the psychology department and their task will be to provide support and advice on study methods to their fellow students with special needs.

## 6. Non-governmental organisations

### *(i) The National Confederation of Persons with special needs (E.S.A.E.A.)*

The National Confederation of Persons with special needs (E.S.A.E.A.) is a social federation of organisations for persons with special needs and their parents. It is the official social partner of the Greek State in matters relating to persons with special needs and their families. It is composed of more than 250 organisations in total. All categories of persons with special need are represented: persons that are blind or with vision impairment, paraplegics, tetraplegics, persons with mobility impairment, persons with hearing disability or deaf persons, hemorophylics, persons with kidney problems, with transplants, with Hansen disease, with anaemia, diabetes as well as the parents of those persons that can not represent themselves (i.e. persons with mental incapacity, autistics, persons with severe psychosomatic, mobility and multiple handicaps. The Confederation (E.S.A.E.A.) as the official social partner is the competent organisation to appoint representatives in Committees regarding the planning and application of measures regarding persons with special needs. Therefore, the Confederation participates in all Committees for the supervision of European Programmes that relate to actions and measures for persons with special needs and it also participates in the National Board of Education. The Confederation co-ordinates the activities of the disability and parent movement both in national and regional level, informs its member organisations, and provides all necessary support and advice for the achievement of their aims and goals.

### *(ii) National Association of Blinds*

The National Association of Blinds was founded in 1932 and is the first organisation created by handicapped people themselves. Its main goal is the support of the rights and the improvement of the quality of life of all people with vision impairment in Greece. In the field of education the National Association of Blinds was the first organisation to found a public library equipped with "talking books" and to make it available to all blinds in both Greece and Cyprus. In the beginning the library aimed firstly to cover the gaps in the education of blind students in all levels and secondly to fill the need to access literature and knowledge in general. This library was the only support for students until 1987, when the Centre for Training and Rehabilitation of Blind Persons undertook the task of distributing this material. Today the Talking Book Service and the Talking Magazine Publishings amount to about two thousand titles. Efforts are made to increase both the quantity and quality of these productions by using modern technology.

### *(iii) Other organisations*

Some other Greek organisations are the following: National Association of Paraplegics, National Association of Paraplegics and Persons with Mobility Problems, Association of Paraplegics "Alexander the Great" in Thessaloniki, Center of Paraplegics in Drama, Association of Persons with Mobility Problems in Karditsa, Association of Paraplegics in Kalymnos, Hellenic Association of Persons with Disseminated Scleriosis, Association for the Protection of Spastics, Parents association with Children with special needs, Parents association with children with Down syndrome, National Organisation of Persons with Kidney Failure, National Association of Persons suffering from anemia etc.

## 7. Research and educational programmes

Greece participates in several educational programmes sponsored by the European Union, as the HELIOS II, the ERASMUS, the Inclusion and the Evident programmes, The University of Patras conducts a research on the Greek Sign Language and has undertaken a project to create an e-book of phrases and vocabulary of sign language. Specifically, the ultimate aim of the Inclusion programme is to provide for the deaf community equal opportunities in training through common planning, effective policies and practices.

TOM BOLAND

# Ireland

## Introduction

The primary objectives of special needs education are:

- The development of potential abilities through quality education which takes the special educational needs (SEN) of children and young people into account.
- The inclusion of children and young people with special educational needs in society.

Special needs education is therefore based on a strong respect for individual differences and not merely linked to a structure of (segregated) special education.

## 1. International law

Convention on the Rights of the Child
Declaration on the Rights of Mentally Retarded Persons
Declaration on the Rights of Disabled Persons
International Covenant on Economic, Social and Cultural Rights
United Nations, Resolution 48/96, The Standard Rules on the equalization of opportunities for persons with disabilities, New York, USA 1994.
UNESCO: The Salamanca statement and framework for action on special needs education, World conference on special needs education: access and quality. Salamanca, Spain, 7–10 June 1994.
European Commission, Helios II programme: European guide of good practice; Towards equal opportunities for disabled people, Brussels, Belgium, 1996.

How have these rules been introduced into national legislation? What influence do non-binding international rules have?

*Answer:* Non-binding international rules can have persuasive influence in an Irish court. That is to say, although they are not binding on the court, the court may

*Jan De Groof and Gracienne Lauwers (eds.), Special Education*, 203–207.

hear argument based on them and may be influenced by them in coming to a conclusion.

## 2. How does your national legislation implement the right to education for children with special educational needs?

*Answer:* The Education Act, 1998 provides the legal basis for education at primary and post primary levels. It sets out the structures for the education system and their powers and functions, including the powers and functions of the Minister. The Act gives specific recognition to the needs of children with special education needs.

### *A. Essentials*

**Right to education/right to access – Which groups are covered by legislation? Who is excluded? (Differences: age, private/public schools)**

*Answer:* No group is excluded, provided the young person is no older than 18. All publicly funded schools are covered.

Are there specific provisions, which give the right to education of children with special needs extra weight? Sum up these provisions and give explicit examples.

*Answer:* While there are no provisions giving "extra weight" to the right of children with special needs the Education Act at a number of key provisions makes specific reference to such children. For example the following is one of the main objects of the Act as stated therein

> to give practical effect to the constitutional rights of children, including children who have a disability or special educational needs, as they relate to education.

The reference to constitutional rights is a reference to the right under the Constitution of Ireland of each child to receive a certain minimum education and the duty of the State to provide for free primary education.

Are there specific provisions to reinforce the right to education for children with special educational needs?

How are they incorporated into standard education and who is excluded from standard education? Who receives education in separate educational institutions/ structures and which pupils receive no education at all?

Which categories of pupils are integrated in standard education and which categories are excluded?

*Answer:* There are no specific provisions for special education at present. However, the Government is committed to bringing forward such legislation in the near future.

The policy approach to the education of children with special needs is that they should be educated in an integrated setting with children who do not have special needs. Only where this is damaging to the child with special needs or to the education of other children are children with special needs educated in special classes in an ordinary school or in special schools.

Can a school refuse to accept children with special needs? Is there a difference between private and state education?

Is a school allowed to refuse children with special educational needs?

*Answer:* The Equal Status Act, 2000 specifically outlaws discrimination in school admissions on grounds of disability. This would apply to all schools whether or not they are publicly funded. However, it is recognised that a school does have a duty towards children who do not have special needs and if exceptionally, the education of those children was to be prejudiced by the admission of a child with special needs then a school could refuse admission. Before doing so however they would have to establish that the child could not be accommodated if additional resources were provided, including staffing. In addition a school is obliged to have an admissions policy, which must state specifically the policy of the school as regards the admission to the school of children with special needs and their participation in the school.

*Answer:* Yes – see above reference to Equal Status Act, 2000

Are the rules concerning non-discrimination (e.g. discrimination on the basis of sex, ethnic background, etc.) applicable to the refusal of children with special educational needs?

Is the principle of freedom of choice also respected for children with special educational needs? (Freedom of choice means that the parents select freely between private and state schools on the basis of their philosophical outlook or other priorities, and that those responsible for running schools are in a position to organise them on the basis of a given philosophical outlook or other priority.)

*Answer:* In principal yes. However, there are serious difficulties in the Irish education system as regards accommodation for children with special needs. There is a shortage of adequately resourced schools. In these circumstances there is a limited choice available to parents and indeed in some cases no publicly funded provision at all. In the latter cases the State has provided funding for private education (that is education which is not normally in receipt of public funds) and has funded the setting up of parent led educational facilities.

## *B. Education and care*

Care provided
How are the legal principles put into practice in terms of the care provided? How is it financed?

*Answer:* In Irish budgetary terms the care and education of children is dealt with in two separate streams. Local health authorities have primary responsibility for health, care and welfare, while the Minister for Education and Science has responsibility for education. The two streams co-operate in delivery of services, although there is some criticism from parents that they do not always do so effectively.

What rights do schools have if they accept pupils with special educational needs?

*Answer:* In general the law does not address the issue of school rights; the focus is on the rights of the child. However, from case law it can be said that a school would have the right not to be forced to accept a child when it objectively could not accommodate him or her, either for reasons of physical space or the nature of the child's disability. It also has the right not to have to apply its own resources (as opposed to those provided by the State) to make accommodation for a child with special needs.

What are the legal duties of public authorities?

*Answer:* The legal duties of public authorities as regards the education of children with special needs derive first and most strongly from the Constitution as referred to above. Under the Constitution the State is required to ensure that all children receive a minimum education appropriate to their needs. This implies that the State has a duty not merely to provide the pure educational inputs, such as trained teachers, but also all of the physical and personnel supports which the child needs to benefit adequately from education – for example speech and language therapists.

## 3. Procedure

**The role of special centres: detection, diagnosis, consultation, referral, advice**
**The role of home counselling services**
What are the rights of parents of children with special educational needs?
What are the rights of the children?

**Legal remedies**
**Rights of appeal: Are the procedures effective?**
Who is allowed to take responsibility for whom? (Authorities, schools, special centres, parents)
**Role of a Special Educational Needs Tribunal**
**Case law: discussion of certain interesting rulings**

*Answer:* The rights of parents with special needs are the same as those of any parents. In particular they have a right to send their child to a school of their choice (subject to what is said above) and they have a right to information on their child's educational progress. While not formally enshrined in law, there is general acceptance that parents have the right to be consulted about their children's education and access to any professional reports concerning their children's disabilities.

Under the Education Act a parent may appeal a refusal to enroll his or her child. This provision has been in operation for less than a year so it is early to say how effective it will be. In addition where the issue is discrimination within the terms of the Equal Status Act a parent may take his or her child's case to the Equality Authority.

## 4. Lifelong learning for children and adults with special educational needs

Is there a need for co-ordination? Is there need for a more structured approach? What is the current situation? (Give a summary of the existing structures.)

*Answer:* There are at present no general special arrangements for the education of adults with special education needs. Third level institutions are required by law to operate in accordance with principles of equality and many have introduced programmes and services aimed at people with disabilities. At other levels of the education system however adults with special needs receive no special treatment over other adult learners. Most local health boards, however, provide some training for young adults up to the age of 21.

## Recommendations to the Council of Ministers

With a view to providing equal opportunities, it should be a policy priority to ensure that schools are as inclusive as possible, and more resources should be made available for implementing such a policy.

ANNEX

# Comparative Analysis of Legislation Regarding Special Education in European Countries[1]

An analysis of the basic articles of the legislation regarding special education of the European nations shows that differences can exist on the one hand and common principles can exist on the other.

## 1. Conceptual differences

In Norway, the education of children with developmental disorders (including those who have been invalids since their childhood years) is regulated by the law regarding compulsory education, which was passed in 1975 (paragraph 8). With the implementation of this law, the law regarding special education that had been in effect since 1951 became defunct and special education was from then on viewed as a part of the general compulsory nine-year education for children aged 7 to 15. The law determines that the education of children with physical or mental disorders strives to achieve the same objectives as general education. It follows from this premise that special education must be involved in the system of general education as fully as possible or at least co-ordinate with it.

Analogically, the base law of 3 October 1990 (chapter 5) regarding the education system in Spain views the most important task of special education as being to ensure certain means and methods for the education of children who (temporarily or permanently) have special educational needs so that these children would be able to achieve the same results as normal students. In that sense, it is considered to be a duty for regular schools to have the necessary experts available (within the school itself) to uncover special educational needs as well as to have special educational materials and the necessary equipment and technical infrastructure.

[1] Reprint. Conclusions of the Flemish-Russian cooperation on special education, De Groof J., Lauwers Gr., *A New Framework of Special Education in the Russian Federation*, Garant, 2000, 242 p.

*Jan De Groof and Gracienne Lauwers (eds.), Special Education*, 209–214.

The Belgian law of 6 July 1970 for special (integrated) education is based on a different approach to education for persons who experience difficulties in receiving education through traditional methods. The law declares the objective of special education to be the development of the physical and intellectual capabilities of such persons, as well as their social adaptation, in particular, (1) preparation for family life, (2) learning suitable trades and jobs, and (3) preparation for work within specially created conditions. The education of these persons in regular schools is in the background and is only permitted on a permanent or provisional basis if the objectives are as follows: ensuring social adaptation or acquiring general education or obtaining a qualification certificate. Placing a student with special educational needs in a regular school is called integrated education and is permitted only upon consent of the schoolmaster involved. In this way, Belgian legislation is found to have more polarised access to general or special education.

The provisional Act of 1 August 1985 regarding special education in the Netherlands provides that the objectives of special education are the development of the emotional sphere, of the intellect and of the creative capacities, as well as the acquisition of essential knowledge and of social, cultural and physical skills. Special education is separated from regular education and is offered in special schools, as is also the case in Belgian legislation.

The common denominator in the legislation of the aforementioned countries is the recognition of the need to ensure special means and methods for the education of persons who are not able to receive education by means of the usual methods or for whom the standard education is too difficult due to shortcomings in their physical, intellectual or emotional development or as a result of disease.

## 2. Typology and classification of special education

According to the various starting points, the regulations differ from the legislation with regard to special education of the various European countries in the matter of classification, types and kinds of establishments for special education and special education in general.

In this way, the classification of the types and kinds of special education according to Norwegian and Spanish legislation is not only not affirmed, but the need for an individual approach in determining the special education needs is even emphasised in every concrete case. In Belgium and in the Netherlands, on the other hand, a fairly fixed classification is laid down.

The Belgian decree in particular provides for eight kinds of special educational establishments for children and adults:

- persons with delayed intellectual development (light mental disorders)
- intellectually disturbed persons (moderate and serious mental disorders)
- persons who suffer from disorders of an emotional nature (personality disorders)

- persons with physical disorders (bodily defects)
- diseases (long-term illnesses)
- persons with visual impairments (sight disorders)
- persons with hearing impairments (auditory disorders)
- persons who suffer from motor function disorders that causes problems when speaking, writing, reading and counting (speech, language and/or serious learning disorders).

Dutch legislation has a more detailed classification. Special education includes schools for the following:

- deaf children
- children who are hard of hearing
- children with serious speech disorders who do not fall under the categories of children who are deaf or hard of hearing
- blind children
- children who are partially sighted
- children with physical disorders
- children who are under clinical treatment
- children with chronic illnesses
- children with learning disorders
- children with serious learning disorders
- children who are not capable of learning
- children with learning and behavioural disorders
- children from schools that fall under the direction of pedagogical institutes
- children with a multitude of disorders
- young children aged 4 to 7 who have delays in their development.

## 3. The Age of the Students

Legislation regarding special education provides for the opportunity to extend the duration of studies for children who are recognised as having a need for special education services, as compared to the duration of studies for normal children.

In Belgium, assistance to persons who require special education is offered to students aged 3 to 21. In the Netherlands, the legislation regarding primary education for pupils aged 3 or 4 to 12 (including special schools for young children aged 4 to 7 who have developmental delays) and secondary education for children aged 12 to 20.

On the other hand, the Norwegian law of 1975 regarding compulsory education views special education as part of the compulsory general nine-year education for children aged 7 to 15. In the event it becomes necessary to extend the duration of the compulsory education for children with developmental deficiencies, this can go to ten years. Young people with developmental deficiencies have the same right as others to continued (complete secondary or higher) education.

## 4. PROCEDURE FOR DIAGNOSING CHILDREN WHO NEED SPECIAL EDUCATION

The legislation of the European countries lays down a mandatory procedure to diagnose and determine the needs for special education of children who have learning problems at a personal level.

In Spain, the rule was laid down according to which a group of experts made up of all necessary specialists is required, for each separate case, to develop a concrete plan of action for the education of that child. Each student who has a need for special education is then subject to an assessment at the end of the school year and the individual plan is then subject to revisions depending on the results of that assessment.

With regard to the conditions for granting special education, Belgian legislation provides that a special document ("report") must be drawn up in which the type of special education which appears to be necessary for the student in question is laid down. The report is drawn up on the basis of a statement from the parents or on the basis of a request from certain organisations or bodies.

In the Netherlands, before sending children to special schools, it is required to have a decision by an appraisal committee as well as the school's agreement to admit the child. The child is then subject to re-evaluation every two years.

## 5. SPECIAL BODIES AND SERVICES

In order to be able to establish the diagnosis and definition of the needs for special education, the European legislation provides for the establishment of special bodies or services on a multidisciplinary (interdepartmental) basis.

In Belgium, such bodies include, in particular, the Centre for Student Councelling which by law must be set up in every community. The duties of these centres are very extensive and range from creating the necessary conditions for the work and education of the students and of the pedagogues who work with these students to intervening, at the request of the persons involved or at their own initiative, in the activities of the education system in the psychological, medical or social fields. The function of these centres is three-fold:

- offering constant support to students throughout their education
- offering urgent help in times of crisis (for acute problems)
- functioning as a support for the compulsory education system.

Norwegian legislation provides for the establishment of psycho-pedagogical services that are responsible for diagnosing individual needs in education and for providing special psycho-pedagogical help to young children with developmental deficiencies.

In the Netherlands and in Spain, groups of experts are brought together with those same objectives.

## 6. Funding of special education

The obligations regarding the financing of special education are either assigned by the legislation of the European countries to local government bodies or local authorities that also are responsible for normal schools, or allocated through centralised sources in the form of donations or direct allowances.

In those countries where the approach to special education is characterised by the development of a network within regular schools (Norway, Spain, USA), the costs for the organisation of special education and the services associated with this (medical services, transportation services, etc.) are borne by the local authority.

In the Netherlands and Belgium, where legal regulations provide for a special form of education, the expenditures incurred by schools for that education and the services related to providing that education are financed by the central government.

## 7. Structure and content of the legislation

The structure of the legislative acts regarding special education in various countries show considerable differences and are practically incomparable. One can discern two approaches: in the first, a legal "framework" is created at the highest level of the legislative power with the general principles and guidelines, after which the executive power and bodies of educational management give shape to the enabling legislation (Belgium, Spain, the Netherlands). In the second, the law is more detailed (Norway), which nonetheless does not preclude the executive power and the bodies of educational management from giving the law more shape. The division of the regulating authority firstly depends on the concrete polity as it was laid down in the constitution.

The content of the legislation on special education, in contrast to its structure, is characterised by greater uniformity. The laws in all countries lay down the following:

- the government policy in the field of special education;
- the definition of the terminology used within the legislation;
- the categories of criteria that must determine whether persons require special education services;
- the forms under which special education can be provided;
- the procedures for evaluating and diagnosing persons who require special education services;
- the regulations for founding and structuring, and for the duty descriptions of multidisciplinary (interdepartmental) bodies and services, in charge of organising special education services;
- the demands made of education programmes;

- the additional rights of the parents whose children receive special education;
- the regulations regarding the funding of special education establishments or regarding other expenditures, which are associated with that education;
- the rules for creating special education establishments;
- the requirements of the staff that are employed within the special education sector, the rights of the pedagogues working in that sector, and so forth.

## Yearbook of the European Association for Education Law and Policy

1. J. De Groof and H. Penneman (eds.): *The Legal Status of Pupils in Europe.* (1996). 1998 ISBN 90-411-0521-2
2. P. Akkermans, J. De Groof and H. Penneman (eds.): *Education Law and Policy in an Urban Society.* (1997). 1999 ISBN 90-411-1146-8
3. W. Berka, J. De Groof and H. Penneman (eds.): *Autonomy in Education.* 2000 ISBN 90-411-1311-8
4. J. De Groof, C. De Smet and H. Penneman (eds.): *Art Meets Law in Education.* 2001 ISBN 90-411-1537-4

KLUWER ACADEMIC PUBLISHERS – DORDRECHT / LONDON / BOSTON